THE CONGRUENCE FRAMEWORK

An opportunity to rethink the future of organisations

THE DEFINITIVE EDITION

Tony Chamberlain

www.**congruence**framework.com

This Book published March 2014 by:

Tony Chamberlain
PO Box 66, Oneroa
Waiheke Island
Auckland, 1081
New Zealand

www.congruenceframework.com

Copyright © 2014 Tony Chamberlain

ISBN 978-0-473-27895-3

Framework motif design by Jeroen ten Berge
(jeroentenberge.com)

We are all visitors to this time, this place.
We are just passing through.
Our purpose here is to observe,
to learn, to grow, to love,
and then we return home.

Aboriginal Australian proverb

Dedication

This book is a tribute to my long-time friend and mentor Barbara Curl, who initiated this conversation more than 25 years ago. She is the most congruent person I know.

This book acknowledges the contribution of many good friends and colleagues who have enriched my personal and professional life journey. These people have also been my teachers and mentors and have played a significant role in shaping the thinking and ideas that are shared in this book.

This book is written for my grandchildren Molly, Rose, Ruby, Mai, Minh and Edie who are my bright lights for the future. If these young people are able to experience congruence within their communities, they may become future ambassadors for peace in their time.

And this book is dedicated to Zara Stanhope, my very best friend and life partner. Without her love and support it would never have been written.

Table of Contents

Preface

About this book

This book marks the conclusion of the first stage of an ongoing project to create an organisational and personal development framework that will assist organisations, communities and individuals to become more congruent. This 'definitive edition' introduces the Congruence Framework, an idea that I will further develop in future concise books, including (if research opportunities become available) one that reviews the experiences of organisations that have applied the Framework to encourage congruency within their stakeholder communities.

Much of the material presented in this book reconnects with, and in some cases reframes, thinking that has been well traversed by many other writers and scholars. Therefore, readers conversant with organisational (and personal) development theories and methodologies will be familiar with many of the concepts discussed. However, it is the definition and integration of these concepts within a new organising (or thinking) framework – the Congruence Framework – that hopefully presents a fresh perspective for interested readers. Defining what we mean by congruence, clarifying the nature of purpose and leadership, emphasising the importance of community, reconnecting with the idea of learning organisations, advocating for more relevant (equitable-shared value) organisational outcomes, and rethinking the notions of corporate responsibility and individual wellbeing, are some of the ways this book tries to present and integrate new thinking about familiar concepts.

How to read this book

If you have selected this book to read, or perhaps to browse, then chances are the notion of congruence (generally understood as a form of harmonious alignment between individuals and/or communities) has caught your interest. You could be simply curious about what congruence actually means and wish to explore how it could be relevant to a community or organisation with which you interact. Maybe your interest is more personal and lies in understanding more about what congruence could mean for you. Or perhaps, on scanning the contents of this book, you discovered that some of the conversation topics are of particular interest to you. Depending on your focus, I can suggest four different ways of approaching this book – **four reader pathways** that provide different entry points for thinking about the notion of congruence.

But first, I suggest you refer to Figure 1 below, which summarises 'The book at a glance' and introduces the notion of congruence. The diagram presents the four conditions for congruence (shared purpose, meaningful relationships, collaborative learning and enabling leadership) and the two shared attitudes they embrace (co-creating the future and embracing difference and diversity). It also summarises what we mean by individual congruence and organisational (or community) congruence and outlines the five key areas of focus (the five factors) that are important in developing congruent organisations, or becoming a more congruent individual.

It is important to appreciate that this book presents a way of thinking about congruence rather than a practical guide on how to achieve congruence.

It presents an organising framework that is intended to focus attention on the key factors that can encourage and enable congruence.

Figure 1: The book at a glance

But it does not provide a methodology for applying that framework to any particular organisation or community. This approach recognises that each organisation (or community) is likely to present a different set of congruence challenges and require an appropriately tailored set of responses to become a more congruent organisation. And that providing a conceptual framework that guides, rather than prescribes or orders the organisation's thinking about congruence, provides the best way to help an organisation become more congruent.

It is also important to understand that achieving individual congruence is not a prerequisite for developing organisational congruence, and therefore you may choose to think quite separately about these two constructs. We can easily imagine how a group of already congruent (harmoniously aligned) individuals could together influence the congruence of their communities and organisations. But we can also imagine how some people could be influenced by their experience within a congruent organisation or community to seek a more congruent individual lifestyle.

Depending on how you choose to think about the notion of congruence, the following reader pathways (or profiles) present different options for navigating the discussions in this book.

A browser's pathway

If you are curious but unsure about whether this book presents any ideas or thinking that is relevant for your personal or professional life, then you could begin by reading any of the chapters or sections that catch your interest. Perhaps make a start by scanning the Contents section and selecting the discussion topics that you are most interested in.

By exploring the ideas and concepts you are familiar with, you will soon discover whether this book presents a useful learning opportunity for yourself or perhaps for someone else you know. But you should also test this view by selecting a few topics with which you are either unfamiliar or that you suspect will present a perspective with which you are unlikely to agree. For it is often in the unfamiliar, or different thinking about the over-familiar, that we uncover the real leaning opportunity.

I am confident that any of the chapter or section discussions can stand alone as a useful commentary on the topic of interest. And I am also confident that they can each provide a helpful entry point for engaging your interest in the notion of congruence; and for encouraging you to consider its potential relevance within your private or public worlds.

A leadership pathway

If you have, or have had, a leadership or management role (including a guiding or consulting role), then you have probably experienced the impacts of organisational dysfunction. However it presents itself, organisational dysfunction is a symptom of incongruence, the existence of a destructive misalignment somewhere within the organisational community.

Such misalignment frequently presents at a relationship level, often as a serious disconnection or dysfunction within the organisation's managerial or operational teams. But the real cause of this misalignment usually reflects a deeper disconnection between some of the organisation's stakeholder communities and its explicit or implicit strategic agenda. That disconnection is frequently all too visible as an inequitable distribution of organisational wealth or the generation of outcomes that preference one stakeholder group (typically the ownership stakeholders), often at the expense of other stakeholder groups (such as staff, suppliers or customers).

If this situation sounds all too familiar and reflects an organisational or community state of affairs that you find disconcerting, then you will appreciate why this book was written. If you think that organisations and communities should strive to create equitable-shared value for all of their stakeholder communities, then you will understand what this book is about. And if you are open to thinking about how you could influence these disconnected organisations and communities to be more congruent and behave as a collective stakeholder community, then I recommend that you read Part One and Part Two in sequence.

Depending on your familiarity with the concepts and ideas presented, you may choose to scan-read some passages and focus on those discussions that have the most relevance for your particular organisation or community. However, I think it is important to have an understanding of the concept of organisational congruence, and an appreciation of the essential conditions and attitudes for its development, before thinking about how you might influence an organisation or community to become more congruent. So I suggest your scan-reading begins with Part One.

A community pathway

If you are involved with an organisation or community that you care about, but you are feeling increasingly disconnected or disengaged with where the organisation is heading or how it is operating, then Part Two will pose some questions that may help you to identify the cause of your concerns.

As you ponder each of the 21 questions, you will be thinking about each of the five factors that encourage and enable organisations (or communities) to achieve congruence with their stakeholders. You will be able to frame your concerns about the organisation in a way that will help you understand what needs to change for it to become more congruent, and to consider if and how that change may be possible. Inevitably, this pathway will lead you to confront the question 'Is this my community?', a question that is addressed in Part Three, and the answer to which may be found, in part, by thinking about your own congruence, which is also the focus of Part Three.

It is important to remember that the questions posed in Part Two are relevant for thinking about the congruence of any organisation or community, even a community of two. The questions provide a framework for thinking about your life partnership, your family community, your workplace community and the social communities you interact with. And, at any point you can choose to shift your focus from the organisational or community level to a more personal level by exploring the same questions in Part Three. Perhaps pondering the question of why the organisation exists (its purpose) will cause you to reflect on how that purpose relates to your own purpose and to consider the question 'why do I exist?'. Pondering the organisational question 'Do we care about our people?' could encourage you to reflect on the related personal question 'Do I love my people?'. In this way you could choose to read Part Two and Part Three in parallel, seeking to personalise your organisational thinking in a way that helps you to see the potential for leading a more congruent life with and within the communities and organisations your care about.

A personal pathway

If you are interested in thinking about your own life journey and how you could make it a more meaningful experience, then I suggest you go directly to **Part Three** and ponder the 21 questions that challenge you to live your life on purpose – to co-create an authentic presence with and within your communities that integrates and aligns who you are with what you do.

These questions will provide a framework for thinking about how you live your life. They will introduce you to the possibility of becoming a more congruent person by focusing your attention on five aspects of your life that influence your potential to be a joyful person. The questions are intended to make you stop and think about who you are, what you know to be true, who you really care about, and how your life can make a real difference.

These are questions that will challenge you to see your life differently; to see the potential for contributing to a different reality for yourself and others. If you are prepared to question the meaning of your life, to challenge the relevance of the communities and organisations you 'belong' to, to openly explore your real potential, and to risk letting go of the things that don't work in your life; then head for Part Three and get a feel for what thinking about congruence could mean for you.

As you join the conversation about individual congruence, you may find some of the concepts and terminology unfamiliar. In that case you could choose to refer to the Concepts and terminology section at the end of the book. Alternatively it could be a signal that you should return to Part One to read more about the four essential conditions for congruence – (individual) purpose, meaningful relationships, collaborative learning and enabling (self) leadership – and the two shared attitudes they embrace – welcoming difference and diversity and co-creating the future.

However and wherever you encounter the notion of congruence, once you have decided to explore what it could mean for you, I am confident you will recognise the potential for the pursuit of congruence to enhance both your personal and organisational worlds.

Part One — Thinking about Congruence

1 | Introduction

Congruent organisations enable new conversations that can change the way our world works.

Never doubt that a small, group of thoughtful, committed citizens can change the world. Indeed, it is the only thing that ever has.

Margaret Mead

The Congruence Framework – an overview

This book presents an idea, a conceptual framework with the potential to change the way organisations and communities think about their stakeholder communities. The Congruence Framework is an organising framework which is intended to influence how organisations interact with their stakeholder communities by influencing the design and implementation of their operating models. The application of this framework is intended to encourage the development of operating models that enable and promote organisational and community congruence, loosely defined as:

> *…the harmonious alignment between individuals and their organisations and communities.*

Although we begin with a focus on organisations and communities, the Congruence Framework can also be applied to enable **individual congruence**, loosely defined as:

> *…the harmonious alignment of people's inner and outer worlds, or the alignment of who they are with what they do.*

One could argue that building congruent organisations is a job for congruent individuals. However, while individual congruence would obviously be influential in promoting organisational (and community) congruence, it is not a prerequisite. Nevertheless, the relevance of individual congruence is admitted in the Congruence Framework, which as we will see, is derived from a 'typical personal operating model'. Clearly, personal and organisational congruence are interrelated and this is why this book includes a discussion on individual congruence in Part Three.

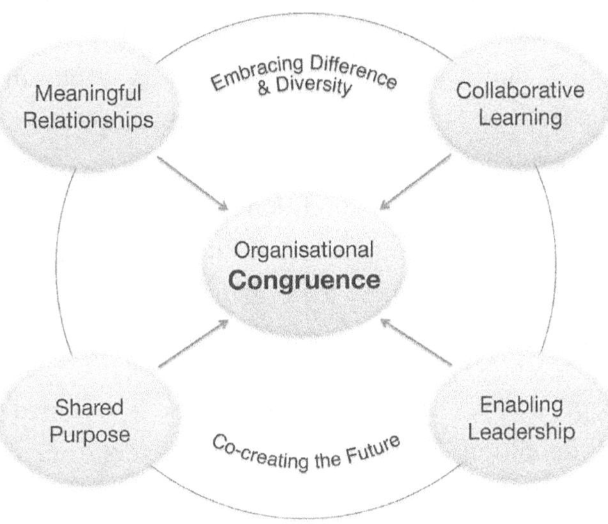

Figure 2: The conditions and attitudes for organisational congruence

Part One of the book discusses what we mean by organisational (and community) congruence, explores the relevance of personal operating models and introduces the Congruence Framework.

Organisational congruence is defined in terms of the four essential conditions (shared purpose, meaningful relationships, collaborative learning and enabling leadership) and the two attitudes (embracing difference and diversity and co-creating the future) that enable it. Each of these four essential conditions, and the two attitudes they embrace, is discussed in some detail to clarify their meaning and why they are important to achieve organisational congruence.

The ecology of personal operating models is introduced as a way of framing organisational operating models. The central idea is that organisational operating models that reflect the characteristics of personal operating models are more likely to enable the alignment and engagement of the organisational community. This discussion draws on traditional mind-body-spirit concepts and the extended family thinking of Indigenous communities to identify the five key factors of effective personal operating models (purpose, people, potential, participation and wellbeing). By integrating the four essential conditions for congruence with these five factors we provide a framework for thinking about congruent operating models. This is how the organising framework, which I have called the Congruence Framework, was conceived.

The concept of the Congruence Framework is outlined with a high-level definition of each of its five factors (purpose and leadership, potential and learning, people and community, participation and contribution, wellbeing and sustainability). For each factor there is a related set of questions designed to stimulate the conversations that will explore the opportunity to create organisational (community or personal) operating models that enable and encourage congruence.

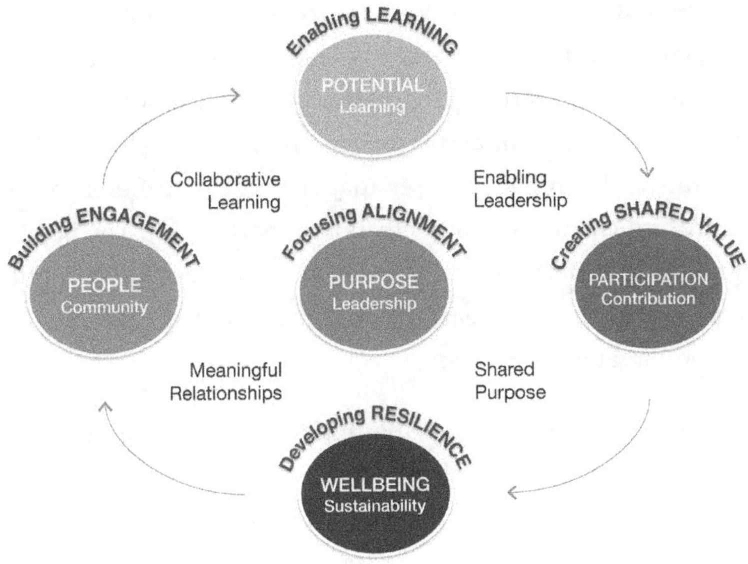

Figure 3: The Congruence Framework

Part Two explores the application of the Congruence Framework to organisations. The discussion responds to a series of 21 questions intended to clarify the meaning and potential application of each factor and to stimulate the thinking and the conversations that encourage the development of organisational congruence.

The **purpose** factor is presented as the lynch pin of the framework. It is fundamental to the definition and application of the other four factors. The existence of a purpose that is shared by the organisation and its stakeholder communities is a precondition for developing a congruent organisation. This shared purpose underpins each of the four essential conditions required for congruence, and is essential for the enabling leadership that is required to build a congruent organisation.

The **potential** factor deals with the collective capability of the organisational community and the requirement for innovation and collaborative learning to create and share knowledge and know-how. The potential of the community is released by a collaborative learning culture that embraces difference and diversity and change as value-creation opportunities. The positive integration of difference and the ability to successfully negotiate change is essential to create the harmony and accordance that congruent organisations enjoy.

The **people** factor focuses on the notion of an organisation as a community of purpose, a collective of its stakeholder communities bound together in the pursuit of a shared purpose. It emphasises the importance of establishing a sense of community to achieve organisational congruence. This sense of community is dependent on the existence of meaningful relationships across and within the total organisational community. Those relationships are created by successful conversations that engage around a shared purpose to create mutual value outcomes for the participants. The shared purpose (commonality) and the creation of mutual benefit or shared-value outcomes (mutuality) are the critical factors that underpin meaningful relationships, and the collaborative learning that develops those relationships.

The **participation** factor focuses on the organisation's contribution to its collective stakeholder communities, which is how the organisation creates value for those communities. Here again, the concepts of commonality and mutuality are important. Relevant contributions are those outcomes that manifest the shared purpose of the organisation and create mutual benefit for the organisation and all of its stakeholder communities.

Organisations that collaborate with their stakeholder communities to co-create their contributions can engage their collective creativity, generate efficiencies in the value creation processes, reduce the risk of failure and increase the collective value generated. The potential for effective co-creation of shared-value outcomes is increased where the organisation has a strong and pervasive presence within its stakeholder communities that is secured by meaningful relationships built on authenticity, trust and mutual benefit.

The **wellbeing** factor focuses on assuring the longer-term sustainability of the organisation and its stakeholder communities. This sustainability is linked to the wellbeing of the organisation and is therefore dependent on the longer-term social, cultural, economic and environmental (ecological) viability of both the organisation and its collective stakeholder community. Responsible organisations recognise this dependency as a necessary part of their commitment to co-creating the organisation's future with their stakeholder community. They engage the collective capabilities of their organisational community to build a resilient, fit-for-purpose and socially responsible organisation, which is sustained by creating outcomes that benefit the organisation and its collective stakeholder community.

Part Three explores the application of the Congruence Framework to individuals. The discussion responds to a series of 21 questions intended to clarify the meaning and potential application of each factor and to stimulate the thinking and the conversations that encourage the development of individual congruence.

Individual **purpose** is presented as the central concept, which embraces and underpins the other four factors, to create a framework within which our individual congruence is enabled and encouraged.

Our purpose expresses the truth of who we are, our deepest understanding of why we exist and our most treasured intentions for our life. It inspires our future ambitions, revealing glimpses of the outcomes that we will create by living our life on purpose. Our purpose also informs and energises the enabling self leadership (from spirit) that is focused on selfless service to others. This is an ethic and an attitude that facilitates our collaborative learning and creates the opportunity for the meaningful relationships that help to make congruence possible.

The **potential** factor is concerned with our capacity for learning, our ability to use our knowledge, intelligence and creativity to continually enhance our 'knowing', to understand who we are and how we can make a uniquely positive difference in the world. By developing a learning orientation that is purpose based, we will embrace difference and diversity and feedback as positive opportunities for learning. We will welcome change as an invitation to explore new pathways and have the courage to risk our future by being who we are in the now.

Our real potential as individuals is to live our life on purpose. We release this potential by using what we know, to make sense of our life; by using our creativity to see new ways of being present in our life; by reframing our life challenges as opportunities for learning and creating the outcomes that keep our life on purpose.

The **people** factor focuses on the importance of seeing our life within a community context and focusing our attention on those communities of people with whom we share a genuine common interest and ambition for the future. These communities of interest can assist our individual congruence by providing an environment where we can be ourselves, a space where our purpose can be productively shared with other like-minded individuals. Within these communities we can develop trust-based relationships, which are anchored by our shared purpose and sustained by the generation of mutual value. These meaningful relationships enable us to engage with our communities in collaborative learning and other co-creative endeavours that expand our fields of knowing, and generate outcomes that manifest our own purpose and also add value for our communities. These relationships also provide the opportunity to cultivate enabling (self) leadership, to co-create a community culture based on selfless service to other. They also provide an opportunity to express and experience the attentive care and support that encourages both individual and community congruence.

The **participation** factor addresses how we participate in our communities, or how we add value within our communities by being purposeful and ensuring that what we do is an authentic expression of who we are.

If we are living our life on purpose, our participation within our communities will be a manifestation of that purpose. And because of our common interest, the commonality and mutuality that underpins our community connections, our purposeful participation will also be in the best interests of our community. If we collaborate with our communities to co-create a future that manifests both our own purpose and the shared purpose of our communities, we are making a contribution that assists both our own congruence and the congruence of our communities.

The **wellbeing** factor recognises our need to be physically, socially, intellectually and spiritually sustainable.

Our sense of wellbeing is influenced by five interdependent settings:

- our clarity of purpose (spiritual wellbeing)
- the nature of our relationships (social wellbeing)
- our capacity for learning (intellectual and emotional wellbeing)
- the nature of our community engagement (occupational wellbeing)
- our physical and mental health condition (situational wellbeing)

These settings are aligned with the five factors in the Congruence Framework – being purposeful, building meaningful relationships, having a positive (collaborative) learning orientation, co-creating shared value, and developing and sustaining our wellbeing. Not surprisingly, our level of individual congruence is directly related to our sense of individual wellbeing. Therefore by focusing our attention on becoming more congruent, we are simultaneously focusing on the things that can improve our wellbeing.

Congruent organisations – why they matter

Put simply, we need to change the way our world works. We need to find new ways to create healthy, peaceful and sustainable communities. We need new ways to share wealth that eliminate poverty. We need new ways to relate to one another that resolve conflict, promote healing and avert wars. We need new ways of learning that embrace difference and diversity to moderate fundamentalism, and to eliminate racism and the abuse of privelege.

To find these new ways we need new conversations that can change how we think and act as individuals and collectively as members of the communities and organisations in which we participate.

Organisations provide the social context for many of our individual and community conversations. We cannot have new conversations about our local or global concerns which exclude organisations. Rather, we need our organisations to be active participants and to host many of the conversations we need to have. For that to happen we need organisations that genuinely care about all of their stakeholder communities. We need organisations that really value the potential of their communities to make a positive contribution to their sustainable future. These are the organisations that will welcome their stakeholder communities to participate in their conversations; set an agenda that admits their ideas and concerns; listen carefully to what they have to say; and facilitate outcomes that create mutual benefits for both the organisations and all of their stakeholder communities.

We need organisations that see their future as inextricably linked to the wellbeing of their total stakeholder community and understand that their longer-term sustainability is dependent on creating equitable-shared value for that community. These are the organisations that behave like communities of purpose, communities that are bound together by their commonality of interest and sustained by the creation of mutual benefit.

We *do not* need organisations that preference one group of stakeholders at the expense of others by limiting the opportunity for some stakeholders to influence the future development of the organisation.

These organisations are typically driven to serve at the pleasure of their ownership community and to maximise the net value created for that community, often by extracting that value from their other stakeholder communities.

We need organisations that value the active participation of their communities in co-creating a shared future. These are the organisations that engage their communities in conversations about their shared purpose and ambitions for the future. Conversations to explore the potential for co-creating the mutual benefits that will sustain the longer-term future of the organisation and its communities.

We *do not* need organisations that preference those stakeholder groups which they perceive to be most valuable in terms of their positional power and influence or as a source of economic value. These are organisations that typically prioritise the creation of their material capital at the expense of their social and environmental capital. The single bottom line (profit) remains the primary focus. There is no serious intention to pursue a triple bottom line (economic, social and environmental) strategy that could address the longer-term sustainability of the whole organisational community.

We need organisations that value the difference and diversity that exists within their stakeholder communities and welcome change as an opportunity for value creation. These organisations foster an organisational culture that enables and supports collaborative learning as a way to positively engage and integrate that difference for the benefit of all stakeholders.

We *do not* need organisations that cannot recognise the value-creation opportunities that difference, diversity and change can present.

Organisations that encourage, sometimes demand, conformity with the 'way things are done around here', discourage new ideas and suppress dissenting opinion. These are not the adaptive learning organisations that can successfully negotiate disruptive change and generate the innovative solutions that can assure their longer-term viability. These are almost certainly not the organisations that work collaboratively with all of their stakeholder communities to expand their capacity for learning and to co-create a more sustainable future. These are usually the 'my-way' organisations that see the future through a lens from the past and use old (tried and trusted) mental models to plan a certain future in uncertain times.

We need organisational leadership which is committed to building cohesion around a shared purpose; encourages community participation and collaboration; continually acknowledges the importance of community and individual contributions; and seeks to achieve success through others. This 'enabling leadership' understands the real potential for positive engagement of the organisational community. In sharp contrast to the fear based command and control leadership that persists in many organisations, enabling leadership is deeply rooted in concern for its communities. It values participative decision making and seeks to co-create shared-value outcomes for all of its stakeholder communities.

We *do not* need the organisational governance and management teams (or the search firms and recruitment companies who are complicit in their appointment) who do not see the wellbeing of all organisational stakeholders as part of their governance responsibility. We do not need risk-averse governance and management which encourage command and control autocracies that are focused on controlling the organisational agenda for the benefit of the ownership stakeholders.

We need courageous and inspirational governance and management to host new conversations that will enable organisations to operate as a truly collaborative community. A community secured by meaningful relationships that are anchored by a shared purpose and sustained by the co-creation of equitable shared-value outcomes that manifest that purpose. We need governance and management that can educate and motivate the organisation to care about the co-creation of a sustainable longer-term future for its total stakeholder community.

To build these congruent organisations we need to change the way that organisations think about their stakeholder communities. We need a new way to frame organisations as collective communities of their stakeholders. And we need to influence these organisational communities to behave in a more congruent way.

In summary, we need organisations that are grounded in a **purpose** that is shared with their stakeholder communities and have a commitment to co-creating their future with those communities. We need organisations to host the conversations that build **meaningful relationships** across and within their communities to enable **collaborative learning** and the positive integration of difference. We need organisations to foster an **enabling leadership** that encourages the positive engagement of the organisational community and the co-creation of valuable outcomes for all stakeholders. These are the **congruent organisations** that we need, to change the way our world works.

Organisation as a community

Before embarking on a discussion about congruent organisations, it is helpful to explore what we mean by the term organisation. Stephen P. Robbins defined an **organisation** as:

> *...a consciously coordinated social entity, with a relatively identifiable boundary, that functions on a relatively continuous basis to achieve a common goal or set of goals.*

This is a helpful definition which identifies and integrates five core attributes of an organisation:

- An organisation is a social entity – it is comprised of a group of people interacting socially (in relationship) with one another.

- An organisation is consciously coordinated – it has some form of deliberate governance, leadership and management structure and processes that coordinates its activities.

- An organisation exists to achieve a common goal or set of goals – the people who comprise the organisation are engaged in pursuing the achievement of a common objective or collective goal.

- An organisation has a relatively identifiable boundary – it is perceived as a distinct entity relative to other organisations and the society within which it operates. There are numerous organisational factors that may contribute to the definition of this boundary (e.g. the organisation's common goal, activities, market or geographic positioning, stakeholder identities etc.).

- An organisation is able to function relatively continuously – it can negotiate continual change in its stakeholders, objectives and operating environment to continue in operation for a significant period of time.

The time attribute is presumably to distinguish organisations from projects or alliances etc. which have many similar attributes to organisations (e.g. social entity, governance, objectives etc.) but usually only exist for a defined period. However we could argue that the lifespan of any organisation is related to the nature of its goals and is therefore not necessarily a defining attribute. As we will note in a later discussion, there is some evidence to suggest that only organisations with a clear and engaging purpose tend to be sustainable in the longer term (tend to function relatively continuously).

Kathleen MacQueen et al defined **community** as:

> *…a group of people with diverse characteristics who are linked by social ties, share common perspectives, attitudes or interests and engage in joint action in geographical locations or settings.*

MacQueen's evidence-based definition has five core elements:

- A community is a group (or a collection of diverse groups) of people who **share common interests** and perspectives.
- A community can be located and described; it has a **locus** denoting a sense of place, locale or boundaries.
- A community is variously involved in **joint action** which is a source of its coherence and identity. Its members are actively engaged in activities that relate to its common interest.
- A community is founded on **social ties**; it is sustained by the interpersonal relationships that exist between its participants. These relationships are underpinned by the community's common interest.
- A community has **diverse characteristics**, meaning it is socially complex. It can involve varying levels of participant engagement and interaction between participants;

accommodate a wide range of demographic and social
diversity; and include sub-groups or sub-communities with
overlapping interests and agendas that are more or less
aligned with the community's common interest. It is
important to recognise that it is the common interest that
provides the necessary focus to positively engage the
community's diversity.

The notion of a common interest is fundamental to this definition. It is the raison d'être for the existence of the community and it gives meaning to the other four elements. The definitional elements of locus, joint action and social ties all need the common interest element to make sense of their relevance to a particular community. The community may be a collective of multiple interconnected communities each with differing community interests, but there needs to be a central common interest to engage the whole community. The relationships that create a sense of community are based in the common interest and the activities of the community will be relevant to that common interest.

It is relevant to note that the geographical locations or settings may be helpful in locating communities that are physically based in a place (e.g. country, city, home, workplace etc.). However, it may not be geographical factors that define the boundaries of the community. For many communities it is their common interests, joint actions or stakeholders, or a combination of these elements, and not their location, that distinguish them from other communities and the larger society (or societies) within which they exist.

Organisations and communities are both social entities with the essential difference being the nature of the common bond that unites them. For the community that bond is their engagement with a common interest, which may or may not be a common goal. For the organisation it is more than just a common interest, it tends to be the achievement of a shared goal.

Both organisations and communities have boundaries variously defined by their focus, positioning, stakeholders and activities, and both will have some form of leadership and management frameworks that govern their activities. Both rely on effective interpersonal relationships that are grounded in a common interest or goal to sustain the active engagement of their people. And both pursue activities that are relevant to the activation of their common interest or the achievement of their common goal.

Thus, an organisation is essentially a community where the common interest is their pursuit of a common goal or set of goals. This may seem a rather trivial assertion but emphasising the community nature of an organisation challenges the current modus operandi of many organisations and underlines the importance of the notion or sense of community as a fundamental building block for achieving organisational congruence.

The people who share a common interest in an organisation are typically referred to as their stakeholders, although some people would argue that interest-holders are different from stakeholders. For the purpose of this discussion we will rely on the Oxford dictionary definition of a stakeholder as *'a person with an interest or concern in something, especially (but not only) a business'*. These stakeholders are usually grouped into clusters of people where their particular common interests are shared (e.g. customers, partners, shareholders, staff etc.). Each of these groups can be distinguished in their own right as communities of interest (they each have their own common interest) and we will refer to them as **stakeholder communities**.

An **organisation** can therefore be defined as a community of stakeholders actively engaged in the coordinated pursuit of a common goal, and is perceived as distinct in some respect from other organisations and the society within which it operates.

This view of organisations as communities of interest is fundamental to the discussion about congruence because it defines the constituency of the organisational community. The definitional focus on a common goal, which we will later redefine as a shared purpose, extends the boundaries of the organisation's stakeholder community to include both internal communities (owners, governance, staff etc.) and external communities (customers, suppliers, business partners etc.) in a single community of purpose.

The notion of an organisation as a collective of stakeholder communities is not a new idea. It has been the subject of much discussion since R. Edward Freedman argued strongly for a stakeholder-biased approach to management in his 1984 book *Strategic Management: A Stakeholder Approach.*

Rajendra Sisodia et al, in their 2003 book *Firms of Endearment*, argue the benefits of a stakeholder (relationship) management model (SRM), which is predicated on treating an organisation's stakeholders as:

> *...part of a complex network of interests that function in a matrix of interdependencies...[where]...no stakeholder group is more important than any other...[and where]...each stakeholder tends to thrive best when all stakeholders thrive.*

Their SRM model expects organisations to:

> *...bring the interests of all stakeholder groups into strategic alignment...[to achieve]...**concinnity**...[where]...the objectives of each stakeholder can be met simultaneously and are in fact strengthened by other stakeholders.*

They argue that organisations that achieve this 'concinnity' can create significant long-term value for all of their stakeholders, including the society within which they operate. They present evidence to suggest that concinnous organisations significantly outperform competitor organisations in terms of their financial performance. But it is not clear how the 'significant long-term value' that these organisations generate represents equitable-shared value for their stakeholder community.

Concinnity, which means 'skillful blending of the parts achieving an elegant harmony', has an interesting resemblance to the notion of congruence, which we have loosely defined as 'accordance or harmonious alignment'.

Commonalities between Sisodia's concinnity and congruence include: the need for a shared understanding and commitment to an organisation's 'vision for its future'; the requirement for leadership from service; the importance of being a learning organisation; and the strong emphasis on the cultural factors that enable and sustain stakeholder relationships.

However, concinnity is not the same as congruence. The key differences can be summarised as follows:

- **Shared purpose**, which defines why an organisation exists, is the lynchpin factor that underpins and enables congruence. Although purpose is frequently referenced in the Sisodia study, it seems to reflect a mix of the often-confused concepts of vision, mission and values. Neither the Sisodia concept of vision (defined as 'where we are going and how we are going to get there') nor values (defined as 'who we are and what makes us tick') answer the central purpose question of why we exist as an organisation.

- **Shared leadership**, which embraces the servant leadership principle of selfless service to others, is an essential condition for congruence. The prevalent leadership model of concinnous organisations is also claimed to be servant (and emotional) leadership inspired. But frequent reference to the leader's personal role (and responsibility) in influencing the strategic alignment of the organisation's stakeholders suggests a leader-follower model of leadership is typically in play.

- **Collaborative learning** enables congruent organisations to positively integrate difference and diversity. The only mention of diversity in the Sisodia book (2010 edition) is in reference to an IKEA family value, which I find very interesting for a study that is concerned with the alignment of diverse stakeholder communities. While Sisodia portrays concinnous organisations as **learning organisations**, it is not clear whether they make any substantial investment in organisational learning as distinct from their investment in skills and competency training.

- **Equitable-shared value** is an outcome that congruent organisations are committed to co-create for all of their stakeholders. As I noted above, it is not clear from the Sisodia study how the significant long-term value that concinnous organisations generate, represents equitable-shared value for their stakeholder community. However, I suggest that, because Sisodia's 'Firms of Endearment' share a capitalist business model, they are more likely to prioritise the economic dimension of stakeholder value. In contrast, congruent organisations embraces a concept of shared value that is meaningful (relevant and valuable) from each stakeholder's perspective, irrespective of the business (or operating) model adopted by the organisation.

While it is important to understand the differences between concinnity and congruence, it is also important to appreciate that the commonalities closely align Sisodia's Firms of Endearment with our notion of a congruent organisation. It is also important to recognise that the outcomes of the Sisodia study confirm the potential for creating significant long-term [stakeholder] value by treating an organisation as a collective stakeholder community.

Acknowledgements

I am indebted to Stephen Robbins[1] and Kathleen McQueen[2] et al for their assistance in defining organisations and communities, and to Rajendra Sisodia et al[3] for their thinking about stakeholder management models.

2 | Congruent Organisations and Communities

Most people want to work with people they like and respect, in organisations with a purpose they care about, and within a culture that enables and acknowledges their personal contribution.

Those organisations who will succeed are those that evoke our greatest human capacities – our need to be in good relationships, and our desire to contribute to something beyond ourselves.

Margaret Wheatley

The meaning of organisational congruence

It is important to state from the outset that being congruent does not mean being the same. The dictionary defines congruence as being harmonious, congruous or in agreement. Congruence is therefore about alignment, but not about homogeneity. It is about celebrating diversity not assimilating diversity; about the positive reconciliation of difference, not the elimination of difference. Congruent organisations welcome difference and diversity as positive opportunities for learning. They have the capacity to engage with their diversity and integrate the difference they encounter in a way that maintains their harmonious alignment.

Organisational congruence is not a perfect or static state. It is a vibrant state of 'being'.

Congruent organisations will experience flows of congruence, periods where they are more or less harmonious and in agreement. Like any other organisation, they will experience unforeseen challenges and periods of disruptive change. It is the response to these challenges that distinguishes the congruent organisation. They have a culture that embraces change in a way that maintains the energy and commitment of their stakeholder communities. The forward momentum of the organisation is maintained and its stakeholder communities remain positively engaged. In this chapter, we will explore some of the factors that enable and encourage such organisational congruence.

Studies in interactional psychology recognise the importance of congruence as a factor that influences the way people behave in organisations. Many of these studies have focused on individual-organisational congruence, which is typically defined as the degree of fit between particular characteristics of the individual and the organisation. The fit analyses are generally based on common or shared characteristics such as values and attitudes; culture, norms and organisation climate; learning styles; goals; and personality-based characteristics.

Much of the individual-organisational congruence research has focused on what is termed 'supplementary congruence'. This is where the influence of organisational characteristics, usually by means of a shared culture (and in most cases shared values), on the individual's behaviour can create increased organisational alignment and commitment. Less seems to be known about 'complementary congruence' where the individual and the organisation both contribute to the fit equation by influencing each other's behaviours to create a positive (usually needs-based) alignment.

I have not conducted a detailed review of the individual-organisational congruence literature, but I believe the following general statements to be consistent with the general research outcomes:

- High levels of individual-organisational congruence:
- usually reflect high levels of individual commitment to the organisation, and
- tend to result in positive outcomes for both employers (productivity, morale etc.) and employees (work satisfaction, low stress etc.)
- Where congruence reflects culture and value alignment we also find higher levels of employee and job satisfaction.
- Where the congruence reflects goal alignment, we also find increased interpersonal congruence (alignment) within the organisation.

It seems sensible to conclude that organisational congruence occurs when there is a positive or harmonious alignment between the goals, culture and values of an organisation and the individuals who comprise its collective stakeholder community. But to understand the factors or conditions that create or encourage the opportunity for this alignment to occur, we need a definition of organisational congruence that identifies (and integrates) its essential components.

Congruence and shared purpose

The existence of a truly **shared purpose** is fundamental for the development of organisational congruence. It provides the source of identity and coherence for building organisational community, and the directional clarity required to enable the positive integration of ongoing organisational change.

Strategy or goal alignment and culture or values alignment between an organisation and the people who comprise its stakeholder communities are clearly conditions that would contribute to individual-organisational congruence. To achieve this alignment, people need to be clear about, and committed to, where the organisation is heading and understand and identify with the organisation's internal culture. They need to believe in what the organisation stands for, share its ambitions for the future and subscribe to its operating principles or values.

An organisation's strategic goals (including its primary goal or vision) and the strategies to achieve those goals indicate the longer-term intentions of the organisation. These goals signal the ambitions of the organisation, but not necessarily what it stands for – why it exists and the principles by which it operates. It is the core purpose (the raison d'être) of the organisation and not the strategic goals or vision that provides the longer-term directional clarity for the organisation and its stakeholder communities. The organisational goals, strategies and values may change over time as the organisation adjusts to shifts in its operating context. But the core purpose of the organisation is a sustaining influence that shapes the organisational culture, guides long-term strategy and enables the integration of ongoing change.

Where individual-organisational 'goal congruence' reflects an alignment with the core purpose of an organisation, rather than with its goals, and that alignment is pervasive throughout the organisation's stakeholder communities, then we have a community with a shared purpose. It is the existence of this shared purpose that creates the potential and the opportunity for organisational congruence.

A shared purpose focuses the organisation's collective agenda. It enables a shared vision (or ambition) for the future and establishes the reference point for the values and operating principles, the operating culture that will frame the organisation's 'modus operandi'. A shared purpose provides the opportunity for building community. It becomes the common interest which enables the interpersonal relationships (the social ties) that develop and sustain the sense of community critical for organisational congruence. A shared purpose also provides the directional clarity to navigate change in a way that maintains the organisation's harmonious alignment. Ongoing changes in organisational context, direction, strategies and form can all be clarified and resolved through a shared purpose.

To continue this discussion: *refer to* **Chapter 3**.

Congruence and meaningful relationships

Meaningful relationships enable the interpersonal congruence that is essential for the development of organisational congruence. These trust-based relationships value honesty and respect difference, encourage cooperation and facilitate collaborative endeavour, and seek mutual benefit from pursuing a shared purpose.

It seems reasonable to assume that interpersonal congruence (the harmonious alignment of individuals) is an important influencing factor in achieving the accordance and harmony that must be evident in congruent organisations. For example, we could expect that high levels of interpersonal congruence would improve social integration within an organisation; be influential in moderating difference and diversity; and create a positive environment for organisational co-operation and collaborative endeavour.

There are many factors that can influence interpersonal congruence such as demographics, personal operating style, organisational status and work profile etc. But the way these factors present as facets of the relationship between two individuals is significantly influenced by the nature of their relationship. For interpersonal relationships to be positive and productive, what I will term **meaningful**, they first of all need to be based on a shared purpose or common intention. It is the existence of this shared purpose that provides the real potential for the relationships to have meaning for its participants. And where that shared purpose is aligned with the core purpose of an organisation, the relationship has the potential to also be meaningful in an organisational sense.

For an interpersonal relationship to be meaningful, it is not enough for the parties to simply have a shared purpose. To be positively productive as a joint or collective endeavour, they need to generate outcomes that are consistent with their shared purpose and which represent value for all participants (where value in this context is as defined by each participant). The relationship must therefore be concerned with the co-creation of mutual benefit and not focused on advantaging only some participants.

A meaningful relationship is essentially a 'win-win' relationship which is sustained by generating mutual benefit outcomes that manifest its shared purpose. For these relationships to be sustainable they must be able to respond to change and deal with difference and diversity in a way that preserves the harmonious alignment of the parties. They need to be collaborative relationships that enable the participants to work together, to identify and explore issues and challenges, and implement solutions that are in the best interest of the whole community.

Effective collaboration not only relies on the existence of a shared purpose. It also requires the participants being open and honest in their dealings with each other and having respect for each other's personal independence and diversity. For relationships to be truly collaborative there must be a deep sense of mutual trust and respect.

Where interpersonal relationships are secured and energised by a shared purpose, focused on the co-creation of mutual value, and enabled by a climate of trust and respect, they have the potential to develop and sustain interpersonal congruence. Where those relationships exist within an organisation, and the common intention on which they are founded is aligned with the organisation's purpose, they provide an agency for the development of organisational congruence.

To continue this discussion: *refer to* **Chapter 4**.

Congruence and collaborative learning

Collaborative learning provides a framework to engage the collective organisational community in the co-creation of its future. It enables organisations to embrace difference and diversity as non-threatening learning opportunities, and to engage the collective intelligence and creativity of stakeholder communities to navigate change. Collaborative learning promotes organisational congruence by enabling the development of positive and productive (meaningful) relationships within and across stakeholder communities.

Dealing with ongoing change is a constant reality for most organisations. An organisation's ability to respond appropriately to significant change in its operating environment, and/or substantial changes in the agendas of its stakeholder communities, will determine its longer-term viability. As the rate of technological, regulatory, socio-economic and environmental change continues to increase, it becomes increasingly important for organisations to make a rapid and incisive response to the impacts of that change. Their change response must be properly informed to address the needs and expectations of their stakeholders, and effectively executed in a timely manner to derive the change benefits. This means they must have the capacity to engage productively with their stakeholder communities to inform, plan and implement their change agenda. They must also know that the changes they intend to make will be in the collective best interests of those communities.

Generally speaking, organisations that successfully negotiate change do so because they have a positive attitude to change. They view the complexity and ambiguity that exists within their operating environments, and the difference and diversity within stakeholder communities, as opportunities for learning. They are proactive learning organisations that endeavour to anticipate and learn from shifts in their operating environment and changes in their stakeholder appetites and priorities. They do not view change as an imposition, or as an involuntary (often latent) reaction to environmental pressures. These organisations have chosen to create their own future.

Organisational congruence is dependent on maintaining a harmonious alignment within and across the organisation's stakeholder communities.

Organisational change can disturb and disrupt that alignment by stressing and severing the relationships that bind those communities. By engaging communities in creating and implementing the change agenda, we can moderate the negative impacts of organisational change.

The positive and collaborative engagement of the communities in identifying, assessing and implementing organisational change initiatives increases the likelihood that the change outcomes will meet their needs and expectations.

Creating and maintaining organisational congruence also depends on being able to positively engage the difference and diversity that exists within and across the organisation's stakeholder communities. For that to happen we need an organisational culture that embraces difference as a learning opportunity. We need a collaborative culture that encourages these communities to embrace their difference and diversity for the benefit of the collective organisational community. We need a culture that enables and supports collaborative learning, a process through which diverse individuals or communities, with a common interest or objective, can interact productively to construct and apply their knowledge and create valuable outcomes for each other.

Organisations that use collaborative learning to engage their stakeholder communities in creating and implementing their response to change, can positively engage the difference and diversity within those communities, and optimise the potential for organisational congruence.

To continue this discussion: *refer to* **Chapter 5**.

Congruence and enabling leadership

Congruent organisations require an **enabling leadership** that champions the organisation's shared purpose and ambitions for the future; facilitates the conversations and interactions that enable meaningful relationships; pursues collaboration as an essential engagement and learning discipline; and openly welcomes difference and diversity as opportunities for learning. This is selfless leadership which is focused on serving the organisational community in a way that creates equitable-shared value for all stakeholders.

Thus far I have proposed that shared purpose, meaningful relationships and collaborative learning are essential conditions for the development of congruent organisations. Now I want to suggest that none of these conditions can exist or flourish without an organisational leadership ethos that enables them.

We need a culture of leadership that believes in the centrality of a shared purpose as the unifying source of energy and direction for an organisation. We need leadership which will enable the organisation to discover and pursue a shared purpose that engages and aligns all of its stakeholder community, and to focus on co-creating outcomes that manifest that purpose and generate equitable-shared value for the membership of that community. For that to happen we need leadership that exemplifies the organisation's shared purpose, has the best interest of the total organisational community at heart, and is a pervasive influence for harmonious alignment within the organisational community. We need enabling leadership.

We need leadership which encourages the development of meaningful relationships across and within the organisational community.

These are the trust-based relationships that underpin interpersonal congruence and are essential for the development of organisational congruence. These relationships are encouraged by a leadership culture which focuses organisational interaction on collective common interest and mutual benefit; a selfless leadership which achieves harmonious alignment by focusing on the needs of others. We need enabling leadership.

We need leadership that is collaborative, which welcomes difference and diversity and engages the whole organisational community to co-create a sustainable future. This leadership fosters organisational congruence by continually acknowledging the potential of its total stakeholder community to create its own future. It fosters collaborative learning as a way of engaging the collective knowledge, intelligence and diversity of the organisational community to integrate difference and navigate change. We need a co-operative and collaborative leadership style that encourages people to work productively together to co-create outcomes that provide equitable-shared value for the whole organisational community. We need enabling leadership.

To continue this discussion: *refer to* **Chapter 6**.

The nature of congruent organisations

I have now identified four essential conditions for the development of organisational congruence. Organisations that have the potential to be congruent, to develop and sustain a harmonious alignment across and within their stakeholder communities, will be able to demonstrate that:

- They know who they are; they know why they exist; they have a **shared purpose** with their stakeholder communities.

- They operate as a community; they develop and sustain **meaningful relationships** that enable their stakeholder communities to collaborate for mutual benefit.

- They are a learning organisation; they embrace **collaborative learning** to engage and integrate the difference and diversity within their stakeholder communities and to successfully navigate organisational change.

- They enjoy **enabling leadership**, a pervasive leadership culture which exemplifies the organisation's shared purpose; promotes an ethic of selfless service to others; and enables the meaningful relationships and collaborative learning that encourages organisational congruence.

These four conditions embrace two powerful shared attitudes which are also important for developing and sustaining organisational congruence.

Organisations that pursue the above conditions have the confidence and the capacity to **embrace the difference and diversity** that exists within their stakeholder communities. The organisation's shared purpose provides a unifying rationale for the integration of organisational difference and a positive focus for the engagement of the diversity within its stakeholder communities.

And a culture of collaborative learning, which frames difference and diversity as positive opportunities for learning, increases the potential for harmonious alignment within the organisational community. Within this culture of collaboration, organisational difference and diversity is welcomed as a vital source of new thinking and new ideas.

Organisations which engage their collective stakeholder community in collaborative endeavour to pursue their shared purpose are essentially **co-creating their future**. They do not see their future as a predetermined vision or strategic goal. Their shared intention is to co-create outcomes that manifest their purpose and create equitable-shared value for their collective stakeholder community. By choosing to co-create their future, they can manifest their purpose in a way that respects the changing needs and expectations of their collective stakeholder community. They can maintain their congruence, the harmonious alignment of the organisational community.

The following definition integrates the four essential conditions of a congruent organisation and the two shared attitudes they embrace.

A **congruent organisation** (or community) is an accordant group of individuals who embrace a shared purpose. They enjoy enabling leadership, which promotes selfless service to others; encourage the development of meaningful relationships that create community; and foster collaborative learning to embrace their difference and diversity. They seek to co-create a future which manifests their shared purpose and creates equitable-shared value for all their stakeholders.

The notion of 'embracing difference and diversity to co-create the future' is possibly a distinctive feature of congruent organisations. It presents a sharp contrast to the behaviour of many incongruent organisations (and communities) where the future is determined by and for the primary benefit of only some stakeholders and difference and diversity often presents as an irritating problem.

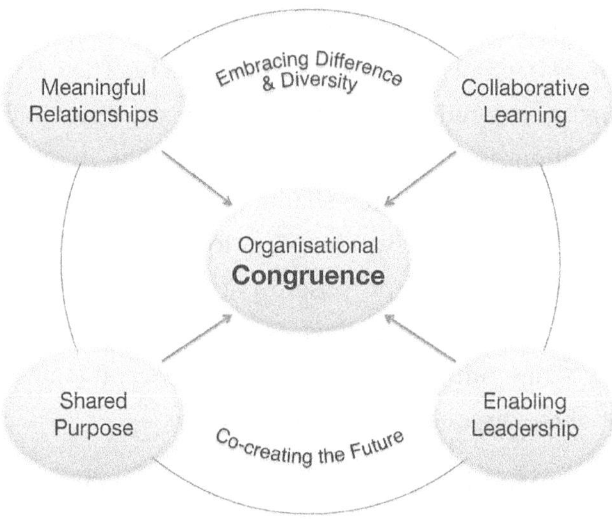

Figure 4: The conditions and attitudes for organisational congruence

Building congruent organisations

To build congruent organisations, we need to find ways to influence the way organisations think about who they are and what they do. We need them to host the conversations that will encourage their stakeholder communities to explore the potential for organisational congruence; to initiate an ongoing community dialogue about the four essential conditions for developing organisational congruence.

We need new conversations about **purpose and ambition** and what we mean by success. We need our organisations (and communities) to discover and understand their shared purpose and to see their future success as the manifestation of that purpose. They need to appreciate that their potential contribution to their stakeholder communities is the co-creation of outcomes that manifest their shared purpose and create equitable-shared value for all of their stakeholders.

We need new conversations about how organisations can **collaborate and participate** with their stakeholder communities, how they can engage with these communities to co-create relevant and valuable contributions.

We need new conversations that influence thinking about how to acknowledge, value and positively engage the **difference and diversity** within these communities. Conversations about how **collaborative learning** can positively engage the collective capability of the organisation's stakeholder communities to integrate difference and navigate change.

But first we need new conversations about **leadership**. The leadership focus needs to shift from problems to possibilities, from command and control to collaboration and creativity, and from self interest to selfless service. We need enabling, authentic and purposeful leadership to host the conversations that will discover a shared purpose, and develop and sustain the trust-based relationships that underpin interpersonal congruence and enable collaborative endeavour.

These four conversations will create fresh opportunities for the social interaction that can build **meaningful relationships**, the social ties that create a sense of 'community' and which are essential for enabling and sustaining organisational congruence.

To be successful, these conversations need to occur in a context that enables and encourages the effective participation of the whole organisational community.

The agenda should connect the community with its shared purpose and foster an open dialogue about organisational potential and future possibilities, and the co-creation of mutual benefit for all participants.

We need new ways of thinking about organisations to frame the conversations. We need a new organising framework that will encourage organisations to have these conversations and think differently about how they design and implement their organisational operating models. Hopefully, the Congruence Framework outlined in this book is such a framework.

Focal points

- An organisation is a community of stakeholders actively engaged in the coordinated pursuit of a common goal and is perceived as distinct in some respect from other organisations and the society within which it operates.

- Organisational congruence occurs when there is a positive or harmonious alignment between the goals, culture and values of an organisation and the individuals who comprise its collective stakeholder community.

- The existence of a truly shared purpose is fundamental for the development of organisational congruence. It provides the source of identity and coherence for building organisational community; and the directional clarity required to enable the positive integration of ongoing organisational change.

- Meaningful relationships enable the interpersonal congruence that is essential for the development of organisational congruence. These trust-based relationships value honesty and respect difference; encourage cooperation and facilitate collaborative endeavour; and seek mutual benefit from pursuing a shared purpose.

- Collaborative learning provides a framework to engage the collective organisational community in the co-creation of its future. It enables organisations to embrace difference and diversity as non-threatening learning opportunities, and to engage the collective intelligence and creativity of stakeholder communities to navigate change. Collaborative learning promotes organisational congruence by enabling the development of positive and productive (meaningful) relationships within and across stakeholder communities.

- A congruent organisation (or community) is an accordant group of individuals who embrace a shared purpose. They enjoy enabling leadership, which promotes selfless service to others; encourage the development of meaningful relationships that create community; and foster collaborative learning to embrace their difference and diversity. They seek to co-create a future which manifests their shared purpose and creates equitable-shared value for all their stakeholders.

- To build congruent organisations we need new conversations that will engage the organisational community in an ongoing dialogue about the four essential conditions and the two shared attitudes for developing and sustaining organisational (and community) congruence:
  - essential conditions:
    - shared purpose
    - meaningful relationships
    - collaborative learning
    - enabling leadership
  - shared attitudes:
    - embracing difference and diversity
    - co-creating the (organisational) future

I am indebted to Amie Southcombe[4] for her summary research analysis about individual-organisational congruence; to Lloyd C. Williams[5] and Mark Esposito[6] for their writings about organisational congruence; to Marvin L. Bouillon et al[7] for their insights about goal congruence; to Jeffery T. Polzer et al[8] for their discussions about interpersonal congruence and to John P. Kotter[9] for his timeless contributions to leading successful change.

3 | Shared Purpose and Ambition

Organisations that pursue a shared purpose can engage the energy, wisdom and commitment of their communities to co-create their future.

Many men go fishing their entire lives without knowing it is not fish they are after.

Henry David Thoreau

Redefining purpose

Purpose – not strategy – is the reason the organisation exists

Christopher Bartlett and Sumantra Goshall

Core purpose is the organisation's reason for being. ... it captures the soul of the organisation.

Jim Collins and Jerry Porras

Although organisational purpose is a term that has been widely referenced in management literature over the last 30 years, it is difficult to find a generally accepted definition that is helpful in explaining its meaning. Purpose is generally defined as the raison d'être, the long-term rationale for the existence of an organisation. But what does that mean? The following discussion will attempt to derive a useful definition of organisational purpose by identifying its essential characteristics.

Purpose is about contribution. For an organisation that knows and understands the reason for its existence (its purpose), I suggest its overarching common goal will be to make that existence meaningful for its stakeholder community. Meaningful in this context means both relevant and valuable. The 'coordinated pursuit' of the organisation's common goal will therefore be the engagement of its community of stakeholders to make its existence (its presence) relevant and valuable to that community. Or, in other words, to engage its organisational community in the manifestation of its purpose in a way that creates or expresses value that is relevant to that community.

Organisational purpose is therefore a statement about the potential value of the organisation as perceived by each and all of its stakeholder communities. It is a statement that describes the organisation's potential to make a valuable contribution that is shared amongst its collective stakeholder community. A contribution that is relevant to each stakeholder community because they define what shared value means within the context of their individual communities. And so relevant must also mean equitable. The valuable and relevant contribution of the organisation is also an equitable contribution to its collective stakeholder community. Each stakeholder community receives a fair share of the value created or expressed by the organisation.

Making organisational contributions that manifest the true purpose of an organisation means creating value for the organisation's total internal and external stakeholder community. The owners, investors, staff, customers, suppliers and business partners etc. all need to identify the equitable value created or expressed for their communities. And because most organisations operate in a public domain, the community at large will also have a general stakeholder interest in their 'responsible citizenry', the (equitable) contribution they make as a participant in the wider public community. Therefore, the purpose of the organisation must also engage the wider public interest – its contributions must include a societal focus.

Purpose is beyond profit. Many business organisations still have the maximisation of profit (the creation of material wealth), as distinct from the maximisation of stakeholder value, as their overarching primary goal. The need for sustainable business organisations (and not-for profit organisations) to make a profit or an operating surplus is not disputed. Profit (or surplus) is required, for example, to fund operational growth, secure intellectual or capital investment and to service risk and/or investment capital. Profit for business organisations can also be an effective measure and motivator of organisational performance. Profit is recognised as a means to an end but it is not accepted as the end game.

Profit itself cannot engage all of the organisation's key stakeholders. It is unlikely to be the primary reason that customers or clients choose to deal with an organisation. Most organisations would not offer their profitability as their customer value proposition. Nor is profit likely to be the primary reason that staff will choose to identify with an organisation. In an increasingly competitive and knowledge-based economy, customer and staff satisfaction and loyalty are fundamental to achieving competitive advantage. The customer's perception of value may well include the viability or sustainability of the organisation, but profit or wealth maximisation for its owner stakeholders is unlikely to be the primary driver for their participation. Product or service attributes, including social attributes (e.g. association, identification etc.) and pricing, are more likely to feature in the customer value proposition.

Similarly the knowledge workers that organisations need are unlikely to be engaged by a purpose concerned with shareholder wealth maximisation. Increasingly they seek meaning from their work which can only be provided by organisations with a purpose that includes caring about them and what they value. An organisational purpose, which seeks to make a contribution that its employees value, is critical to achieving the loyalty and commitment that will enable superior longer-term organisational performance.

As Bartlett and Ghoshal observed in their 1994 article *Beyond Strategy to Purpose:*

> *Purpose is the embodiment of an organisation's recognition that its relationships with its diverse stakeholders are interdependent. In short purpose is the statement of a company's moral response to its broadly defined responsibilities, not an amoral plan for exploiting commercial opportunity... If corporate ambition begins to focus on the company's narrow self interest it eventually loses the excitement, commitment and support (of its stakeholders) that emerges when objectives are linked to broader human aspirations.*

Profit may be a necessary outcome of pursuing a purpose, but purpose is beyond profit.

Purpose lives in the present; it is not a future state. Purpose is not the organisation's aspirational vision or mission statement. Nor is it the organisation's statement of intent (which is often a synthesis of both vision and mission). A typical organisational vision defines a desired future state of the organisation and its mission is usually about how it will achieve that vision. Organisational visions of the future, however defined, are in essence longer-term strategic goals or objectives.

Unlike purpose, these goals change over time as stakeholder influences and operating environments fluctuate and change organisational priorities.

Purpose is the long-term unifying and sustaining force that informs strategy and enables change. It is not the result of strategy or change. Purpose is a constant and vibrant force and is always relevant in the present. Purpose is not about what the organisation wants to become. It is a statement about what the organisation is, what it stands for and what it believes in. Purpose-driven organisations make contributions to their stakeholder communities that are always relevant in the present.

Purpose is enabling and inspiring, it is not a constraint. Purpose is not a destination. It enables a journey, guiding and influencing outcomes that are consistent with its core proposition. Purpose informs strategy and guides decision making, but its influence is not constraining or limiting. Rather, purpose enlightens organisational strategy by creating a context within which new ideas and insights are welcome as the organisation seeks to respond to change in a way that keeps it 'on purpose'.

Purpose can be a powerful influence in creating an organisation's presence, shaping its brand values, enabling its distinctive achievements and inspiring good citizenship. An organisation's brand, reputation and performance over time may well reflect its purpose, but they do not define or limit that purpose.

Purpose may champion ethical and principled organisational behaviours, but it is not a set of ethics or principles. Purpose can influence the organisational culture and values, but it does not impose a set of organisational behaviours.

It influences the development of the organisational culture; it is not influenced by that culture. Purpose captures the hearts and minds of the organisation's people. It is a proposition that connects with their personal values, the deeply held beliefs that give meaning to their lives. It is an aspirational statement which they recognise as an expression of their own ambitions for the future.

By embracing an organisational purpose, people feel like they are part of something bigger than themselves, something they really care about, something they believe can make a positive difference in the world. Purpose engages and energises the organisational community by presenting the opportunity for them to collaborate with others to co-create a future that they feel deeply passionate about. An opportunity to be who they are within a community with a purpose they really care about. Purpose enables and inspires.

Purpose is not easily chosen, it is usually discovered with difficulty. It is not a simple choice between rational alternatives. For example, purpose is not easily defined by strategic analysis. It is not a strategic response to stakeholder pressures or environmental challenges. It is not about selecting the best market opportunity or deciding to prefer the creation of shareholder wealth. Purpose is not simply choosing to maximise customer value or to create the best company to work for. These may all be valid strategic options but purpose is not a strategic option. Purpose may inform, mould and sustain these strategic choices but it will not be one of them.

There are a number of characteristics that help to describe the essential nature of purpose:

- purpose expresses the **raison d'être** of an organisation
- purpose is concerned with **equitable contribution**
- purpose has a **societal focus**
- purpose lives in the **present**
- purpose is beyond profit
- purpose informs strategy and sustains change
- purpose is enabling and inspiring
- purpose is energising and engaging
- purpose is **discovered** not crafted

The following definition integrates these characteristics to create a useful definition of organisational purpose.

Organisational purpose is the reason the organisation exists. It articulates the organisation's primary value proposition (it's 'why'), its equitable contribution to its collective stakeholder community. Organisational purpose is beyond profit and expresses a raison d'être that inspires all of the organisational community to engage in manifesting its true presence. It sustains the organisation by shaping its strategic agenda and guiding its purposeful response to change.

This definition includes the wider community within its 'collective stakeholder community' and therefore a 'societal focus' is assumed. The reference to 'beyond profit' is a deliberate challenge to those who would prioritise the maximisation of profit and shareholder wealth as the purpose of business organisations. These people may care to note the following evidence that suggests where organisations focus on a purpose that is beyond profit, they often enjoy superior financial performance.

Christine Arena's 2007 research about corporate responsibility identified that 'high-purpose' companies (companies dedicated to achieving societal outcomes) create profitable outcomes for shareholders while at the same time making significant contributions to their other stakeholder groups. These companies are committed to the pursuit of value propositions which recognise and respect the interdependence of the organisation (business), the physical environment and society at large. In essence, they pursue a purpose that is shared with many of their stakeholder communities.

Porras and Collins, 1994 *'Good to Great'* analysis of over 60 large US companies observed that those with strong underlying values, and purposes that went beyond making profits, had significantly out-performed their peers (in terms of stock market value) over a long period of time. And Richard Ellsworth's 2002 review of 23 companies with clear purpose statements showed that those with a focus on providing value for customers performed better (in terms of stock market value) than those with a focus on maximising shareholder wealth.

In 2010 Rajendra Sisodia et al published the results of their study of 28 companies called *Firms of Endearment*. The financial performance of these companies, which were selected on the basis that they endeavour to make relevant and valuable contributions to all of their stakeholder communities, adds further evidence to our beyond-profit argument. All of these companies outperformed the S&P 500 by significant margins over 10, 5 and 3-year horizons. Interestingly, these companies also outperformed the Porras and Collins group by up to three times over the 10 year horizon.

The discovery of organisational purpose is concerned with finding an answer to a tough set of questions.

- Why do we exist?
- What would be lost if we ceased to exist?
- What do we contribute to the world?
- How do we add value for all of our stakeholder communities?
- Why should people believe in us?
- What is it about our organisation that engages and motivates our stakeholders?

Posing these questions is the responsibility of the organisational governance team, but unfolding the answers is the collaborative responsibility of the whole organisational community.

Unlocking the real potential of an organisation begins with expressing its core value, its raison d'être, its true purpose. Discovering that purpose requires a conversation which engages the collective knowledge, wisdom and humanity of the organisational community. It may be a challenging conversation, but it is the most important conversation the organisation will ever host.

Shared purpose

A study by Joel Kurtzman of organisations that have survived for over 100 years found that their long-term viability related to their ability to continually align individual, mutual and organisational interests.

> *To greater or lesser degrees...they (all) had a sense of common purpose. ...They had cultures that made people feel part of something bigger, which made the people who worked there feel*

special...they shared their wealth in ways that were deemed fair within their industry sectors.

In contrast, those organisations that failed to survive the test of time lacked a common (or shared) purpose, common vision or common goals. He found that the failed organisations did not suffer from having inferior technologies or methodologies. Nor did they have inferior products. They failed to positively engage their stakeholders in a shared strategy for the future.

Most organisations have multiple stakeholder communities. Identifying a shared purpose that has the potential to express the value of an organisation to a diverse group of internal, external and public stakeholders is a real challenge. Each of these stakeholder communities is likely to have differing perspectives of what constitutes value for their own stakeholders. But, in order for an organisation to have a shared purpose, there needs to be a single-value proposition that engages all of its stakeholder communities.

Some people seem to think that navigating the potential conflicts between competing stakeholder interests (e.g. ownership, employee, customer, and supplier interests) can be achieved by prioritising the interest of particular stakeholder groups. For example, some proponents of customer-focused strategies suggest that prioritising the customer community will create the greatest long-term value for all stakeholders. Others still insist that maximising shareholder or owner wealth is in the longer-term best interests of both the organisational and public communities. In my view these are risky assumptions, especially where stakeholder value is usually measured in terms of economic benefit.

Organisational strategies that preference particular stakeholder communities will almost certainly lead to inequitable value sharing that marginalises some stakeholder groups in favour of others.

Failure to deliver equitable value for all stakeholder groups will create unproductive, and potentially destructive, tensions within the organisational community. To engage the full collective potential of their stakeholder communities, organisations need to discover and pursue a shared purpose that balances the equitable interests of all their stakeholder communities.

A shared purpose is discovered by engaging the whole organisational community in conversations to find a common rationale for their participation in the organisation; conversations to reveal and understand the basis for their common sense of belonging. This deep connection with the 'hearts and minds' of the organisational community cannot be discovered by a board or executive leadership team alone. They cannot presume to 'know' the 'common sense' of their organisational community without listening to its voice.

Organisations that are serious about discovering their shared purpose will make a significant investment in hosting community conversations, which engage the collective knowledge, intelligence and wisdom of their stakeholders, to answer the question – why do we exist (as an organisation)?. They recognise that these conversations are an essential part of the most important collaborative learning journey they will ever undertake. For, without an answer to this question, they have no real understanding of who they are, or the potential for their presence in the world.

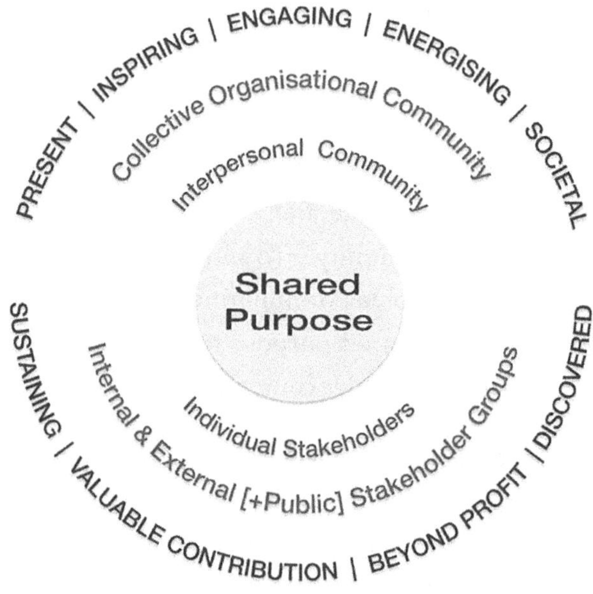

Figure 5: Shared purpose

Purpose with ambition

The manifestation of a shared purpose is evident in an organisation's contributions to its stakeholder communities over time. The pursuit of this purpose is unlikely to be a linear process; most organisations are constantly navigating change resulting from environmental and stakeholder pressures. Keeping the organisation's stakeholder community 'on purpose' requires a flexible planning model that can adapt the organisational strategy to accommodate changes in its operating environment and stakeholder agendas. The organisation needs to be able to refocus its goals and refresh its strategies to ensure that its contributions remain relevant and valuable manifestations of its shared purpose.

Purpose expresses the core value of an organisation, and its strategic plan or blueprint shows how it intends to share that value with its stakeholder communities over time. That plan, which is anchored and shaped by the organisation's shared purpose, will typically focus an organisation on a vision for the future. That vision, which is intended to represent the best view of what a successful manifestation of its shared purpose would be like in the medium term (say 5-10 years), can also be described as the organisation's **ambition** for its future.

Concepts of strategic intent or organisational vision are often used as medium-term summary goals for organisations. Ambition is a subtly different concept and has been deliberately chosen to differentiate the purpose-ambition model. Vision (or strategic intent)-based models tend to rely on a compelling statement about the future state of an organisation to 'pull' the organisation's communities forward to achieve that state. In a sense, the vision or intent is the end goal, at least until it changes (as it often does). These models encourage organisational cohesion around a future that has not yet been experienced. In contrast, purpose-based models encourage cohesion around the 'presence' of a shared purpose that already exists, and allows the future to unfold as an ongoing manifestation of that purpose.

For the purpose-ambition model, the organisation is 'driven' (inspired, engaged and energised) by a higher shared purpose which provides a constant and consistent source of cohesive guidance for the organisation. Ambition is not the end goal, but a glimpse of the organisation's shared purpose in action, a 'bright light' that illuminates the future potential of a journey in pursuit of its shared purpose.

An organisation's ambition must be a realistic expression of its future potential, which has meaning for all of its stakeholder communities, and is clearly derived from (and a constant reminder of) its shared purpose. And it must be measurable in terms of the equitable value created for each stakeholder community. Organisational ambition provides a focus for the strategic plan or blueprint that describes the strategic goals and pathways that map the organisation's journey in pursuit of its purpose.

An organisation's ambition may change over time as its direction and focus is adjusted to respond to changes in its operating environment and/or stakeholder agendas. However, it is important to recognise that these shifts do not reflect a change in its core purpose. They simply signal a change in the way that purpose needs to be manifested in order to maintain the value (and relevance) of the organisation's contribution to its stakeholder communities. That is why purpose-driven organisations are confident in their ability to navigate change. Shifts in their focus and direction do not undermine the organisational cohesion that is secured by the constancy of their shared purpose.

Purpose and values

The core values of an organisation can be defined as a set of guiding principles, which reflect deeply held beliefs of the organisational community.

They are usually described as the preferred modes of interpersonal behaviour that will enable the organisation to achieve its objectives. These principles are typically referenced within the organisational community by brief descriptors (called value statements) that summarise these preferred behaviours and/or organisational practices that embody them. According to this definition, the guiding principles of a purpose-driven organisation are the set of preferred organisational behaviours and practices that enable it to achieve its primary objective, the manifestation of its shared purpose.

If we understand shared purpose to be the fundamental guiding principle of an organisation and its core values to be a set of guiding principles that enable the manifestation of that purpose, then we must also accept that organisational values are not a constant. They are purposefully crafted by the organisation and can be re-crafted to emphasise new behaviours and/or practices that are required to support changes in the way the organisation needs to operate and interact with its organisational community.

Establishing the guiding principles of a shared-purpose organisation is not the preserve of the organisational governance group. These principles should be crafted in collaborative conversation with the whole organisational community. By inviting the organisational community to participate in these conversations, we are:

- acknowledging that their collective knowledge and wisdom is required to determine the preferred behaviours and practices that will be relevant to the whole community
- creating a shared ownership and therefore responsibility to observe the guiding principles that have been co-created by that community

- increasing the organisational community's understanding of
  the meaning of these principles and why they are necessary,
  which increases the likelihood that they will become part of
  the organisational culture

Values are often linked with purpose (and/or vision and mission) as a key influence in the formation of organisational culture, which we will later define as:

The complex set of explicit and implicit practices and behaviours that affect the way the organisation operates and interacts with its stakeholder communities.

Obviously, an organisation that wishes to pursue a shared purpose needs a culture which enables the manifestation of that purpose. The culture needs to embrace a set of guiding principles that encourages organisational practices and behaviours that enable the organisation to collaborate with its stakeholder communities to realise their ambition for the future.

It helps to embed the organisation's guiding principles as part of the operating culture if they are expressed in the vernacular of the organisation. If the descriptors that trigger the recognition of the guiding principles are expressed in a language that is commonly used throughout the organisational community, then two things are likely to happen. Firstly, people will more easily remember the principles and what they mean. And secondly, they will feel more able to reference these principles as part of their everyday interaction with their colleagues.

Where an organisation's guiding principles are crafted in collaboration with the organisational community, are clearly relevant to the manifestation of its shared purpose, and are expressed in language that reflects the organisation's common vernacular, then it is more likely that those principles will become an integral part of the organisational culture.

Focal points

- The essential nature of organisational (or community) purpose:
    - o expresses the **raison d'être** of an organisation
    - o is concerned with equitable contribution
    - o has a societal focus
    - o lives in the **present**
    - o is beyond profit
    - o informs strategy and sustains change
    - o is enabling and inspiring
    - o is energising and engaging
    - o is **discovered** not crafted
- Organisational purpose is the reason the organisation exists (it's 'why'). It articulates the organisation's primary-value proposition, its equitable contribution to its collective stakeholder community. Organisational purpose is beyond profit and expresses a raison d'être that inspires the organisational community to engage in manifesting its true presence. It sustains the organisation by shaping its strategic agenda and guiding its purposeful response to change.
- Purpose will be truly shared by the collective organisational community when it represents the potential for the co-creation and sharing of equitable value that is relevant to each and all of its stakeholder communities.
- An organisation's ambition for the future is a glimpse of its manifest purpose. It reveals and illuminates the future

potential of a pursuing a shared purpose to all of its stakeholder communities.

- The guiding principles (core values) of an organisation with a shared purpose are the shared behaviours and practices that will enable and encourage the manifestation of that purpose. They should be crafted in conversation with the organisational community and expressed in their common vernacular.

- A truly shared purpose is the essential requirement for achieving organisational congruence. It underpins and enables the organisational leadership, meaningful relationships and collaborative learning that are necessary to create and sustain harmonious alignment within an organisational community.

Acknowledgements

I am indebted to Nikos Mourkogiannis[10], Richard R. Ellsworth[11] and Christopher Bartlett and Sumantra Ghoshal[12] for their writings about corporate purpose; to Jerry Porras and Jim Collins[13], and Joel Kurtzman[14] for their writings and research about shared purpose and performance; and to Christine Arena[15] for her writing about corporate responsibility (and corporate health).

4 | Meaningful Relationships

Successful conversations enable meaningful relationships that increase productive engagement between individuals and their communities and organisations.

In organisations, real power and energy is generated through relationships. The patterns of relationships and the capacities to form them are more important than tasks, functions, roles, and positions.

Margaret Wheatley

Relationships as learning opportunities

We travel through life as unique individuals moving in and out of relationships with other people. Some of these relationships we choose to participate in and others require our participation because of our circumstances. By way of example, we may choose our life partner but we do not choose their parents, siblings or their friends that we find ourselves in relationship with. We may also choose some of the organisations that we interact with (our workplace, our educational, social and cultural institutions) and the relationships they bring. But our circumstances can also dictate our job choice, place us within a particular community, or require that we use the services of an organisation and hence place us in relationships that we have not chosen. Similarly, the communities we live in or interact with will involve us in a mix of chosen and imposed relationships.

Our relationships change continually during our lifetime as we interact with other people (individuals, organisations and communities) to negotiate the challenges and opportunities that shape our personal lives. The challenge is to view all of our relationships as learning opportunities, no matter when and where they occur or whether they are chosen or imposed. While we are more likely to engage within our chosen relationships, we should not ignore the learning opportunities within our imposed relationships. In some cases it is the imposed relationships that will present the greatest learning opportunities, challenging us to learn what we need to learn rather than what we choose or want to learn. The imposition of relationships that present us with adversity or engage us with diversity and difference can stimulate the reflective learning that can change our thinking, our actions and our future.

Even relationships that, due to their very nature and/or the circumstances that created them, we would characterise as oppressive or destructive, have the potential to provide learning. Even though they may profoundly alter our lives in ways that we would not have chosen, we can choose to extract productive personal meaning from these relationships. The words of Friedrich Nietzsche, *'If you gaze for long into an abyss, the abyss gazes also into you'* and *'That which does not kill us makes us stronger'*, remind us that even the most difficult, empty or one-sided relationships have the potential for reflective learning.

Meaningful relationships

A relationship is loosely defined as a particular type of connection existing between two or more people. Where that connection has a particular significance (meaning) for all of the relationship parties, a shared connection with an important or useful quality or purpose, then the relationship has the potential to be meaningful.

Relationships that are 'full of meaning' are enabled and sustained by a strong commitment to a mutual interest. That interest could be a shared problem or concern, a commitment to a common goal, objective or journey, or a shared understanding, appreciation or passion for an aspect of work, life or play etc. The meaningfulness of the relationship will depend fundamentally on the strength of the shared attachment to this mutual interest. But it will also be influenced by the attitudes and behaviours that characterise the conduct of the relationship parties.

There are four conditions of engagement which can influence the conduct of the relationship and enhance its potential to become more meaningful for the relationship parties:

- **Trust:** creating an atmosphere of trust and goodwill; building a relationship that is based on mutual respect, honesty and integrity; creating a mutual sense of responsibility and accountability; establishing reliability and dependability as relationship norms.

- **Acknowledgement:** creating an environment which acknowledges the potential and contributions of others; demonstrating a genuine interest and concern for the views and concerns of other people; building relationships based on empathy and goodwill.

- **Collaboration:** fostering interdependence and co-creativity; valuing the individuality (independence, difference and diversity) of other people; creating relationships that value collaborative learning and expect to co-create win-win outcomes.

- **Communication:** enabling open communication through conversations that are welcoming and inclusive; empathetic conversations that listen to create mutual understanding about matters of interest or concern; learning conversations that

encourage enquiry and feedback, and endeavour to create
mutually beneficial outcomes for the participants.

In a sense, all of these conditions of engagement are about
acknowledgment. An environment that is trusting, empathetic
and collaborative will be acknowledging for its inhabitants.
Communication that is welcoming, fosters understanding, and is
concerned with achieving mutual benefit is likewise
acknowledging for its participants.

Meaningful relationships continually acknowledge the value of
their participants. They find their meaning in a strong mutual
interest or shared purpose. These relationships are nurtured
within an atmosphere of mutual trust and goodwill. They
welcome conversations that embrace difference and diversity,
promote understanding, and encourage learning and collaborative
engagement to co-create outcomes that generate equitable value
for all participants.

Conversation creates the potential for relationships and the means
by which relationships can be developed and sustained.
Conversations that focus on a common interest (such as a shared
purpose) and mutual benefit create the potential for meaningful
relationships. And meaningful relationships create the
opportunity for a strong sense of community and the harmonious
alignment of a group of individuals that a congruent community
enjoys. An organisation that embraces a shared purpose has the
potential to develop the meaningful relationships that will
strengthen its sense of community and increase the opportunity
for organisational congruence. Thus the conversations that
stimulate the growth of meaningful relationships are also the
conversations that we need to develop and sustain organisational
or community congruence.

Given the apparent lack of congruent organisations and communities that exist in the world, it seems reasonable to assume that organisations and communities are not good at hosting (initiating and facilitating) these conversations. If they do, they are obviously not good at creating the environments that enable these conversations to be successful, authentic and create mutual value for all the participants.

If we are to develop more congruent organisations and communities, we need to understand what makes conversations work and how they can facilitate the productive dialogue that enables congruence.

The nature of conversation

Conversation, which is defined as the informal interchange through spoken words of thoughts, information, sentiments, ideas etc., is more than what is said between two or more people. The conversational meaning that is expressed by the words and language used can be significantly influenced by the environment (the space) within which the interchange occurs and the nature of the relationships that exist between the participants. The nature of the conversation space is not only influenced by its physical characteristics, but also by the positional and emotional presence of the participants.

Positional presence references factors such as participant power and authority, cultural beliefs and attitudes, knowledge, experience etc., all or any of which can operate to enhance or constrain the conversation opportunity.

Emotional presence can also have a negative or positive impact on the conversation by affecting the ambience and aesthetic of the conversation space and/or contaminating or illuminating the words and language chosen to communicate meaning.

The factors that facilitate meaningful relationships – trust, acknowledgement, collaboration and communication – are also important for the development of productive conversations. While these factors are clearly inter-dependent, it is the level of trust that exists between the conversational participants that is the critical determinant of the positional and emotional nature of the conversation space.

The level of trust that exists within a conversational space will directly influence the authenticity of the conversations, and therefore the behaviours that take place within that space. Trust-based relationships are enabled and sustained by authentic conversations. Trust between the participants is progressively developed and validated through authentic conversational actions – behaviours, actions and outcomes that constantly demonstrate a consistent alignment between the participant's expectations and experiences. Conversations where the language and behaviours (what they see and hear) are consistent with the outcomes they experience (what they actually get in practice).

Authentic conversations occur when the participants are all able to be who they really are and say what they really think about a topic they care about.

For conversations to create real value or elicit real meaning for the participants, or in other words to be successful, they need to be authentic. These conversations can only occur in a safe place – a trusted conversational environment where the concern for the collective wellbeing of the participants overrides the pursuit of self interest; where there is a common commitment to truth and transparency, and a common interest or shared purpose; and where collaboration and co-creation are the overarching and genuine aim of the participants.

Unfortunately, too many of our conversations are not authentic. They may involve a matter of deep mutual interest or concern, but they do not progress to a level where that interest or concern can be converted to a positive outcome. These are the conversations that fail to progress beyond an opening cursory discussion, or get stuck in positional or ideological debate before they can unfold into a meaningful exploration of the topic. They are often blocked by defensive and offensive behaviours, used to mask participant doubts and insecurities; or by the prior experiences or 'positioning' of participants which can 'infect' the conversational space. These conversations are disabled by a lack of trust within the conversational space.

In these situations, the conversations will tend to be contained (for safety reasons) within the participant's personal spaces. The participants will not have the confidence to let the conversation expand into a more collaborative space where they can share their true thoughts and feelings. Meaningful relationships are trust-based relationships that provide a context for conversations to transcend personal (selfish) space and enjoy a communal (collective) space where the conversational focus can move from self interest to mutual interest.

Otto Scharmer, in his book *Theory U*, suggests that there are four different fields of conversation that describe the typical patterns of participant interaction:

- **downloading** – talking nice, speaking from 'what they want to hear'
- **debate** – talking tough, speaking from 'what I think'

- **dialogue** – reflective enquiry, speaking from 'seeing myself as part of the whole'
- **presencing** – essential emergence, speaking from 'what is moving through'

These four levels or phases of conversation can also characterise the different levels of relationship and engagement between participants as the conversation moves from the field of downloading, or what I call **creating context**, through to the more complex and challenging field of presencing, or what I call **co-creating community**.

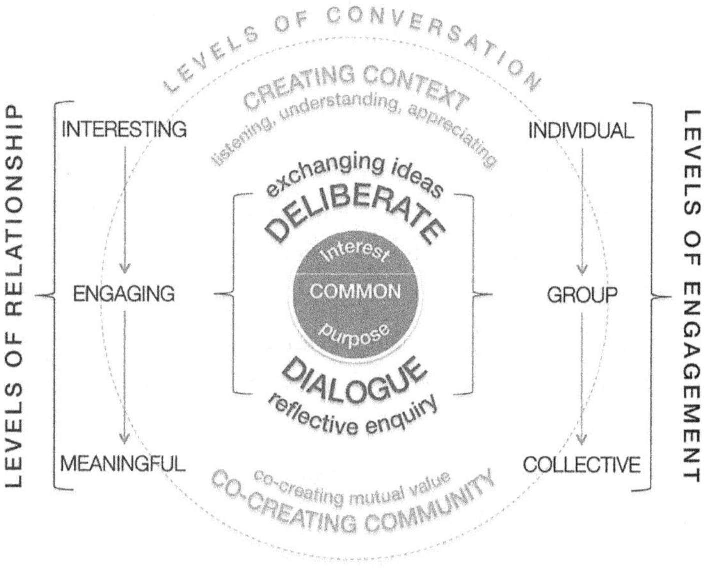

Figure 6: Levels of conversation

The above diagram shows three levels of engagement as the conversations move progressively from a more selfish focus on the personal (individual) to include selective engagement with the views of others (group) and finally to a level of engagement which includes the total conversational community (collective). The engagement focus shifts from the interest of the individual to the interest of the group and finally to that of the community.

Similarly, the level of relationship moves from being aware of and interested in others (interesting) to enabling and encouraging others to participate (engaging) and finally to collaboration with the total community to co-create mutual value (meaningful) outcomes. The raison d'être for the relationship changes from self interest to selfless interest as it moves from a focus on individual benefit to a focus on mutual benefit.

At the **interesting-individual** level the conversation is about creating context and becoming familiar with the topic (the mutual interest or shared purpose) and the participants by listening to, understanding and appreciating the different conversational perspectives.

At the **engaging-group** level we engage in deliberation and dialogue as the more vigorous exchange of ideas softens to a more reflective enquiry mode – the shift from 'talking tough' to 'speaking together' that signals we are strengthening the level of engagement, and preferring dialogue as the relevant conversational mode. And the conversation shifts its focus to topics and themes clearly derivative of the common interest or shared purpose.

At the **meaningful-collective** level we are in Scharmer's presencing space, where the conversation is all about co-creating coherent outcomes. The dialogue shifts from reflective to generative and the relationships become more meaningful as there is a wider collective engagement of the conversational community with the co-creation of mutual value – in essence the collective manifestation of the shared community interest or purpose.

The levels of conversation diagram suggests that the four phases of conversation may occur sequentially. However, they represent a set of dynamic conversational layers that are most often continually in play as participants traverse and explore the mutual interest or shared purpose that holds the conversation together. All four conversational phases (context, deliberation, dialogue and community) are important for the development of meaningful relationships. However it is only when the conversational focus shifts from creating context through deliberation to dialogue that participants move into a space where they can access the real potential of their relationship.

It is through reflective dialogue (reflective enquiry) that people are able to engage in the generative dialogue (co-creating mutual value) which explores and develops the mutual-value outcomes that give their relationships real meaning. Where that dialogue is focused on a common or collective interest or purpose, it is building a community around that interest or purpose. Hence, we refer to the achievement of this level of collective engagement and meaningful relationships as co-creating community.

Getting into dialogue

William Isaacs, in his book on *Dialogue,* defines dialogue as:

> *...a conversation with a centre not sides. It is a way of taking the energy of our differences and channeling it towards something that has not been created before...it is a conversation in which people think together in relationship.*

Creating the opportunity for dialogue, for thinking together to produce coherent outcomes, requires paying attention not only to the physical, positional and emotional elements of the space within which the conversations will take place, but also to the conduct of the participants.

Isaacs argues that the following participant behaviours foster a form of dialogue that has the potential to generate coherent outcomes:

- **Listening**: the capacity to listen 'carefully' to ourselves and others; to create an inner silence that expands our capacity to listen – to hear what is said and not said; and through listening to connect with and admit the wider horizons and perspectives of the world in which we live.

- **Respecting**: the capacity to observe and see others, and their opinions and beliefs, as legitimate in their own right; to honour the boundaries that establish and protect that legitimacy; to be able to see the potential in others and be always open to their unique voice; to generally appreciate and acknowledge the importance of each individual in a global community.

- **Suspending**: the capacity to suspend our opinion and assumptions – to stop, step back and see things with new eyes; to acknowledge our thoughts and feelings without being compelled to act on them; to loosen our grip on our own convictions and acknowledge the potential for uncertainty and ignorance; and to expect conversation to inform us and influence our thinking.

- **Voicing**: the capacity to understand the need to be still and allow your inner thoughts and feelings to unfold their meaning; to say what you actually think rather than what you think you should say; to access and trust what you 'know' to be true and make your authentic voice heard; and to be patient, remain quiet and resist the urge to speak when your voice is not required.

These conversational behaviour sets can also be aligned with our levels of conversation to provide a relatively consistent dialogical track, to guide conversations towards dialogue – to shift the conversation focus from creating context through to co-creating community:

- **Listening** is about **creating context** – continually contextualising the conversation by remaining open and attentive to the emergent views and opinions of ourselves and others.

- **Respecting** is about enabling the authentic and free **exchange of ideas** – including, recognising and respecting the potential and contribution of all participants.

- **Suspending** is how we enable **reflective enquiry** – stepping back, suspending judgement and action, and allowing time to see new possibilities and alternatives.

- **Voicing** is how we presence our thinking – how we voice our thoughts and opinions in a way that contributes to the **co-creation of cohesive outcomes**.

It is interesting to observe that these behaviour sets are also aligned with the conditions of engagement for the development of meaningful relationships. The trust, acknowledgement, collaboration and communication factors which enable meaningful relationships are clearly 'in synch' with the listening, respecting, suspending and voicing behaviours that encourage dialogue. Thus, it is no real surprise that conversations which move into dialogue are more likely to create the conditions for the development of meaningful relationships.

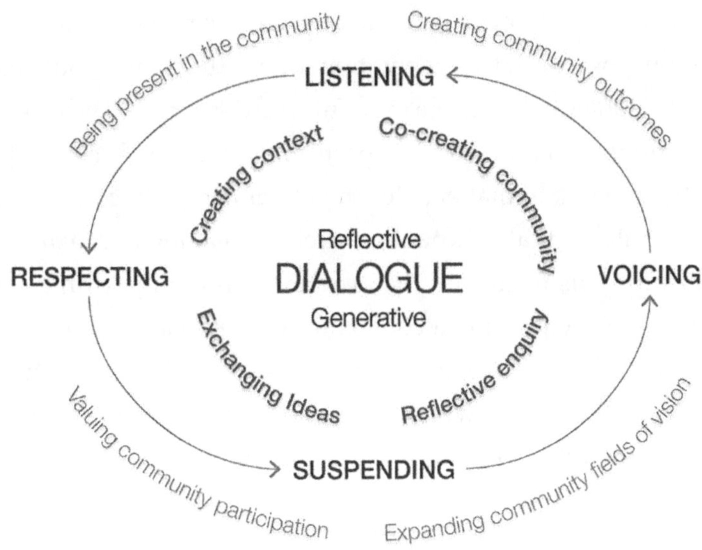

Figure 7: Towards dialogue

Creating a positive opportunity for organisational dialogue is concerned with providing an appropriate physical and cultural context for community conversations to take place. It is about encouraging the behaviours that will move those conversations into dialogue and providing the conversational leadership which will ensure that the transition to dialogue actually happens.

Enabling leadership creates the positive organisational climate or 'safe place' for such conversations to occur. It also supports the participative and collaborative behaviours that are consistent with the conversational behaviours that enable the transition to positive community dialogue. And enabling leadership has the necessary focus on cohesion around a shared purpose to guide reflective and generative dialogue towards co-creating relevant and valuable outcomes for all stakeholders.

Enabling successful conversations

Conversations that focus participants on a common interest or shared purpose and the generation of mutual value outcomes create the potential for meaningful relationships. These same conversations create the opportunity for (reflective and generative) dialogue that enables the relationships to co-create the mutual value that expands their meaning. Meaningful relationships also create the context and opportunity for community. They provide a context for dialogue about the shared purpose on which the relationship is based, and the opportunity to generate outcomes which manifest that purpose; cohesive outcomes that build a strong sense of community.

Such conversations enable congruence. We will call them successful because they enable relationships, communities and organisations to be successful.

They engage individuals (in relationships), communities and organisational communities in positive dialogue about the co-creation of their future, generating outcomes that manifest their shared purpose.

Successful conversations occur when two or more people (or communities) enter into dialogue about a common interest or shared purpose and co-create outcomes that manifest that interest or purpose and create equitable value for all participants. Successful conversations are also authentic conversations in which participants are all able to be who they really are and say what they really think about a topic they care about.

Value in this context can take many forms and is particular to the individual, group and/or the collective participants' perspectives of the conversation and their perception of the value created.

The value created may be the opportunity to contribute, the acknowledgment of listening, the sense of belonging, the learning that occurs, or the understandings, actions and agreements that result from the conversation. What constitutes equitable or fair value is also judged from the perspective of the participants.

Enabling successful conversations is about creating the opportunity and the space for them to take place, encouraging their authenticity and fostering the conversational behaviours that promote dialogue and the generation of outcomes that hold mutual value for all of the participants.

Creating the **space** for successful conversations means creating an organisational context that lets people show up as who they are, to say what they want to say, about something they really care about. Establishing this context means paying careful attention to the following settings:

- **Environmental** settings: Establishing a physical environment that is enabling. Providing an appropriate physical or virtual space with a relevant range of interaction and communication options, and the people, information and systems support that enables people to interact in a way that best suits 'who they are'. The interaction options should enable participants to engage remotely to address space or time constraints, and/or to participate from a personal space where they feel more comfortable.

- **Cultural** settings: Ensuring that the organisation has the enabling leadership and collaborative culture to create a conversational space which encourages positive interactional behaviours. These are behaviours that create the opportunity for positive dialogue and moderate the emotional and positional behaviours that can disrupt and block the

opportunity for successful conversations. These behaviours
may be encouraged by appropriate procedural and
participation settings, but they will not prevail without the
pervasive influence of a truly collaborative organisational
culture.

- **Procedural** settings: Understanding who needs to be part of
the conversation; issuing a welcoming invitation that allows
invitees the freedom to accept or decline or choose another
way of participating; and an agenda which frames the
conversation topic as a possibility rather than a problem, and
makes it clear what is expected of the participants.

- **Engagement** settings: Providing effective conversational
leadership, preferably a guiding coalition of participants, that
has the capacity to host the conversation; encouraging
authentic participation and positive collaboration;
accommodating difference and dissent by maintaining a focus
on possibilities; moderate negative emotional and positional
participant behaviour; and facilitate the generation of
equitable shared-value outcomes.

The engagement settings also need to enable the conversation
to be continued and expanded by providing **open feedback
loops** which facilitate the ongoing reflective enquiry and
related discussions that will quality-assure the outcome. These
feedback loops extend the invitation to participate by
communicating the conversation and its outcomes to people
who may not be directly engaged. And they can accommodate
different styles of participation, for example the introvert
thinkers who may be less communicative in a direct face-to-
face setting, but have a valuable contribution to make.

- **Focus** settings: Positioning the conversation within the wider
context of the organisation to clearly establish its relevance

and potential for meaning; and connecting the topic with the shared purpose of the organisation to increase the potential for a unifying, engaging and hopefully inspiring conversation.

Creating the **opportunities** for successful conversations is the role of organisational (or community) leadership, not governance or management. This means the whole organisational community has a shared responsibility to host the successful conversations which move the community into dialogue that results in the co-creation of mutual-value outcomes.

Organisational meetings, workshops, forums and discussions need to become successful conversations. Organisational communications including emails, phone calls and correspondence, should also be framed within the context of a successful conversation.

Successful conversations need to become part of the organisational culture, 'the way we do things around here'. The organisation's interactions with its external stakeholder groups, its customers, suppliers and business partners etc., should also be framed in a similar context. The interactions should have a focus on the shared purpose and the generation of equitable-shared value. They should occur in a space which encourages authentic and collaborative behaviours, welcomes and acknowledges the input of all stakeholders, and encourages people to be open to new ideas and the possibility of different futures.

If the interactions of an organisational community are continually framed by a culture of enabling leadership and collaboration, and focused on the manifestation of a shared purpose, they will stimulate the community dialogue that enables and sustains meaningful relationships and encourages organisational congruence.

Building organisational engagement

Communities and organisations are not discrete entities. An organisation can be a community (and vice versa) and it can consist of multiple communities (internal stakeholder groups) who may also share different common interests. An organisation's external stakeholder groups (customers, suppliers etc.) are also separate communities with a common interest and the total (internal and external) stakeholder group for any organisation is yet another single community of interest. Thus, an organisation operates with and within many different communities of interest, each with their own diverse stakeholder relationships.

An organisation is essentially a construct which connects individuals through and with their communities of interest to pursue and manifest a shared purpose. These stakeholder communities are comprised of people connected by relationships which have their basis in common characteristics, interests or attitudes. It is these shared and potentially meaningful relationships within and across all of these communities that present the wider opportunity for an organisation to engage its full potential and achieve its ambition for the future.

Increasing organisational engagement is therefore concerned with strengthening the relationships that connect an organisation with and within its stakeholder communities. It is concerned with hosting the successful conversations that build and strengthen the networks of meaningful relationships which operate across and within those communities. It is through these meaningful relationships that the organisation can engage its stakeholder communities to create outcomes that manifest their shared purpose and thus sustain their ongoing commitment to the organisation.

Engaging the relationships that span the organisation's boundaries and connect it with other stakeholder communities provides an important opportunity to inform and enrich the organisational conversations. By extending the invitation to converse it is acknowledging the potential of the wider organisational community to amplify and enlighten the conversation. It is welcoming the inclusion of fresh perspectives and new ideas which are vital conversational ingredients for the longer-term sustainability of the organisation. Therefore, when an organisation hosts conversations to explore opportunities to manifest its shared purpose, it needs to acknowledge the potential of its collective stakeholder community to participate and make a valuable contribution.

It is important to realise that engagement with organisations and communities is elective even when participation may not be. We do not 'belong' to organisations or communities. We may identify with them (embrace a shared purpose or common interest) but they do not 'own' us. The engagement conversations need to recognise and reflect this observation. They need to invite, encourage and enable, but not coerce or purchase our participation.

We should also remember that like people, organisations and communities are born, flourish, decline and die. They have periods of sickness and sometimes they have terminal disorders. Nevertheless, they can also outlive the people who sometimes comprise their stakeholder communities. Enduring organisations maintain their engagement with their evolving stakeholder communities. They do this by changing the way they manifest their purpose, maintaining the relevance of their contributions (the shared value they add) to these diverse communities. Enduring organisations enable and maintain successful long-term conversations within their stakeholder communities. Conversations about their shared purpose, hosted within an enabling and collaborative culture, which develop the meaningful relationships that build strong congruent organisational communities.

Focal points

- The challenge is to view all of our relationships as learning opportunities, no matter when and where they occur or whether they are chosen or imposed.

- Meaningful relationships continually acknowledge the value of their participants. They find their meaning in a strong mutual interest or shared purpose. These relationships are nurtured within an atmosphere of mutual trust and goodwill, by welcoming conversations that embrace difference, promote understanding, and encourage learning and collaborative engagement to co-create outcomes that have value for all participants.

- Conversations that focus on a common interest (such as a shared purpose) and the creation of mutual benefit create the potential for meaningful relationships. And meaningful relationships create the opportunity for the harmonious alignment of a group of individuals that a congruent community enjoys.

- Authentic conversations occur when the participants are all able to be who they really are and say what they really think about a topic they care about. Trust-based relationships are enabled and sustained by authentic conversations.

- There are three different levels of conversational interaction that reflect the connection between the levels of participant engagement and the nature of their relationships:

- At the interesting-individual level, the conversation is about creating context and becoming familiar with the topic.
    - At the engaging-group level, the conversation engages in deliberation and dialogue as the more vigorous exchange of ideas softens to a more reflective enquiry mode.
    - At the meaningful-collective level, the conversation is about co-creating coherent outcomes. The dialogue shifts from reflective to generative and the relationships become more meaningful.
- It is only when the conversational focus shifts from creating context through deliberation to dialogue that participants have the potential to advance the focus of the conversation to co-creating community by generating outcomes that manifest the community's common interest or shared purpose.
- Creating a positive opportunity for organisational dialogue is concerned with providing an appropriate physical and cultural context for community conversations to take place; encouraging the behaviours that will move those conversations into dialogue; and providing the enabling conversational leadership which will ensure the transition to dialogue actually happens.
- Genuine organisational or community dialogue is enabled by the following behaviours:
    - Listening: remaining open and attentive to the emergent views and opinions of others.
    - Respecting: enabling, recognising and respecting the potential and the contributions of all participants.

- o Suspending: stepping back, suspending judgement and action, and allowing time to see new possibilities and alternatives.
  - o Voicing: offering our thoughts and opinions in a way that contributes to the co-creation of cohesive outcomes.
- Successful conversations occur when two or more people (or communities) enter into dialogue about a common interest or shared purpose and co-create outcomes that manifest that interest or purpose and create equitable value for all participants. Successful conversations are also authentic conversations.
- Creating the space for successful conversations means creating an organisational context that lets people 'show up as who they are, to say what they want to say, about something they really care about'.
- The engagement settings for successful conversations need to provide for open feedback loops which enable the conversation to facilitate ongoing reflective enquiry that quality-assures the outcome. These loops also enable different styles of participation and extend the invitation to participate to people who may not be directly engaged but have a valuable contribution to make.
- Creating the opportunities for successful conversations is the role of the shared leadership of the organisational community. Organisational interactions (meetings, workshops, forums, discussions) and communications should be framed within the context of a successful conversation. Successful conversations need to become part of the organisational culture.
- Increasing organisational engagement is concerned with hosting the successful conversations that build and strengthen

the networks of meaningful relationships which operate
across and within stakeholder communities.

- Enduring organisations enable and maintain successful long-
term conversations within their stakeholder communities;
conversations about their shared purpose, hosted within an
enabling and collaborative culture, which develop the
meaningful relationships that build strong congruent
organisational communities.

Acknowledgments

I am again indebted to Peter Block[16] and also to Paul Born[17] for
their writing about community conversations; to Otto Scharmer[18]
for his perspectives on conversational action; to Jamie and Maren
Showkeir[19] for their writing about authentic conversations; and to
William Isaacs[20] for his discussion about dialogue. All of these
writings have informed this discussion.

5 | Collaborative Learning

Organisations that collaborate to welcome difference and diversity as learning opportunities can engage the full potential of their stakeholder communities.

If we are to achieve a richer culture, rich in contrasting values, we must recognize the whole gamut of human potentialities, and so weave a less arbitrary social fabric, one in which each diverse human gift will find a fitting place.

Margaret Mead

Learning organisations

In order for congruent organisations to maintain their harmonious alignment they must be able to successfully navigate disruptive change and to positively integrate the difference and diversity they encounter within their stakeholder communities. This requires an organisational capacity to frame change and to contextualise difference as opportunities for learning. Congruent organisations must also be learning organisations.

Much has been written about learning organisations but arguably the 1990 publication by Peter Senge, *The Fifth Discipline* (together with its related and subsequent publications), remains the seminal writing on this topic. In his book, Senge defined learning organisations as:

Organisations where people continually expand their capacity to create the results they truly desire, where new and expansive

*patterns of thinking are nurtured, where collective aspiration is set
free, and where people are continuously learning to see the whole
together.*

Senge proposed that the capacity of learning organisations to successfully adapt to change and remain competitive was dependent on an ensemble of five interrelated (leadership) disciplines:

- Personal mastery – a commitment to personal growth and learning; the discipline of continually clarifying and deepening our personal vision, of focusing our energies, of developing patience, and of seeing reality objectively.

- Mental models – being open to new ideas and new ways of thinking; the discipline of surfacing and rigorously challenging our preconceptions, assumptions and generalisations about how the world works.

- Shared vision – a commitment to a shared vision for the future; the discipline of discovering and committing to a common aspiration for the future and agreeing on the principles and practices to realise that aspiration.

- Team learning – the capacity to enter into dialogue and participate in collective learning; the discipline of suspending personal assumptions and entering into genuine thinking together.

- Systems thinking (the fifth discipline that integrates the other four disciplines) – the capacity to see an organisation as a whole rather than as a collection of its segmented parts; the ability to see the 'big picture' and frame the organisation's interrelationships and patterns of change as parts of the whole.

It is interesting to correlate these five disciplines in a way that enables us to see the similarity between the attributes of Senge's learning organisation and the characteristics of a congruent organisation. By reframing the five disciplines, we are able to make a comparison with our definition of a congruent organisation.

A **learning organisation** is a community of individuals and groups that can operate as an integrated 'whole' (systems thinking) to successfully adapt to change and sustain the pursuit of its shared purpose for the future ('shared vision'). A learning organisation has a capacity for collective learning (derived from 'personal mastery') that is enabled by genuine dialogue ('team learning') and an ability to embrace new ways of thinking ('mental models'). It has leadership that embraces its shared purpose, encourages a collective view of its capacity for organisational learning, and fosters the dialogue and thinking which enables that learning.

Therefore, the characteristics of congruent organisations are very similar to the attributes of Senge's learning organisations. Congruent organisations are learning organisations that are sustained by their shared purpose. They enjoy enabling leadership, which embraces that purpose, and encourages the genuine dialogue that develops meaningful relationships and enables collaborative learning to integrate new and different ways of thinking.

Not everyone agrees with Senge's characterisation of the learning organisation. Other scholars and writers, seeking to advance management thinking about learning organisations (and organisational learning) have proposed alternative definitions or constructs of a learning organisation.

A 2008 paper by David Garvin et al, and a review of the literature by Greenan and Lorenz in 2009, are helpful in identifying some common ground in these definitional differences. The following 'building blocks' are suggested as the essential common characteristics of a learning organisation:

- **Learning orientation**: an ability to adapt to change and sustain the pursuit of a shared vision (shared purpose) through learning.

- **Learning leadership**: a leadership style that fosters productive interrelationships between individual, team and organisational learning and encourages positive learning outcomes (enabling leadership).

- **Learning environment**: a supportive learning environment; a set of shared beliefs, values and attitudes, practices and behaviours favourable to learning (a learning culture).

- **Learning processes**: a set of learning practices or methodologies that enable collective (collaborative) learning.

Congruent organisations foster (an environment of) collaborative learning to embrace their difference and diversity and engage their collective capability to successfully adapt to change and sustain the pursuit of their shared purpose. Their collaborative learning is facilitated by enabling leadership that:

> *fosters organisational cohesion around a shared purpose...builds meaningful relationships within its stakeholder communities...(and)...encourages participation and collaboration.*

Congruent organisations are a particular type of learning organisation. They are distinguished by their collaborative culture of community and the congruence factors (shared purpose, enabling leadership and meaningful relationships) that enable their collaborative learning processes.

Fostering a learning culture

The culture of an organisation can influence the way that organisational learning occurs. It can affect the mandate, approach and practice of organisational learning.

The **culture of an organisation** is a complex set of explicit and implicit practices and behaviours (or social practices) that affect the way the organisation operates and interacts with its stakeholder communities. These behaviours are the manifestation of shared understandings, norms, beliefs and symbols which have developed over time and are considered by the organisation to be valid or 'correct'. The beliefs derive from a set of (usually tacitly held) core values or assumptions.

This general definition recognises a three-layered model of organisational culture – practices and behaviours; norms, beliefs and symbols; and core values and assumptions. The underlying strength of the culture will usually reflect the extent to which the core values and assumptions are shared and embraced across the organisation.

In most organisations, the general or summary culture will be a combination of numerous subcultures that operate within the organisation. The interrelationship of these subcultures is complex and their influence will vary across stakeholder groups. Also, the boundaries between the three layers of the culture model are often blurred. However, we will assume that the culture of most organisations can be defined by a set of common themes (typically evidenced by common practices and behaviours) that we can reference as its general culture.

Much has been written about the culture of organisations. There is a substantial body of thinking and research about how to define, measure, manage and change organisational culture. In recent years, there has been increasing interest in how these cultures may enable (or disable) organisational learning. In particular, there is interest in what values, beliefs, and related or consequential behaviours encourage organisational learning. The diagram below (Figure 8) is an attempt to synthesise some of the more recent thinking about learning cultures.

Figure 8: The layered cultures of organisations

At the base level (**core values and assumptions**) a climate of trust, respect and responsibility is required to enable collaborative interaction. The learning participants must trust and respect each other and accept responsibility for their own learning and their active participation in the learning process. The assumption that all knowledge is valuable, and shared knowledge increases the potential for learning, enables participants to be positive about the potential for difference and diversity, innovation and change to provide important learning opportunities.

At the intermediate level (**beliefs and norms**) there needs to be a strongly held view that knowledge is an important shared resource; that people have a responsibility to acquire knowledge and an obligation to ensure that it is shared. There also needs to be a shared understanding that proactive learning enables positive change; that learning benefits from experimentation and is enriched by diversity and difference; and that collaboration is the most effective way of engaging the whole organisational community in learning activities.

At the upper level (**practices and behaviours**) the organisation needs to operate as an inclusive community, enabling and encouraging collaborative, flexible and adaptive ways of working, and supporting open and participative decision processes. Learning must be accepted as a valued personal and community practice and facilitated by effective knowledge management systems and appropriate learning and feedback processes. Reasonable risk taking assumes that failures will be expected and accepted as valid learning outcomes. And the organisational community should have a practice of acknowledging learning contributions and celebrating learning outcomes.

A 2004 study by Lopez et al concluded that collaborative cultures have a significant and positive impact on organisational learning. Collaborative culture in this study was defined by eight dimensions: change orientation; open communication; people focus; individual participation; risk tolerance; positive attitude to diversity; collaborative and cooperative working style; and customer focus. These dimensions are largely consistent with the dimensions of the cultural model described in Figure 8 above. This suggests that the most important feature of our learning culture model is its collaborative style; that genuine collaboration is the key cultural practice which facilitates the other dimensions of a culture that enables organisational learning.

Collaboration enables knowledge acquisition and sharing, and the positive engagement of difference and diversity. Collaboration enables the proactive navigation of change and the collective confidence to risk experimentation. It also provides an effective way to embrace learning as a community process.

The Lopez study also observed that for a collaborative culture to:

> *...leverage knowledge through organisational learning...the learning participants...must adopt a sharing position and commit themselves to meeting the aims of the organisation.*

This finding suggests that the commitment of learning participants to a shared organisational purpose is also an important factor in the collaborative learning process. Organisational learning is, therefore, enabled by fostering a culture of collaboration around a shared purpose. Such a culture values collective learning as a way of leveraging the knowledge and intelligence of the organisational community to sustain the pursuit of its shared purpose.

It is interesting to note the complementarity that exists between the conditions that enable an organisational learning culture and the conditions that enable organisational congruence.

Enabling a learning culture

- An inclusive community that embraces its difference and diversity and has a positive attitude to change.
- Learning and knowledge acquisition and sharing is a valued personal and community practice.

- Ways of working are collaborative, flexible and adaptive, and experimentation (reasonable risk taking) is encouraged.
- Decision processes are open and participative.
- Learning contributions and outcomes are acknowledged.

Enabling congruence

- An organisation bound together by a commitment to a shared purpose – an inclusive community of purpose.
- Collaborative learning that values and engages the collective knowledge and capacity of the organisational community to integrate difference and diversity and adapt to change.
- Meaningful relationships that create a climate of trust, responsibility and mutual respect to enable genuine collaboration and support experimentation.
- Enabling leadership which fosters a culture of collaborative community, which supports shared responsibility for decisions and acknowledges individual participation and contribution.

Enabling collaborative learning

Collaboration can be broadly defined as the effective interaction of two or more diverse and independent (autonomous) participants, who share a common interest or purpose, using an agreed set of generated or negotiated processes (rules or guidelines) to pursue a shared-value outcome. By working together, collaborators can share their collective capability (resources, knowledge, intelligence and experience) to co-create a 'more valuable' outcome.

Assuming there is a will to collaborate, and the collaborators share a genuine common interest in the collaboration, the challenge is to enable an effective interaction that delivers a shared-value outcome. An effective collaboration is enabled by three process imperatives:

- **Mutuality**: maintaining the focus of the collaboration on the common interest or shared purpose (objective, concern or problem) and the pursuit of a shared-value outcome; a possibility agenda which is anchored in the common ground, but enables the conversations to be open to spontaneous and divergent thinking.

- **Interdependence**: respecting the independence (autonomy), diversity and difference of the participants, encouraging and enabling their individual contributions and facilitating the positive integration of divergent views and opinions. It is the combination of mutuality and interdependence that creates the opportunity for a positive shared-value outcome.

- **Governance**: ensuring the application of mutually agreed rules of engagement or modus operandi, which encourage and enable equitable participation, open communication and transparent, participative decision mechanisms. The formality of these rules will depend on the maturity and familiarity of the participants. Naive or unfamiliar participants will need more process guidance than familiar and experienced groups who may operate best in an open and less formal framework.

Collaborative learning is essentially collaboration that uses a learning framework to achieve a common objective.

Collaborative learning is a relationship among learners that requires positive interdependence, individual accountability, and interaction to complete a common task. It is a process of constructing knowledge and meaning through interaction with others.

The idea of positive interdependence recognises that the participants may have independent (different and diverse) views but, by having a common focus, those views can be positively engaged and integrated to achieve a mutually beneficial outcome. This positive interdependence enables collaborative learning to engage the diversity and integrate the difference within an organisational community in a way that maintains its harmonious alignment. By valuing diversity and difference within the organisational community, we are acknowledging the potential for individual contribution in a way that confirms inclusion and builds trust and respect amongst the learning participants.

The notion of individual accountability reinforces the importance of each participant's role in achieving a meaningful outcome. It recognises the individual responsibility for commitment, participation and personal contribution to the learning process and its outcomes. However, the individual accountability aspect also includes the responsibility for 'learning alone', recognising that personal learning is essential to inform and integrate group learning and ultimately community or organisational learning.

The collaborative learning model shown in Figure 9 below summarises the essential conditions to enable and support collaborative learning. The four building blocks or common attributes of a learning organisation (learning leadership, orientation, processes and environment) link to the four essential conditions for organisational congruence (shared purpose, meaningful relationships, collaborative learning and enabling leadership) and create a context for the three collaborative process imperatives (mutuality, interdependence and governance).

Figure 9: A collaborative learning model

The development of collaborative learning processes will obviously need to respond to the particular learning and environmental context of the organisation. However, in the two sections that follow, we will focus on two collaborative process factors that are important for collaborative learning interactions to be effective:

- **Collaborative opportunity**: providing participant access to an appropriate collaborative time and space for the collaborative learning interaction to occur.

- **Feedback loops**: implementing the feedback loops that sustain collaborative learning by providing continual acknowledgement of participant contributions and reinforcement of the collaborative learning outcomes.

If you want to continue thinking about collaborative learning processes, you may find Amy Edmondson's discussion about 'teaming' helpful.

Her book, *Teaming: How Organisations Learn, Innovate and Compete in the Knowledge Economy,* provides an interesting discussion on how collaborative learning processes can be organised and engaged to help organisations learn. Edmondson's discussion about the teaming process provides useful insights into how collaborative learning processes can span the physical, status and knowledge boundaries in complex organisations. She emphasises the importance of effective learning leadership (framing and enabling the learning opportunities) and the need to provide a safe learning environment (collaborative space). And she reminds us again that failure is an essential part of the learning process

Providing collaborative opportunity

An essential feature of collaboration is the positive and interactive engagement of participants to negotiate and co-create outcomes. It differs from cooperation in the way the collaborative endeavour is shared. Cooperative endeavours typically involve the division of workloads by allocation to distinct owners or workplaces with processes to qualify and synthesise or aggregate outcomes.

In contrast collaboration expects participants to be engaged in the same 'workspace' with processes to enable a shared responsibility for the outcome. This understanding is important when considering the context for collaborative learning.

The interactive nature of the collaborative learning process has implications for both the space within which the learning is enabled and the time required to achieve a learning outcome. The learning process must accommodate multiple levels of learning (personal, group and organisational/community), with each level requiring an appropriate space and time for research, dialogue, reflection and integration or synthesis.

Thus, it is clear that collaborative learning requires a significant organisational investment in both the time and space for the learning to occur.

It is difficult to find evidence to support a suspicion that most organisations are reluctant to make the necessary investment in the time that effective collaborative learning requires. I suggest that the 'learning' imperative is most often focused directly on the bottom line, with occupational training investment prioritised to harvest the value of (internally or externally) defined operational improvements. This is the learning that may enable the organisation to capitalise on derivative change, but it will not adequately prepare the organisation to anticipate or deal with the impacts of disruptive change.

The organisational learning that expands the capacity of the organisation to continually understand and adapt to its environment is typically a less-invested management activity, which is often restricted to a specialist organisational group (the leadership team, innovation forum etc.). This approach risks undervaluing the potential of the organisational community to contribute to the learning outcomes. It narrows and restricts the feedback loops that are critical to informing a longer-term learning agenda, including relevant occupational training.

In the absence of any specific data on levels of investment in collaborative learning, perhaps we can infer from two recent training and development surveys that the typical investment in any organisational learning is relatively low.

A 2012 survey of US organisations by Bersin and Associates (now Bersin by Deloitte) observed that during 2011, noted as a year of significant increase in learning and development investment, 'high impact learning organisations' delivered an above the national average 20 hours' training per employee per annum.

A 2011 European training survey (Cegos Group) observed that, on average, employees received only nine hours' training per year. These annual training commitments represent less than 1% of the average employee's available work time. Interestingly, both surveys observed a shift towards more informal training, including social and collaborative processes. However, I suspect that this shift is probably attributable to the need for increased efficiencies rather than any move to serious organisational learning, as training and development comes under continuing pressure to deliver directly to the organisation's 'bottom line'.

The findings of a 2010 study by Rajendra Sisodia et al show that companies who have a focus on engaging their total organisational community make a serious investment in training. However, based on the case study commentaries, much of this training seems to be role focused rather than organisational (or collaborative) learning. Nevertheless, the study provides some evidence that organisations that have a determined intention to engage the collective capacity of their stakeholder community make a substantial investment in training.

Collaboration requires work-spaces that enable interaction, social environments with effective participant interfaces. It requires the systems and processes that enable open dialogue, contemporaneous knowledge sharing (including feedback and reflection) and effective tracking of the learning processes. The form of the space will vary to suit the circumstances. It may be an actual physical location for face-to-face encounters or a web-based space which can extend the spatial and temporal parameters of the learning encounter.

Collaborative learning depends on positive interactivity between the learning participants. It is therefore concerned with meaningful relationships and the successful conversations that enable them. We know from our previous discussions that these conversations require an appropriate context to encourage participation. They require the appropriate environmental, cultural, procedural and engagement settings to enable 'people to show up as who they are, to say what they want to say about something they really care about'. Only then can we expect learning participants to engage in the genuine dialogue that is necessary for effective collaboration.

A **collaborative space** is a social context which enables and encourages positive interactions between individuals and groups. This context promotes learning outcomes by providing the opportunity for effective knowledge sharing and dialogue about the mutual interests or concerns of participants.

The social aspects of the collaborative space are fundamentally important for the participants' interactions to be productive. Providing an environment enabled by interactive learning methodologies and sophisticated communication technologies is not enough.

The participants need to feel that they belong to a community of learners who are connected by a common interest (shared purpose or concern). They need to share a climate of mutual trust and respect that enables them to feel safe and empowered to participate without fear of failure. This means paying attention to the behaviours and practices of the learning participants, ensuring that the collaborative space is supported by a learning culture and learning leadership which encourages positive collaborative interaction.

The requirement for the collaborative space to be safe should not be underrated. If the occupants of that space do not believe that they can be who they really are and say what they really want to say, they will not feel confident to voice differing opinions, to critique the views of others or to venture fresh thinking and new ideas. The collaborative conversation will lack authenticity and the opportunity for productive collaborative learning will be disabled.

The importance of feedback loops

According to Senge et al, feedback loops operate in learning organisations to detect and close gaps between desired and measured organisational outcomes. They operate similarly in quality systems to inform and enable the continuous improvement learning cycles. Action-outcome feedback loops operate in all forms of learning systems to inform and focus the learning process and quality-assure the outcome.

Margaret Wheatley reminds us that feedback is essential for the sustenance of all living systems:

> *Through the constant exchange of feedback, the individual and their environment co-evolve towards mutual sustainability.*

Feedback tells us how we interact with our environment and when adaptation and growth is necessary for our wellbeing and ultimately our survival. Organisations as living systems are also dependent on the feedback loops with their stakeholder communities (their people) and their operating environment. These feedback loops are powerful catalysts in the organisational learning processes that sustain the organisation. Not only do they guide the learning process, they increase the engagement and participation of the learning participants by providing a constant source of acknowledgement about the value of organisational learning.

While the value of feedback loops may seem obvious, it is my experience that organisational learning opportunities are often lost or disabled because the need for effective feedback loops was not properly considered. This happens especially where learning is not recognised as an important, ongoing and integrated organisational activity or where the learning agenda is reactively instructional (focused on an immediate need) rather than proactively educational (focused on the long-term future). In other words, the importance of feedback as a necessary mechanism to sustain an ongoing learning conversation is simply not in focus. Unfortunately, this is probably due to the fact that organisational learning is most often not viewed as a fundamental and continuing community conversation.

Without an effective feedback system, the learning opportunity is likely to be:

- **Constrained** by the lack of opportunity for an ongoing critical dialogue amongst the original learning participants – a feedback system provides an effective way of enabling the learning conversation to continue.

- **Contained** within its participant envelope – a feedback system is a productive way of enabling the learning conversation to expand and connect productively with other participants and to interconnect with other learning conversations and opportunities.

- **Unsustainable** due to a loss of engagement – a feedback systems ensures participants remain productively engaged with the learning conversation and the continuing critical commentary means participant interest is unlikely to wane.

- **Unqualified** due to the lack of an effective quality assurance process – a feedback system can provide access to challenging new ideas and alternative ways of thinking that continue to improve the learning.

- **Unproductive** as an opportunity to reinforce the value of organisational learning – a feedback system provides the opportunity for acknowledgement flows that recognise learning contributions and help to build a learning culture.

Collaborative learning within organisations should be a multilevel or multilayered process. It can enable the productive connection (integration or synthesis) of individual, group and community/organisation learning to inform and consolidate organisational learning outcomes. Feedback, which occurs at all levels of the learning process, is enriched by the context, scope and focus of individual and team learning processes.

A multilevel, multilayered feedback system not only ensures that organisational learning outcomes are appropriately informed, but it also increases the likelihood that resultant adaptation strategies are understood and supported by the organisational community. This latter observation is particularly important for organisations where the learning is intended to be a catalyst for change.

Again, this may also seem rather obvious, but how often is organisational learning managed as a set of isolated activities for specific organisational groups? How many organisations understand the importance of including the 'organisational edges and interfaces' in their learning conversations? How often, therefore, are the organisational learning conversations so contained within specific groups that the opportunity for stimulating and engaging feedback from 'outsiders' is lost? And what does this say about the organisation's attitude to learning and the value they place on the potential of their people to contribute to organisational learning?

Collaborative learning initiatives by their very nature are an open acknowledgement of the value and potential contribution of the invited participants. If the collaboration opportunity is appropriately resourced and supported, it signals that the organisation is seriously committed to the learning process. Supporting organisational learning not only increases the opportunities for participation, but also the potential for a valuable outcome. It also strengthens participant engagement by reinforcing the value the organisation attaches to organisational learning and their participation.

Because learning collaboration concerns a mutual interest of the participants, it is important that they are involved in the integration and/or disposition of the learning outcomes. The organisational communication and decision processes should ensure that learning participants understand how the outcome relates to their personal contribution. Agreement with the outcome is not the issue. It is an appropriate level of inclusion in the decision process that will maintain the participant's sense of value as a contributor and ensure their ongoing commitment to organisational learning.

Acknowledging organisational learning outcomes is concerned with establishing and sustaining learning feedback loops. This includes the feedback loops inherent within the learning process to inform, focus, assure and confirm the value of the learning outcome. And the overarching organisational feedback loops that engage and sustain effective participation by acknowledging and affirming the role of learning participants and the value of organisational learning.

Focal points

- Learning organisations are 'organisations where people expand their capacity to create the results they truly desire, where new and expansive patterns of thinking are nurtured, where collective aspiration is set free, and where people are continuously learning to see the whole together' (Peter Senge).
- Learning organisations share the following common attributes:
    - an ability to adapt to change and sustain the pursuit of a shared vision (learning orientation)
    - a leadership style that fosters productive interrelationships between individual, team and organisational learning (learning leadership)
    - a supportive learning environment (learning culture)
    - a set of processes or methodologies that enables collective learning (collaborative learning processes)
- Congruent organisations are learning organisations, which are distinguished by their collaborative culture and the congruence factors (shared purpose, enabling leadership and meaningful relationships) that enable their collaborative learning processes.
- Collaboration is the effective interaction of diverse and independent participants who embrace a shared purpose, using an agreed set of guidelines to pursue a shared-value outcome (where value is determined by the participants).
- Collaborative learning is a relationship among learners that requires positive interdependence, individual accountability, and collaborative interaction to complete a common task. It is a process of constructing knowledge and meaning through interaction with others.

- Collaborative learning is enabled by the four common attributes of a learning organisation (learning orientation, leadership, culture and methodology); and the four essential conditions for organisational congruence (shared purpose, enabling leadership, meaningful relationships and collaborative learning); which create a context for the three collaborative process imperatives (mutuality, interdependence and governance).
- Developing a culture of collaborative learning requires a focus on building an inclusive organisational community that:
  - embraces its difference and diversity and has a positive attitude to change
  - values learning and knowledge acquisition and sharing as a personal and community practice
  - encourages ways of working that are collaborative, flexible and adaptive
  - encourages and supports experimentation (reasonable risk taking)
  - supports open and participative decision processes
  - acknowledges learning contributions and outcomes
- Effective collaboration is enabled by three process imperatives:
  - maintaining focus on a shared objective and the pursuit of a shared-value outcome (mutuality)
  - respecting the independence and diversity of the participants, and enabling and encouraging their individual contribution (interdependence)
  - ensuring the application of co-created 'rules of engagement' which provide for equitable participation, open communication and transparent participative decision mechanisms (governance)

- The space required for collaborative learning is a social context which enables and encourages positive interactions between individuals and groups. A collaborative space must attend to the environmental, cultural, procedural and engagement settings, which make it 'safe' and enable 'people to show up as who they are, to say what they want to say about something they really care about'.

- Without effective feedback loops, learning opportunities are likely to be:
    - constrained – by a lack of ongoing critical dialogue
    - contained – within the original participant envelope
    - unsustainable – due to waning participant engagement
    - unqualified – due to limited quality assurance opportunity
    - unproductive – in reinforcing the relevance and importance of organisational learning

- Acknowledging organisational learning outcomes is dependent on having effective feedback loops that inform, focus and confirm the value of the learning outcome, and overarching organisational feedback loops that engage and sustain effective participation in the learning process.

- The opportunity for collaborative learning is typically constrained by low levels of investment in the opportunity (time and space) for organisational learning to occur; thus the organisation is less equipped to anticipate and deal with the impacts of major disruptive change.

Acknowledgements

I am indebted to Peter Senge[21] for his seminal writing about learning organisations; David A. Garvin et al[22] for their thinking about the attributes of a learning organisation; Nathalie Greenan and Edward Lorenz[23] for their review of the literature; Pierre Dillenbourg[24] for his writing about collaborative learning; Amy C. Edmondson[25] for her writing about 'teaming'; Daniel Bishop et al[26] for their review of the research about learning and culture and to S. P. Lopez et al[27] whose collaborative culture study is included in that review; Margaret Wheatley and Myron Kellner-Roger[28] for their helpful observations about feedback systems.

6 | Enabling Leadership

Leadership is about helping other people to succeed. It is concerned with selfless service by individuals to each other and to their communities. Thus, leadership involves everyone.

To lead people, walk beside them ... As for the best leaders, the people do not notice their existence... When the best leader's work is done the people say, 'We did it ourselves!'

Lao Tsu

The sense of leadership

Leadership is defined as a process whereby groups of individuals are influenced to achieve a common goal or to pursue a common interest or shared purpose. But defining the influencing process of leadership is not so simple. There are multiple theoretical **models** (behavioural, contingency, trait, power and influence etc.) and **styles** (autocratic, authentic, bureaucratic, charismatic, democratic, laissez-faire, servant, transactional etc.) of leadership. And newer theories of leadership (complexity, collective, emergent) continue to attract discussion and debate as scholars and practitioners search for new ways to understand and codify the leadership process (often for leadership assessment and development purposes).

There is also continuing discussion about the **leadership-management** divide, the idea that leadership is not management and vice versa.

This discussion is typically framed by a dichotomous analysis. Leaders have followers; managers have subordinates. Leadership is transformational; management is transactional. Leadership is charismatic; management is authoritative etc. Obviously, the distinction between management and leadership is not that clear cut. Depending on which model and style you select, these leadership-management differences become more of a dynamic continuum with dimensions of **influence versus authority**.

And the discussion becomes even more complex when we consider different types of organisations and the different leadership and management models and styles that may be required to sustain their development life cycles. For example the influencing or guiding dimension of leadership may be more important during the more creative growth and revitalising stages in the organisational life cycle. While the authority or controlling dimensions of management may be more appropriate to sustain the birth and maturity stages of the organisation.

Then there is the discussion about the distinction between leaders and leadership and the emerging notion that effective leadership is not dependent on the attributes or facilities of an individual (or group of individuals) but on a collective influencing force operating across and within the organisation. The idea that the values or attributes that attach to the leadership model or construct are more important as an organisational influence than the traits or behaviours exhibited by individual leaders. And, where those leadership values and attributes are owned and expressed collectively by the organisation as a community, we then have a form of collective or shared leadership in play. This thinking challenges the prevalent leader-follower models of leadership which typically assume that the guiding and influencing functions are the mandate and responsibility of certain individuals within the organisation. Inevitably, leader-follower models become part of the organisational management structure and are thus more concerned with authority and direction.

I have Peter Block to thank for a view of leadership that has enriched and sustained my professional career over many years. His writing in 1993 about leadership in his book *Stewardship, Choosing Service over Self Interest* changed my view of what leadership was really about. Block introduced me to the concept of **servant leadership**, which challenged the traditional notions of authoritative, directing and controlling leadership. It defined leadership in a way that was inclusive. Leadership was no longer simply about one individual or group of individuals influencing others to achieve an outcome. It was more a collective, democratic notion, a privilege, and an obligation that could and should be embraced by everyone in the organisation (or community).

In the words of Robert Greanleaf, who first introduced the concept in 1970:

> *The servant-leader is servant first…It begins with the natural feeling that one wants to serve, to serve first. Then conscious choice brings one to aspire to lead. That person is sharply different from one who is leader first, perhaps because of the need to assuage an unusual power drive or to acquire material possessions…The leader-first and the servant-first are two extreme types. Between them there are shadings and blends that are part of the infinite variety of human nature.*

Servant leadership is not about personal power, achieving distinction or amassing personal wealth. It is about serving others to pursue a common interest and to create shared outcomes with mutual value. Servant-leaders are empathetic listeners who understand the needs and concerns of their community.

They build commitment to a shared purpose and encourage collaboration to discover and negotiate their community's pathways for change. Servant leadership is focused on building community by discovering a shared purpose, developing relationships that work, sharing information, encouraging participation, and fostering high levels of interdependence. It is about enabling success through others.

I have found the concept of servant leadership particularly helpful in situations that have involved building organisational capability and facilitating significant organisational change. It is a style or process of leadership that imposes mutual service obligations on all of the participants in a change situation. It reminds everyone involved that a selfless focus on achieving mutually beneficial outcomes (helping others to succeed) is a critical ingredient for negotiating a change outcome that is in the best interests of the organisational community.

Inevitably some change outcomes will alter the shape and nature of an organisation and the constituency of its community may change. Often this can be a traumatic process for the whole organisational community, not only for those that may leave the organisation but also for those who remain and must adapt to the changes. In such circumstances it is important that the change process demonstrates the integrity, goodwill and genuine concern for everyone involved. These qualities are implicit in a servant leadership approach.

There are views that the servant leadership model is less suited to organisations experiencing levels of dynamic change common to highly competitive environments; that the model is more suited to mature organisations that operate in more stable environments.

This view reflects leader-follower thinking and confuses leadership with management. It also tends to ignore the potential of servant-led organisations to cope with environmental uncertainty and respond positively to ongoing change. The servant-led organisation has a strong attachment to its shared purpose. That attachment can underpin the organisation's ability to confidently adapt to major environmental change and temporal shifts in organisational focus and goals. Change becomes an opportunity for the organisation to manifest its shared purpose differently rather than being seen as a threat to individual or organisational survival. Servant-led organisations are concerned with achieving mutually beneficial outcomes for the whole community. Some change outcomes may be inevitable, but their impacts on the community will be more palatable where 'selfless service to others' is clearly evident in the change processes and outcomes.

Frames of leadership

The diagram below presents a schematic of some of the predominant leadership styles and models (frameworks). The diagram frames a typical dichotomy between the command and control approaches (controlling frameworks) and the collaborative, agile and adaptive approaches (enabling frameworks). The controlling leadership frameworks are viewed as more applicable to compliant-reactive and risk-averse organisations that typically have tight-controlling management frameworks. The enabling leadership frameworks are viewed as more applicable to the proactive-creative and enterprising organisations that typically have more loose-allowing management frameworks.

This schematic view is obviously an oversimplification of a much more complex and dynamic leadership picture. Nevertheless it is a useful way to think about the management-leadership continuum within a diagram that also has organisational dimensions (loose-tight, proactive-reactive etc.).

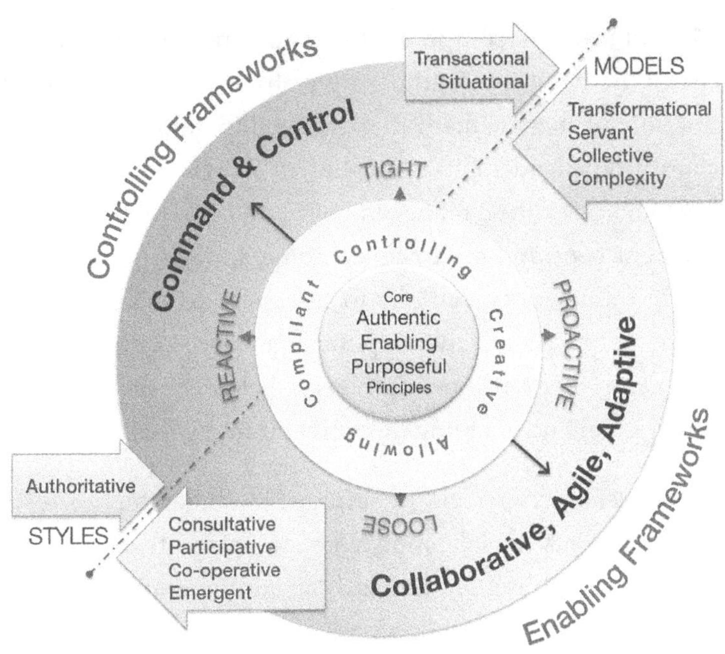

Figure 10: Leadership paradigms

I have previously defined leadership as 'a process that influences and guides groups of people to pursue a shared purpose or intent'. The leadership notions of 'influencing' and 'guiding' (in the sense of assisting and supporting) are generally not associated with controlling or coercive concepts. Rather, they are persuasive and aligning concepts that fit more easily with the enabling leadership models and styles.

How the enabling influence of leadership is translated and applied to achieve organisational outcomes is the function of the organisation's management structures and processes. The organisation deploys management (and control) frameworks to ensure that its objectives are realised. Leadership retains its influencing and guiding role in that process, but it is not the implementer.

This view of leadership supports the argument that the controlling leadership frameworks (authoritative, transactional, situational) are more about management than leadership, and that command and control-type leadership is more often associated with coercion and belongs at the management end of the leadership-management continuum. However, some supporters of enabling leadership frameworks continue to search for a leadership model that can span the leadership-management continuum and accommodate the tensions that exist between the controlling (administrative) and enabling (adaptive) frameworks.

Collective leadership and complexity leadership are two leadership models which endeavour to integrate the adaptive features of the enabling models and the administrative features of the controlling models. While neither of these models provides a substitute for the enabling leadership, which is an essential condition for organisational congruence, they each present an approach to adaptive leadership which can amplify our leadership discussion.

Collective leadership

Obviously, organisations are not homogeneous entities. There are many different types of organisations with many different raisons d'être and potentially all with different development life cycles.

There are also multiple leadership models and styles, each purporting to be more-or-less applicable to particular organisational types and situations.

Some argue that we should adopt a 'horses for courses' approach to leadership which admits that the influencing and guiding process needs to be adaptable to meet the requirements of different organisations at different stages in their life cycles. Even organisations operating contemporaneously in the same spheres of activity may experience completely different environmental or stakeholder influences. Effective organisational responses to changing circumstances may require a mix of different leadership styles to be present at different times.

For example, organisations under significant stress may benefit from a more authoritative and controlling leadership to manage risk-and-recovery strategies. Organisations in a predominant growth or positive change cycle may be better enabled by charismatic and/or transformational leadership. Organisations in a longer-term mature and/or stable phase of their development may benefit more from the servant leadership approach. And organisations that experience all of these life-cycle patterns on a continuing basis may need a mixed leadership style to sustain their development and growth.

The **collective leadership** model, as defined by James Quigley and Mehrdad Baghai in their book, *As One: Individual Action, Collective Power*, attempts to embrace a multi-faceted definition of leadership which accepts a mix of different models or styles as applicable to different organisations and/or situations. As its name suggests, there is intended to be a sense of community and participative engagement in the leadership process.

Collective leadership is seen as a way for individuals, leaders and organisations to interact cohesively in order to achieve common goals. In contrast to servant leadership, collective leadership is a leader-follower model which also includes a significant emphasis on management. Indeed, one could choose to regard it as more of a collective management model which applies a mix of management models and styles to guide and influence the co-operative interaction of a diverse organisational community.

Collective leadership is similar to servant leadership in its emphasis on co-operation and collaboration. But its focus on organisational goals and multiple leadership and management styles contrast with the singular shared purpose focus on service to others and the shared leadership style of the servant leadership approach. However, the contrast reminds us that leadership must also be about outcomes. Sustaining a shared purpose requires the continual achievement of outcomes that manifest the relevance of that purpose to the organisational community. An effective shared leadership model must also have an emphasis on the achievement of mutual benefit outcomes. This is necessary to reinforce the presence and currency (meaning and relevance) of the organisation's shared purpose to its constituent stakeholder communities.

Complexity leadership

In recent years there has been increasing research on the potential for organisations and communities to implement a sustainable operating model that reflects the nature of self-organising systems that exist within the natural environment. To implement such a model, organisations need to create a context for the development of complex adaptive (self-organising) systems and the interdependent-interactive organisational networks that enable and sustain them. Some people suggest that to create and sustain such a context requires a particular leadership model or style.

Complexity leadership is seen as having the potential to balance the controlling and enabling influences within an organisation so that adaptive behaviours are encouraged in a way that does not endanger the long-term sustainability of the organisation. Complexity leadership encompasses three intertwined leadership roles – adaptive leadership, enabling leadership, and administrative leadership. This blended leadership model is considered appropriate to focus and facilitate the dynamic relationship between the controlling (administrative), adaptive, and enabling functions of an organisation.

Administrative leadership provides the effective planning, management and control frameworks that maintain the stability, operating efficiency and performance focus of the organisation. This leadership role is akin to the traditional command and control leadership that I have previously referenced as more of a management function and could describe as the 'leadership implementation' function.

Adaptive leadership enables the organisation's response to emergent change in its operating environment. This is the 'collaborative change' element that engages difference and diversity within the organisation. Adaptive leadership ensures that the rational, authoritative disciplines of administrative leadership do not frustrate the need to admit the new ideas and knowledge that facilitate creative problem solving (adaptive solutions) and organisational learning.

Enabling leadership, as defined in this model, fosters the conditions that enable creative problem solving and adaptive learning. Its role is to manage the intertwining of administrative and adaptive leadership so that the opportunities for creativity, adaptability and learning across the organisation are discovered, explored and enabled. Enabling leadership has the responsibility of 'loosening' the organisation's controlling systems and structures so that new thinking and new ways of doing things can emerge and influence organisational learning (e.g. influence change within the organisation's formal systems).

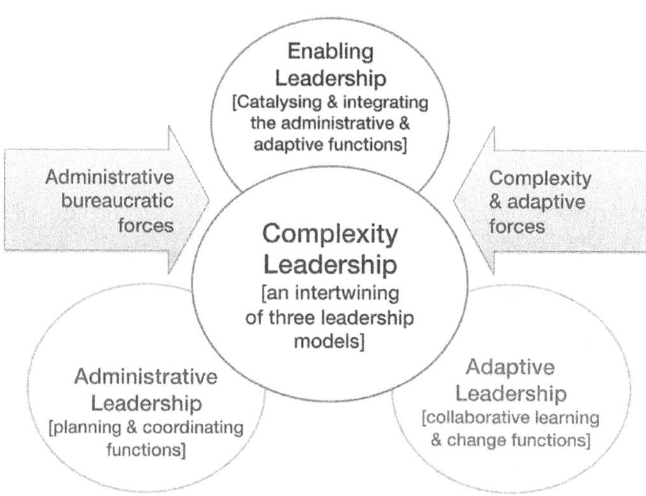

Figure 11: Complexity leadership model

Complexity leadership appears to be critically dependent on its enabling leadership factor for its success. It is the enabling factor that creates the organisational culture which contains and moderates the application of the mechanisms or systems of administrative leadership and adaptive leadership. That culture fosters the development of interactive and interdependent relationships which span typical administrative control boundaries to enable and encourage information sharing and collaboration.

It welcomes difference and diversity as stimulants for adaptive learning which challenge and transform the organisation's administrative norms. This positive focus on interactivity, interdependence and diversity stimulates the creative tensions within the organisational culture that are necessary to encourage new learning and build the relationships that can facilitate the deployment of learning outcomes.

If we ignore the administrative leadership factor, which is essentially the management and control element of this model, then complexity leadership has much in common with servant leadership. The creation of a culture (enabling leadership) that enables people to learn and adapt (adaptive leadership) is consistent with the creation of a culture of shared leadership which *'encourages collaboration to discover and negotiate positive pathways for change'*.

An essential and important difference from the servant leadership model is the apparent absence of an underlying shared purpose which binds the organisation or community. Presumably, in the absence of a shared purpose, it is the directional goals within the organisational plans created by the administrative leadership that provide the unifying theme for complexity leadership.

However the temporal nature of these directional goals (or ambitions), mean that they are unreliable as guides to the future. They are no substitute for a shared purpose which provides the organisational community with a sustaining common interest and underpins its capacity to negotiate changes in direction. This directional reliance on administrative leadership also suggests that the complexity model is another form of leader-follower model.

Emergent leadership

The need to shift from controlling to enabling leadership models, and the concept of leadership as a shared participatory responsibility of the total organisational community, is recognised in the writing of Donde Plowman and Dennis Duchon. They argue that, in order to deal effectively with the increasing complexity of our organisational operating environments, leadership must shift its focus and emphasis from a centralised 'cybernetic' (regulating and controlling) approach to a more flexible decentralised 'emergent' approach that can deal with the uncertainty, unpredictability and self-organising nature of human systems.

Plowman and Duchon view **emergent leadership** as a shared behaviour that emerges as it is required to guide and influence the complex interactions of an organisational community adapting (self-organising) in response to its changing circumstances. These emergent leadership behaviours are viewed as an integral part of an operating culture that exists at all levels and localities within the organisation. They enable the organisation to respond to localised change by making sense of patterns in small changes and making the appropriate internal and external linkages and connections to negotiate that change.

Emergent leadership is presented as a 'new reality' which responds to complexity theory principles and dispels four perceived myths of traditional top-down (cybernetic) leadership models. Like complexity leadership, emergent leadership is about enabling continual adaptation to complex change. By creating an 'enabling' culture of shared leadership behaviours, an appropriate leadership response can emerge as it is needed anywhere in the organisation. These shared behaviours are reflected in the 'new realities' in the following table.

Complexity Theory Principles	Cybernetic Leadership [Myths]	Emergent Leadership [New Realities]
Emergent self organisation: order emerges as independent agents act, exchange information and adapt to feedback	**Leaders specify desired futures**	**Leaders provide linkages and enhance connections**
Sensitivity to initial conditions: small fluctuations can have huge, unpredictable consequences	**Leaders direct change**	**Leaders make sense of patterns in small changes**
Far-from-equilibrium is where change can occur: system imports and dissipates energy and information, creating disorder and new order	**Leaders eliminate disorder and close gap between intention and reality**	**Leaders encourage disequilibrium and disrupt existing patterns of behaviours**
Nonlinear interactions in dynamic system occur because multiple players with diverse agendas are interconnected and affect each others actions	**Leaders influence others to enact desired futures**	**Leaders encourage processes that enable emergent order**
[Table 6.3, Plowman and Duchon [2008]]		

Figure 12: Emergent leadership and complexity theory

To the extent that emergent leadership presents as a shared participatory model which values relationships (linkages and connections) and has a focus on adaptive learning, it is similar to servant leadership. The notion that leadership can emerge as it is needed and therefore everyone has the potential for leadership is also consistent with servant leadership. But, like complexity leadership, the emergent leadership model does not appear to presume the need for any unifying shared purpose.

The notion that order will emerge as people interact and respond to change is consistent with the way an organisation's shared purpose will unfold and be manifested over time. This emergent order references the shifts in the organisation's direction as it responds to changes in its internal and external environment. However the raison d'être of the organisation, which is a constant unifying force that enables and secures that change, is not an emergent order. It is the shared purpose of the organisational community that, in a servant-led community, continues to underpin and enable the ongoing co-creation of the organisation.

The importance of authenticity

Our discussion so far has been about leadership as a shared organisational ethic or set of shared behaviours rather than a leader-follower process. This concept of leadership, as a pervasive and essential part of a shared organisational culture, views everyone as part of 'the leadership team'. To consider the importance of authenticity as an attribute of shared leadership it is informative to consider how authenticity is typically presented within the leader-follower models.

Not surprisingly there are differing definitions of **authentic leadership**. However there seems to be general agreement that authentic leaders, like transformational and charismatic leaders, are confident optimistic and resilient individuals. Their authenticity is considered to derive from two core behaviours. They operate in an open and transparent manner and consistently align their actions with deeply held values and convictions. This authenticity enables them to win the trust and respect of their followers. It also enables them to build the collaborative networks through which they can influence and encourage their followers to adopt a strong moral perspective, and to create a positive ethical climate within their organisations.

Authentic leaders are positive people who know who they are (self aware). They are true to themselves (self regulated), motivated by deep personal convictions (independent), are without bias or prejudice (hold balanced opinions) and behave in a manner consistent with their personal values and beliefs (authentic action).

The importance of authenticity in a shared leadership model relates to the nature of the relationships that it engenders within the organisational community. Authenticity in these relationships reflects a deep alignment with and commitment to a shared organisational purpose. It also reflects the trust and respect that exists between individuals within the community; trust that encourages open participation and respect for each individual's diversity and potential contribution that is essential for collaboration and community learning.

Authenticity is a key attribute in all of the leadership models we have discussed. It is clearly important to enable the adaptive linkages and connections within complexity and emergent leadership and the co-operative relationships in collective leadership. Authenticity is also a critical ingredient in servant leadership where authentic service to the community depends on a deeply shared commitment to a shared purpose; and a shared ethic of selfless service that respects independence and welcomes their difference and diversity in community conversations.

Purposeful leadership

All of our discussions about enabling forms of leadership have acknowledged the need for a strong sense of shared (common) purpose to provide the central cohesive force for a shared leadership model. This shared purpose, which is central to the notion of servant leadership, is not evident as a core construct in the collective and complexity leadership models where the substitute construct is probably seen as an overarching strategic goal, statement of strategic intent or compelling vision for the future.

It is important to reinforce the fact that a shared purpose is not a shared vision and that a statement of purpose is also different from a statement of intent. Unlike purpose, visions change as organisations shift their focus and goals in response to changes in their operating environments and fluctuations in stakeholder requirements. Purpose is the constant that underpins and enables that change. This is why attachment to purpose, and cohesion around a shared purpose, is a powerful sustaining force within a shared leadership model. Enrolment in a shared vision can foster organisational cohesion around a shared future, but that cohesion is more sustainable if it is based on a collective attachment to (or belief in) a shared purpose.

It is also important to note that a shared purpose is different from shared intention. Although the dictionary definitions of purpose and intention cross-reference each other as synonyms, their meanings are subtly different. Intention suggests what you have in mind to do, while purpose suggests the reason behind the intention.

In this respect, intention equates more with ambition (and vision), what we seek to achieve in the medium term, and so is more to do with organisational goals than organisational purpose.

Shared leadership that is grounded in a common or shared organisational or community purpose (and therefore purposeful leadership) creates a foundation for the development of:

- authentic trust-based organisational relationships that welcome difference, respect diversity, and enable and encourage collaboration

- a flexible and adaptive organisational culture that responds positively to change as a learning opportunity

- a participative organisational culture that supports a decentralised and localised response to change which often occurs at the organisation's edges and interfaces

Enabling leadership

The servant, collective, complexity and emergent leadership models all appear to have much in common. They all seek to engage and empower people to achieve a common organisational or community goal. All models have a strong focus on the importance of relationships as the linkages and connections that enable cooperation and collaboration. They all recognise the importance of fostering adaptive learning as a mechanism for successfully negotiating change. The essential differences relate to the degree to which leadership continues to be viewed through a leader-follower lens, how leadership is actually shared, and how that sharing is enabled and supported.

I would argue that servant leadership holds the key to synthesising these different leadership models and creates the foundation stone for a new, integrated shared leadership model which I will call **enabling leadership**. This is because I consider the notion of a shared purpose as essential for a shared leadership model.

I agree with the emergent leadership rejection of 'cybernetic' or top down controlling leadership models (including leader-follower models) as unsustainable in an unpredictable operating environment. But, I cannot envisage an organisation or community with a totally emerging (and therefore totally unpredictable) sense of direction.

And I do not think that the organisational goal focus of the collective and complexity models resolves this challenge.

I find the attachment to organisational visions, mission and strategic goals, which will change over time, equally unsustainable as a cohesive agency for the organisational community. In my view it is the **shared purpose** of the organisation (or community) that provides the sustaining long-term force that binds the community or organisation in pursuit of its ambition for the future. This shared purpose underpins shifts in organisational direction and focus and provides the platform for organisational (and community) cohesion.

I would also argue that the **selfless service** ethic of servant leadership is essential for a truly shared leadership model. The reality of an organisation or community-wide commitment to 'helping others to succeed' is only feasible within a shared purpose community. Community purpose takes priority over personal agendas and a selfless focus on others defeats the imposition of personal power and advantage. Pursuing mutual benefit, the essence of sharing, becomes the only option. Truly shared leadership becomes possible because the focus of the people involved is achieving outcomes that manifest the shared purpose. Their participation is concerned with achieving purposeful mutual advantage and not personal 'success'.

A shared purpose combined with adherence to an ethic of selfless service also encourages authentic leadership. Participation in a shared purpose organisation derives from a deep personal and organisational commitment to that shared purpose. This attachment will encourage both personal and organisational behaviours that are purpose-aligned and therefore authentic. And the pursuit of selfless service, because of its emphasis on the importance of others (all people in the community), and a focus on creating mutual advantage, will contribute to building a culture of mutual trust and respect within the organisational community.

The complexity and emergent leadership models place an emphasis on the need for **adaptive leadership** to continually navigate and respond to unpredictable futures. The complexity model is underpinned by an 'enabling leadership' component that intertwines with the administrative and adaptive leadership components 'so that the opportunities for creativity, adaptability and learning across the organisation are discovered, explored and enabled'. Complexity leadership fosters 'the development of interactive and interdependent relationships which span typical administrative control boundaries to enable and encourage information sharing and collaboration'. It is the collaborative learning emphasis within this model that is important for our enabling leadership model.

The contribution of the **emergent leadership** model to this discussion is to remind us that enabling leadership must be able to emerge as a shared behaviour wherever it is needed to guide and influence the complex interactions of an organisational community as it adapts (self-organises) in response to its changing circumstances. Learning leadership cannot be a centrally controlled function. It must enable the organisation to sense and respond appropriately to internal and external change which occurs at the edges and interfaces of the organisational community.

The **collective leadership** model reminds us that shared outcomes are also an important focus for any shared leadership model. For a purpose enabled organisation, these outcomes represent the manifestation of their shared purpose. They are the contributions that the organisational community co-creates for its stakeholder communities.

Because they are expressions of the shared purpose and are the product of a shared selfless service ethic, these contributions represent mutual value outcomes for the whole organisational community.

Enabling leadership is not proposed as a simple fusion of these leadership models. It remains firmly rooted in the servant leadership model, but it also recognises and benefits from contrasting elements within the collective, complexity, and emergent leadership models.

The following definition attempts to capture the essence of that commonality and integrate a necessary emphasis on the important model differences. It embraces the purposeful, authentic and shared service ethic of the servant leadership model and also recognises a necessary focus on adaptation (localised collaborative learning) and the achievement of outcomes (mutual value contributions).

Enabling leadership is about contribution through service. It fosters organisational cohesion around a shared purpose; creates a positive and ethical organisational climate and builds meaningful relationships within its stakeholder communities. Enabling leadership encourages participation and collaboration to discover, co-create and deliver relevant and valuable outcomes for all stakeholders; and always acknowledges the potential of the organisation's people.

The critical component of enabling leadership is the focus on a **shared purpose**. As we have discussed previously a shared purpose is not just an organisational goal that secures the strategic focus and guides the management control activities to prevent the organisation spinning out of control.

Shared purpose is the fundamental 'community glue' which enables the productive relationships that span the organisation's internal and external boundaries and engage its total stakeholder community in creating mutual-value outcomes. Enabling leadership ensures that the organisation's shared purpose is always present and referenced as a defining factor that guides and influences the life of the organisation.

Enabling leadership encourages the linkages and connections within the organisational community that create the opportunity to build meaningful relationships. It is these relationships, based on a shared purpose and the co-creation of mutual benefit, that enable an emergent order within the organisational community. They bind the organisation in a way that can sustain on-going evolution in organisational structures and processes and the emergence of new forms and formats of working.

Enabling leadership allows and encourages the organisation to embrace change and choose different pathways to manifest its shared purpose. It creates the opportunities for continual adaptation by supporting a culture of collaborative learning which embraces difference and diversity; a culture that engages the organisation's collective intelligence to make sense of patterns of change and enable the positive negotiation of disruptive change.

Enabling leadership finds its power in the credibility of its voice: it does not need to shout authority; it can speak softly because it enjoys the respect and loyalty of a listening community.

Figure 13: Enabling leadership model

The context for enabling leadership

It is important to recognise that this discussion about enabling leadership is framed within the context of an overarching discussion about congruent organisations. Enabling leadership is one of the four interdependent conditions for achieving organisational congruence. It is the catalyst that interacts with shared purpose, meaningful relationships and collaborative learning to develop an organisational culture within which leadership is a shared responsibility. Enabling leadership fosters and reflects a culture of sharing that is underpinned by a shared purpose, supported by meaningful relationships that are based on mutual trust and respect, and enabled by collaborative learning that values difference and is predicated on the co-creation of mutual value.

This is an enabling and adaptive (learning) culture where the emphasis on mutuality is entirely consistent with the servant leadership ethic of selfless service to others. It is a culture that can exist in a congruent organisation or community where the alignment between stakeholders reflects their common commitment to co-create their future. Such a future is the manifestation of their shared purpose; a future that is enabled by collaborative behaviours that are motivated by selfless service to others and seek outcomes that benefit the total stakeholder community. Enabling leadership is the catalyst that enables such a culture.

To conclude this discussion about enabling leadership I would like to reflect on a definition of leadership that has been my personal pocket-book definition for many years. Not surprisingly it embraces enabling leadership, highlights its servant leader origins, emphasises the importance of authenticity and reinforces the focus on purpose.

Leadership is about helping other people to succeed. It is concerned with selfless service to individuals and by individuals to their communities. Thus, leadership involves everyone. Success is achieved by manifesting purpose and so effective leadership must be purposeful. Authentic leaders are those who act in accordance with their purpose. In doing so, they build the personal credibility that wins the respect and trust of their communities. It is this collective trust that enables and supports organisational (and community) congruence. We are all leaders. We must all be authentic.

In my experience, people readily grasp this concept of leadership. They immediately recognise its potential as an enabling alternative to the disabling command and control leadership that continues to dominate many organisations and communities.

Finally, for leadership to become a shared ethic within an organisation, it must become a shared attitude or state of mind of the organisational community. We need to view leadership as a concept that is more concerned with 'being' and less with 'doing'. For that to happen, we need to replace the traditional leader-follower constructs, which rely on influential power and confuse leadership with management, with a belief that leadership is a shared privilege and responsibility of the whole organisational community. Perhaps the idea that we are all leaders can only become a reality in a truly congruent community?

Focal points

- Leadership is commonly defined as a process whereby groups of individuals are influenced to achieve a common goal or to pursue a shared purpose or common interest.

- Leadership is not about one individual or group of individuals influencing others to achieve an outcome. It is a collective, democratic notion, a privilege, and an obligation that should be embraced by everyone in the organisation (or community). This thinking reflects a servant leadership ethos and conflicts with the leader-follower construct embraced by many leadership models.

- Different leadership models and styles can be framed within a dynamic leadership-management continuum. The controlling leadership frameworks (authoritative, transactional, situational) are more about management than leadership. They reflect a command and control type leadership which is more often associated with coercion and belongs at the management end of the leadership-management continuum.

- The leadership notions of 'influencing' and 'guiding' (in the sense of assisting and supporting) are generally not associated with controlling or coercive concepts. Rather they are persuasive and aligning concepts that fit more easily with the enabling leadership frameworks (transformational, servant, collective, complexity). How the enabling influence of leadership is translated and applied to achieve organisational outcomes is the function of the organisation's management structures and processes.

- The collective leadership model proposes a multi-faceted definition of leadership; a way for individuals, leaders and organisations to interact cohesively in order to achieve common goals. This model has an emphasis on co-operation and collaboration, but is essentially a leader-follower construct, which is more akin to a collective management model. It applies a mix of management models and styles to align the co-operative interaction of a diverse organisational community to achieve organisational goals (as distinct from the pursuit of a shared purpose).

- The complexity leadership model proposes a blend of administrative, adaptive and enabling leadership to balance the controlling and enabling influences within an organisation, so that adaptive behaviours are encouraged in a way that does not endanger the long-term sustainability of the organisation. This model has much in common with servant leadership. The essential difference is the absence of a unifying and sustaining shared purpose which is replaced by the directional goals and plans provided by the 'administrative leadership' to assure 'long-term sustainability'.

- Like complexity leadership, emergent leadership is about enabling continual adaptation to complex change. By creating an 'enabling' culture of shared leadership behaviours, an appropriate leadership response can emerge as it is needed anywhere in the organisation. But, like complexity leadership, the emergent leadership model does not appear to presume the need for any unifying shared purpose.

- Authenticity, which is an important element of all of these shared leadership models, reflects a shared alignment with and commitment to a shared organisational purpose. It also reflects the existence of the high level of interpersonal trust and respect for individual difference and diversity essential for collaboration and community learning.

- Servant leadership provides the foundation for integrating the enabling (persuasive and aligning) and adaptive aspects of the collective, complexity and emergent leadership models to create a new shared leadership model called enabling leadership. Enabling leadership is distinguished from the other models by its dependence on a shared purpose (not shared goals or interests) to provide the unifying and cohesive influence that enables and sustains a truly collaborative organisational community.

- Enabling leadership embraces the selfless service ethos of servant leadership; integrates the adaptive and enabling aspects of complexity leadership; adopts the shared nature of emergent leadership; endorses the collective leadership focus on collaborative outcomes; and includes the concept of authenticity present in all of these models.

- Enabling leadership is about contribution through service. It fosters organisational cohesion around a shared purpose; creates a positive and ethical organisational climate; builds meaningful relationships within its stakeholder communities;

encourages participation and collaboration to discover, co-create and deliver relevant and valuable outcomes for all stakeholders; and always acknowledges the potential of the organisation's people.

- Enabling leadership provides the catalyst for organisational (and community) congruence.

Acknowledgements

I am indebted to Peter Block[29] (and to Robert Greanleaf) for their writings on leadership; to Mehrdad Baghai and James Quigley et al[30] for their writing about collective leadership; to A. Gregory Stone et al[31] and Brien N. Smith et al[32] for their comparative research summaries about transformational and servant leadership; to Fred Walumbwa, Bruce Avolio and William Gardner et al[33] for their summary of, and contributions to, authentic leadership research; to Gregory D. Dess and Joseph C. Picken[34] and Donde A. Plowman and Dennis Duchon[35] for their writings about complexity leadership and emergent leadership.

7 | The Congruence Framework

If we can influence the design of operating models that enable organisational congruence, we have created the opportunity to build better organisations.

The way we frame the opportunities and challenges in front of us matters. In fact, it can be one of our most important choices. When we rely on established framing, our ideas generally evolve in linear, incremental and increasingly predictable ways. But when we use a new lens on an old problem, we allow creativity back into the process, and this can enable us to make major leaps forward.

Ted London and Stuart L Hart

Organisational operating models

The way organisations frame their thinking about who they are and how they operate has a significant impact on how people interact with them. The interfaces that channel and manage individual interactions with organisations are typically a manifestation of the way the organisation has decided to structure its operating model. Whether we are owners, investors or employees; business partners, collaborators, contractors or suppliers; customers, fans or followers, the way that an organisation designs and enables its operating model significantly influences the way we behave as actual or potential stakeholders.

An organisational operating model is usually defined by a schematic, which illustrates the structural relationships between various business or operating units and internal and external stakeholder groups. It also incorporates and a set of guidelines that detail how the model is intended to work. The function of an operating model is to engage the organisation's stakeholder communities in the pursuit of its ambition for the future. To engage those communities, the operating model must be designed to embrace (recognise, value and engage) the diversity they present. It must enable and encourage each community (and its individual members) to participate positively as a collective organisational community. The operating model must be able to cater for the multiplicity of interests and motivations of these diverse communities as well as accommodating the functional requirements of the organisation it is intended to enable.

The commonality available to the model designer is the human factor. The design possibility is to focus on the connecting relationships; to create an operating model that reflects the way individuals prefer to relate to one another and with their communities and organisations. The idea is therefore to design organisational operating models that reflect the way we prefer to operate as individuals; to mimic 'the natural ecology of a typical personal (or human) operating model'. The expectation is that such models will create the potential for better alignment and engagement between the organisation, its diverse communities of interest and the individuals who belong to those communities.

By creating these personalised operating models we should enable and encourage the congruence of those organisations and their stakeholder communities.

To explore this, we need to define what we mean by the ecology of a typical personal operating model, and to understand why the characteristics of such a model, deployed in an organisational (or community) context, could enable increased alignment and engagement and therefore congruence.

Personal operating models

The notion of 'natural (human) ecology' envisages people as living (self-organising) systems, continuously interacting with and adapting to their physical and social environments, and exhibiting a level of autonomy in the way they balance complex environmental interdependencies to sustain their life. Organisations (and communities), which can also be viewed as living systems, comprise an important part of the complex and constantly changing social environments that people interact with. Ongoing organisational (and community) change is a constant source of personal environmental change requiring a mutually adaptive learning response from both individuals and organisations.

People are connected to their social environments (other people, organisations and communities) through their relationships. It is these relationships that provide the opportunity for a positive response to change. They create the opportunity for adaptive learning and they enable the co-creation of change outcomes, which are mutually sustaining for the individual and the organisations that form part of their social environment. It seems more likely that individual and organisational adaptation strategies will be aligned and result in mutually beneficial outcomes if both entities think and operate in a similar way; if their respective operating models are 'in synch'.

So what are the characteristics of personal operating models that, if applied to the design of organisational operating models, could create better individual-organisation alignment and increase the opportunity for increased stakeholder engagement and organisational congruence?

The notion of a 'personal operating model' is drawn from the mind-body-spirit constructs that typically underpin the thinking in many personal growth and development models and wellness or wellbeing frameworks. This thinking frames human wellbeing around a central concept of leadership from spirit, unique purpose and personal values. The construct of mind typically embodies concepts of knowledge, intelligence and learning (adaptation). And the construct of body includes a focus on sustainability and the (spiritual, mental, physical) health and wealth that sustain our lives. These personal frameworks are often used to encourage people to express their spirituality or manifest their unique purpose (roles, activities and behaviours) in a way that achieves life balance and wellbeing.

Similar thinking is evident in the human-physical-sacred world concepts from the dreamtime model of the Australian Indigenous people and the wellbeing model for the New Zealand Maori people. Both models use similar physical-mental-spiritual-family (Te Tanaha, Te Hinengaro, Te Wairua and Te Whanau) concepts to frame their approach to life and wellbeing. These indigenous models enrich the definition of a personal operating model with their emphasis on the importance of relationship with extended family and therefore personal community.

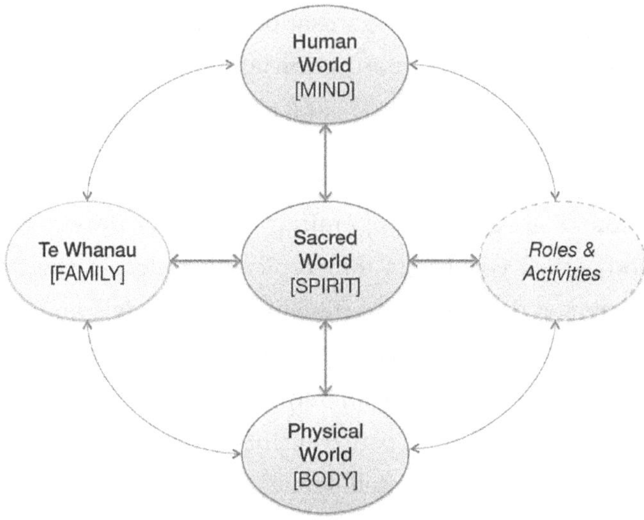

Figure 14: Personal operating model

Integrating these notions of natural (human) ecology and personal operating models identifies five key characteristics or concepts that could be important when thinking about how we design organisational operating models to be more like personal operating models.

The three primary concepts are:

- the concept of unique **purpose** (drawn from spirit or sacred), with its emphasis on self leadership (from spirit)
- the concept of **potential** (drawn from mind, mental or human), with its emphasis on knowledge, learning and adaptation
- the concept of **wellbeing** (drawn from body or physical) with its emphasis on sustainability – health and wealth or resources.

The fourth concept of **people**, with its emphasis on family and community, is drawn primarily from the Australian and New Zealand indigenous models, which like many other societal models, encourage a focus on extended family and personal community.

The recognition that we each participate differently in our communities admits the fifth concept of **participation**, with its emphasis on contribution. Each of us participates in many different communities (e.g. family, work, social etc.) where we have a particular role or we engage in a particular activity. This is how we make our unique contribution to our communities.

These five concepts are embraced and integrated by the following definition of a personal operating model.

The **natural ecology** of a personal operating model is **people** as living organisms; **participating** with and within their communities of interest; each making a contribution according to their unique **purpose**; continually increasing their knowledge and expanding their **potential** to adapt to change; and renewing the resources that enable and sustain their **wellbeing**.

This definition identifies the five key elements that could focus the design of organisation or community operating models to reflect the natural ecology of personal operating models, and thus increase the opportunity for individual-organisational alignment. The next question is how would a focus on these five factors increase the opportunity for the productive engagement of the individuals and communities that comprise an organisation's collective stakeholder community?

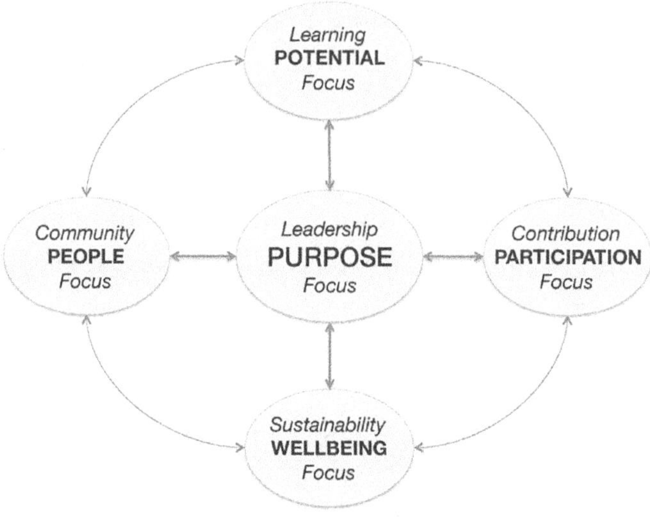

Figure 15: Personal operating model factors

Engaging the organisational community

For an operating model to be a useful mechanism to increase the engagement of an organisation's stakeholder community, it must first recognise the collective nature of that community and provide a focus to align its diverse interests. Secondly, it must provide an effective framework for engaging that community in the pursuit of the organisation's shared purpose and its ambition for the future. This means in effect that the operating model must enable and assist the organisation to build and sustain a community of purpose.

An organisation's collective stakeholder community includes all the people who share an interest in the organisation. Thus, it includes a wide variety of internal and external stakeholder communities (groups sharing common characteristics or having interests in common).

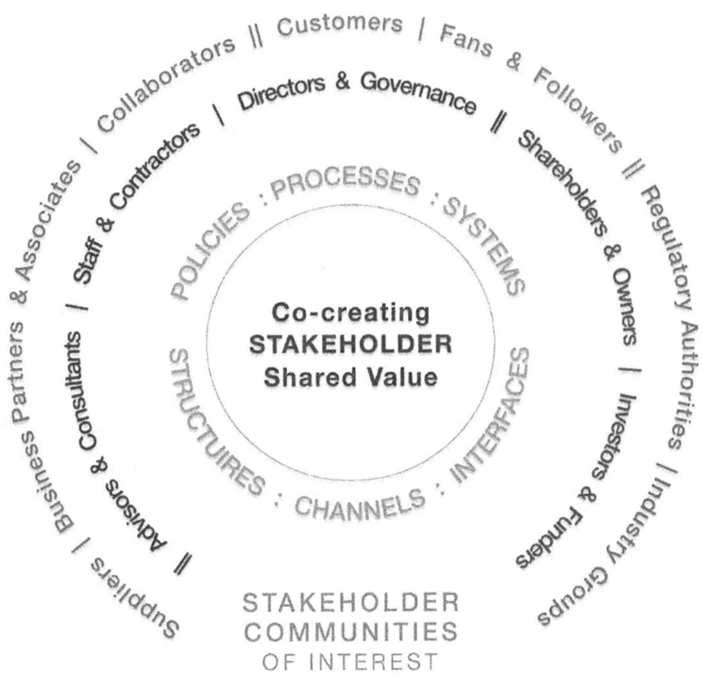

Figure 16: Internal and external stakeholder communities

For an organisational operating model to engage such a diverse group of stakeholders it must frame the group as a single community. Instead of dealing with each stakeholder community (e.g. customers, suppliers, staff etc.) as distinctly partitioned groups, the operating model must view these groups as part of one collective organisational community.

This approach contrasts sharply with the way many organisations are structured. Partitioning an organisational community by role or activity can seem efficient, but it may not be the most effective way to engage the collective capability of an organisation's stakeholder communities. Unfortunately, the network relationship structures, which offer organisations a more flexible and adaptive way of engaging with stakeholders, are often defeated by the command and control leadership that remains focused on directing community interactions. Organisations that embrace shared leadership and encourage a culture of collaboration can rethink their traditional partitioning. They can sustain an emergent organisational order of interconnections (networks) that respond to the changing operational needs of the community.

Irrespective of how an organisation is structured, a community viewpoint is enabled by a focus on the common interest or shared purpose of its organisational community. An operating model anchored by the shared purpose of an organisation has the opportunity to align the diverse interests of its stakeholder communities with the primary interest of the organisation. An organisational purpose, which is truly shared by the organisational community, is the critical connection between the organisation's operating model and the personal operating models of its collective stakeholder community.

Thus, purpose, which is the centrepoint of our personal operating model, is also the aligning central focus for our organisational operating model.

By treating the organisation as a **community** and focusing alignment on its **shared purpose**, the operating model helps to frame the organisation as a community of purpose. The emphasis on community acknowledges that **people**, both individually and collectively, are central to the life of the organisation. It recognises that people, through their community relationships, provide the social infrastructure for building organisational cohesion and engagement. These relationships, which are grounded in the organisation's shared purpose and sustained by the co-creation of mutual value, are the social ties that bind the community. They provide the collaborative networks which enable the organisation to engage its people in activities that manifest its shared purpose and generate equitable-shared value for its stakeholder community. It is through these **meaningful relationships** that the organisation can build and sustain a community of purpose.

We know from our previous discussion that meaningful relationships are developed through successful community conversations about their shared purpose, hosted within an enabling and collaborative culture. We also know that this culture is cultivated by a focus on enabling (shared) leadership and collaborative learning. Thus, for an operating model to create a positive context for the community conversations that build meaningful relationships and enable stakeholder engagement, it must support shared leadership and collaborative learning.

A focus on **collaborative learning** acknowledges the potential of the individuals in the community to make a valuable contribution to the organisational community.

It connects organisational and individual learning in a way that values the diversity of the organisational community and provides a framework for the collaborative engagement of individuals and their communities in organisational activities. Collaborative learning builds community by enabling the positive integration of community difference and diversity, and facilitating a positive collective response to disruptive change. Where that learning is facilitated through meaningful (trust-based) relationships, it will be purposeful in its intent, and generate outcomes that create shared value for the learning participants. Thus, collaborative learning helps to build communities of purpose.

A focus on **enabling leadership** (as I have defined it) helps build communities of purpose. It encourages a culture of collaborative community by making selfless service to others a shared leadership responsibility of the organisational community. Individual self leadership and organisational leadership are aligned by a common ethic of selfless service to others, which provides a basis for building true community and enabling genuine collaboration around a shared purpose. An operating model that embraces shared (enabling) leadership:

> *'fosters cohesion around a shared purpose...(and)... encourages participation and collaboration (engagement) to discover, co-create and deliver relevant and valuable outcomes for all stakeholders.'*

A culture of collaborative community encourages the participation (engagement) of individuals in organisational activities. Sustaining such a culture requires the organisation to participate with its organisational community to generate outcomes that reinforce the value of collaborative engagement and the benefits of belonging to that community.

This participation requires an organisational operating model that can encourage the co-creation of outcomes (contributions) that manifest the organisation's shared purpose and represent equitable-shared value for its stakeholder community. These outcomes encourage engagement by connecting personal and organisational contributions through their shared purpose, and acknowledging the potential of the individual to make a difference as an active participant in the organisational community. Shared-value outcomes also strengthen and sustain the relationships of the people that co-created them and thus help to build their community of purpose.

An operating model must also have a focus on enabling and sustaining the capacity of the organisation to operate effectively as a collective stakeholder community to co-create purposeful outcomes. In addition to engaging the necessary material (infrastructural and monetary) capital and intellectual (information, knowledge and know-how) capital to sustain organisational activities, it must pay attention to the development of the social capital it needs to function as an effective community.

This returns us to a focus on the organisation's people and the connection between organisational and personal (individual) wellbeing. A truly collaborative community, centred on its shared purpose and co-creating equitable-shared value for all of its stakeholders is an engaged and caring community, which will ensure the wellbeing of its constituents.

In summary, for an operating model to enable and encourage the productive engagement of an organisation's collective stakeholder community, it must have a focus on:

- the **shared purpose** that enables the organisation to align the diverse interests of its stakeholder community and frame the organisation as a community of purpose;

- including all of the **people** who comprise the organisation's stakeholder community and the development of their **meaningful relationships**, which provide the social infrastructure for building organisational cohesion and engagement;

- fostering **collaborative learning** and **enabling leadership** to create a culture of collaborative community, which enables the positive integration of difference and diversity and the successful navigation of disruptive change;

- enabling the organisation to operate as a community of purpose by collaborating with its stakeholder community to co-create outcomes (**contributions**) that manifest its shared purpose, and create equitable-shared value for all stakeholders;

- assuring organisational sustainability by caring about the long-term **wellbeing** of the people that comprise its collective stakeholder community.

Thus, an organisational operating model that provides a framework for encouraging organisational alignment and engagement will embrace the essential conditions (shared purpose, enabling leadership, meaningful relationships, and collaborative learning) for developing and sustaining organisational congruence.

It will also have a focus on the essential elements of our personal operating model (purpose and leadership, people and community, potential and learning, participation and contribution, wellbeing and sustainability).

Framing organisational congruence

This book is about exploring ways to increase organisational (and community) congruence. The opportunity is to create a new organising framework which has the potential to influence the design and deployment of operating models that enable and encourage organisational congruence. The assumption is that, because organisational operating models influence the way organisations interact with their stakeholder communities, we could design operating models which preference the interactions (the actions and behaviours) that enable and encourage organisational congruence.

An **organising framework** is a conceptual model designed to frame, structure, systematise, or give character to a situation or group of entities. It is essentially a way of thinking about the organisational structures and processes that influence how entities operate.

In the current context, we are interested in organising frameworks as a way of thinking about the design and implementation of organisational operating models. Although an organising framework could provide the skeletal structure for an operating model, it is not in itself an operating model. An organising framework may persuade the inclusion of certain ideas and concepts within the model design, but the final design and deployment will be tailored to meet particular organisational (and community) requirements.

An organising framework can be used to influence or map the design of new operating models or to critique existing models. And because they are conceptual thinking frameworks, they can be applied to any type of organisation or community.

They can also assist individuals to think about how their personal operating models should work.

The Congruence Framework is an organising framework which is intended to influence the design of organisational, community and individual operating models that will enable and encourage congruence. In developing the thinking that informs the design of this organising framework, I have considered the following questions:

- What do we mean by **organisational congruence** and why is it important?
- Why is a **shared purpose and ambition** for the future fundamental to organisational congruence?
- How do we develop **relationships** that increase congruence (alignment and engagement) between individuals and their communities and organisations?
- How do we use **collaborative learning** to develop and sustain congruence?
- Which **leadership** framework (model and style) is most likely to foster organisational congruence?
- What characteristics of an **operating model** increase the potential for the alignment and engagement (and therefore congruence) of and organisation's stakeholder communities?

In responding to these questions, I have identified the essential characteristics of congruent organisations, which are embraced by the following definition.

A **congruent organisation** (or community) is an accordant group of individuals who embrace a shared purpose. They enjoy enabling leadership, which promotes selfless service to others; encourage the development of meaningful relationships that create community; and foster collaborative learning to embrace their difference and diversity. They seek to co-create a future which manifests their shared purpose and creates equitable-shared value for all their stakeholders.

The key components of this definition, presented in the following diagram, suggest the potential overarching focus for an organising framework that would encourage organisational congruence.

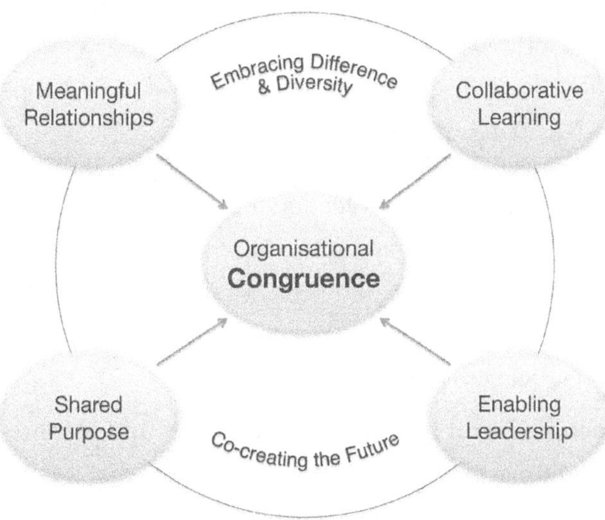

Figure 17: The conditions and attitudes for organisational congruence

Our discussion about operating models identified the possibility that personal operating models could provide a useful blueprint for the design of organisational operating models.

We identified the five key elements of personal operating models (purpose and leadership, potential and learning, people and community, participation and contribution, and wellbeing and sustainability) that encourage increased individual-organisational alignment and thus foster organisational congruence. By integrating the four essential conditions for organisational congruence with the five key elements of our personal operating model, we can create an organising framework that has the potential to influence the design of operating models that enable and encourage congruence. This is how the organising framework, which I have called the Congruence Framework, was conceived.

---

is an organising framework; it has five factors each of which provide an influencing focus for organisations (communities or individuals) designing and implementing operating models that enable and sustain organisational congruence.

- The **purpose factor** has a leadership focus and is concerned with aligning and engaging the organisation's stakeholder communities with a shared purpose, and fostering shared enabling leadership that encourages an organisational ethic of selfless service to others.

- The **people factor** has a community focus and is concerned with building the meaningful relationships that increase community (and individual) engagement and enable genuine collaboration.

- The **potential factor** has a learning focus and is concerned with encouraging collaborative learning to embrace difference and diversity and promote positive response to change.

- The **participation factor** has a contribution focus and is concerned with promoting the co-creation of equitable-shared value (mutually-beneficial) outcomes for stakeholders.

- The **wellbeing factor** has a sustainability focus and is concerned with providing access to the frameworks, systems, and resources that enable growth and sustain the collective wellbeing of the organisational community.

Figure 18:

Each factor in the framework has a particular focus (e.g. participation with a contribution focus). The framework expects each focus to be enabled and supported by a set of organisational activities, which will be configured to reflect the organisation's particular operating context.

For each factor, the framework poses a set of questions to stimulate operational model design thinking.

The expectation is that these questions will enable conversations which will influence the way we think about ourselves and our organisations (and communities). The presumption is that this thinking will then influence the design and implementation of operating models in a way that increases the opportunity for organisational (community or personal) engagement and congruence.

The **six focus questions**, which are intended to stimulate the conversations that unlock and focus thinking about each framework factor, are listed in Figure 19 below. Each focus question is accompanied by subsidiary questions designed to generate conversations about the organisational activities that could support the factor focus. These subsidiary questions are clearly not the only questions that we could ask, and they may need to be tailored to reflect the particular circumstances of the organisation (or community). These focus and subsidiary questions are the subject of further discussion in Part Two.

The framework does not ask the question 'do we have a particular organisational focus centre?'. Rather, it poses the question 'how does our organisation design, enable and sustain this focus?'. The framework does assume that the five foci are necessary elements of the operating model design, but it does not specify how or where these foci are to be framed or delivered. It assumes that the activities that enable and support a particular focus will be configured to reflect the organisation's particular operating context.

Factor	Focus Questions	Subsidiary Questions
PURPOSE & leadership CONGRUENCE FACTOR Shared Purpose & Enabling Leadership	What is our unique **purpose**? What is our **ambition** for the future?	Is our **leadership** enabling? Can our organisation tell its **story**? How do we respond to **change**?
PEOPLE & community CONGRUENCE FACTOR Meaningful Relationships *– Embracing difference and diversity*	Who are 'our people'; who is **our community**?	How do we **engage** our stakeholder communities? Do we value **difference** in our organisation? Do we care about our **people**?
POTENTIAL & learning CONGRUENCE FACTOR Collaborative Learning *– Co-creating the future*	Do we have a **learning centre**?	How do we **know** what we know? How do we generate **new ideas**? Do we create opportunities for **learning**?
PARTICIPATION & contribution CONGRUENCE FACTOR *Mutual value outcomes; manifesting purpose*	How do we **add value** within our communities?	How do we know our **contributions** are relevant? Are we a **connected** community? Does our **brand** resonate within our community?
WELLBEING & sustainability	How **sustainable** is our organisational community?	Is our organisation 'fit-for-purpose'? Is our organisation **resilient**? Does our organisation behave **responsibly**?

Figure 19: Focus questions for organisations

The Congreunce Framework is not dependent on any particular organisation or management structures. It can be usefully applied to any public, private or not-for-profit organisation or community, and can accommodate hierarchal, portfolio, matrix, network and organic (self-organising) management structures. However, the framework is dependent on how these organisation and management structures are implemented, especially the degree to which they enable the organisational community to embrace the framework's five factor foci.

Successful implementation of the Congruence Framework requires purposeful, authentic and enabling leadership. Command and control autocracies will simply disable the framework's potential. The structures that typically emanate from control-based leadership will not enable the culture of collaborative community that is essential for encouraging organisational and community congruence. Controlling leadership frameworks are also likely to impact organisational sustainability, as they constrain the level of flexibility and agility that enable the organisation to adapt to change. Nor will they enable the level of community interaction that strengthens engagement and enables collaborative learning.

Individual congruence

Because the Congruence Framework is based on a personal operating model it will also be useful for people who want to increase their individual congruence; the alignment between who they are and what they do.

A **congruent individual** is a person who lives their life on purpose. They seek to co-create an authentic presence with and within their communities that integrates and aligns who they are with what they do. They have a learning orientation that welcomes difference and diversity, and continually seeks opportunities for personal development and renewal. And they develop and sustain their communities of interest by building meaningful relationships that are based on selfless service and the generation of mutual value.

Achieving individual congruence is, therefore, about creating an authentic presence in the world. It is about being aligned with our true purpose and making valuable contributions to our personal communities (family and friends), local communities (educational, social and occupational) and to the universal community of which we are also an integral part. Being 'purposefully present' in the world means having the courage and the confidence to be who we are in what we do; aligning our inner and outer worlds to engage us in a positive way with our communities to co-create our life on earth. To be purposefully present:

- we must know and understand our true purpose
- have a capacity for personal and collaborative learning
- create meaningful relationships with our family, friends and colleagues
- make a positive difference within each of our communities
- ensure we have the wellbeing to sustain our authentic presence during our life on earth

The framework can help us to think about how to configure our personal operating model so that we are able to embrace these five challenges.

It encourages us to ask the questions that will stimulate honest reflection on our current reality and our ambitions for the future; invites us to initiate conversations with ourselves and others to discover and pursue our purpose in life. It challenges us to release our true potential for the sake of others, to make a real difference by simply showing up as who we are.

The set of focus and subsidiary questions, which are relevant for the personal application of the Congruence Framework are listed in Figure 20 below and discussed in further detail in Part Three. These are tough questions which do not expect simple answers. Rather they expect to stimulate our thinking and the ongoing conversations that will help us to unfold a purposeful life journey.

Hopefully, if the factors that influence thinking about individual and organisational congruence are the same, then increasing the application of the framework at a personal level could also enable community congruence by strengthening the authentic presence of individuals within the communities and organisations they belong to and interact with.

Factor	Focus Questions	Subsidiary Questions
PURPOSE & **being** CONGRUENCE FACTOR Personal Purpose & Self Leadership	What is my unique **purpose**? (Why do I exist?) What is my **ambition** for the future?	What will be my **legacy**? How **authentic** am I? Am I **joyful**?
PEOPLE & **community** CONGRUENCE FACTOR Meaningful Relationships *– Embracing difference and diversity*	Is this my **community**?	Are my **relationships** meaningful? How do I deal with **difference**? Do I love my **people**?
POTENTIAL & **knowing** CONGRUENCE FACTOR Collaborative Learning *– Co-creating the future*	How do I release my **potential**?	What is my capacity for **knowing**? Where is my **creative space**? How do I sharpen my **life focus**?
PARTICIPATION **& contribution** CONGRUENCE FACTOR *Mutual value outcomes; manifesting purpose*	Do I make a **difference** in my communities?	Is my community profile **authentic**? Do I **collaborate** with my community? Is my life on **purpose**?
WELLBEING & **sustainability**	How do I improve my **wellbeing**?	Do I have a **healthy** attitude? Do I have the **wealth** I need to be well? Am I a **sustainable** person?

Figure 20: Focus questions for individuals

- An organising framework is a conceptual model designed to frame, structure, systematise, or give character to a situation, or group of entities; It is essentially a way of thinking about the organisational structures and processes that influence how entities operate.

- The way organisations frame their thinking about who they are, how they operate and why they exist, has a significant impact on how people interact with them. The interfaces that channel and manage individual interactions with organisations are typically a manifestation of the way the organisation has decided to structure its operating model.

- The idea is to design organisational operating models that reflect the way we prefer to operate as individuals i.e. to mimic 'the natural ecology of a typical personal (or human) operating model'. Such models can create the potential for better alignment and engagement between the organisation, its diverse communities of interest and the individuals who belong to those communities.

- The **natural ecology** of a personal operating model is **people** as living organisms; **participating** with and within their communities of interest; each making a contribution according to their unique **purpose**; continually increasing their knowledge and expanding their **potential** to adapt to change; and renewing the resources that enable and sustain their **wellbeing**.

- The above definition embraces five interrelated concepts:
    - the concept of unique purpose (drawn from spirit or sacred), with its emphasis on leadership

- o the concept of potential (drawn from mind, mental or human), with its emphasis on knowledge, learning and adaptation
  - o the concept of wellbeing (drawn from body or physical), with its emphasis on sustainability – health, wealth and wellbeing
  - o the concept of people, with its emphasis on family and community (drawn from indigenous models that focus on extended family)
  - o the concept of participation with its emphasis on contribution (reflecting our multiple community roles and activities)
- An organisation's collective stakeholder community includes all the people who share an interest in the organisation. Thus, it includes a wide variety of internal and external stakeholder communities.
- To increase its engagement with its collective stakeholder community, an organisation should focus the design of its operating model on:
  - o embracing the shared purpose that enables the organisation to align the diverse interests of its stakeholder community
  - o developing the meaningful relationships of all of the people who comprise the organisation's stakeholder community
  - o fostering collaborative learning and enabling leadership to create a culture of collaborative community
  - o enabling the organisation to co-create outcomes (contributions) that manifest its shared purpose, and create equitable-shared value for all stakeholders

- o caring about the long-term wellbeing of the people that comprise its collective stakeholder community

- An organising framework intending to influence the design of operating models that promote organisational congruence must also address these same factors. Because they also embrace the key elements of our personal operating model definition, an organising framework that addresses these factors has the potential to influence the design of organisational operating models which create the potential for better alignment and engagement between the organisation, its diverse stakeholder communities and the individuals who belong to those communities.

- The Congruence Framework is an organising framework; it has five factors, each of which provides an influencing focus for organisations (communities or individuals) designing and implementing operating models that enable and sustain organisational congruence.

  - o The purpose factor has a leadership focus and is concerned with aligning and engaging the organisation's stakeholder communities with a shared purpose, and fostering shared enabling leadership that encourages an organisational ethic of selfless service to others.

  - o The people factor has a community focus and is concerned with building the meaningful relationships that increase community (and individual) engagement and enable genuine collaboration.

  - o The potential factor has a learning focus and is concerned with encouraging collaborative learning to embrace difference and diversity and promote positive response to change.

- o The participation factor has a contribution focus and is concerned with promoting the co-creation of equitable-shared value (mutually-beneficial) outcomes for stakeholders

- o The wellbeing factor has a sustainability focus and is concerned with providing access to the frameworks, systems, and resources that enable growth and sustain the collective wellbeing of the organisational community.

Part Two – Thinking about Congruent Organisations

A congruent organisation (or community) is an accordant group of individuals who embrace a shared purpose. They enjoy enabling leadership, which promotes selfless service to others; encourage the development of meaningful relationships that create community; and foster collaborative learning to embrace their difference and diversity. They seek to co-create a future which manifests their shared purpose and creates equitable-shared value for all their stakeholders.

8 | Our Purpose

Only organisations that enjoy clarity of purpose and foster enabling leadership can build the congruence that enables extraordinary outcomes.

Figure 21: Organisational purpose

Organisations that are clear at their core hold themselves together because of their deep congruence.

Margaret Wheatley

What is our purpose?

Organisational purpose is concerned with adding value within, or making a contribution to, an organisation's multiple (stakeholder) communities of interest. Those communities (owners, employees, customers, suppliers etc.) will most likely have differing perspectives of value, but a shared purpose requires a common sense of the core value proposition (the purpose) of the organisation. There may be multiple subsidiary or derived-value propositions that more directly engage each community group, but there needs to be a single proposition that engages all of an organisation's communities for its core purpose to be truly shared.

Where an organisation's future plans are underpinned by a shared purpose then its stakeholder communities will more readily accept relevant shifts in the organisation's direction because these changes do not alter the primary reason they choose to participate. It is purpose, not vision, that anchors the organisational community and enables ongoing adaptation and change. It is purpose-driven organisations that create the level of stakeholder engagement that builds organisational (and community) congruence and enables longer-term sustainability.

The emphasis on 'beyond profit' in the definition of purpose is important. It asserts that notions of profit (or shareholder wealth) maximisation do not enjoy any primacy of place in the purpose statements of congruent organisations, which are focused on achieving longer-term sustainability. This is consistent with an emerging view that organisations that emphasise profit (often termed shareholder wealth) in their vision (or high level goals) for the future are often not the most profitable. Rather organisations that pursue a core purpose as their primary goal may prove to be more profitable and sustainable in the longer term.

This does not mean that profitability (or financial surplus in the case of not-for-profit communities) is unimportant. Providing adequate financial returns for capital provision, generating development capital and funding risk and intellectual property investment is clearly important for longer-term sustainability. Thus, a focus on profitability is more about sustaining an organisational platform for the future and less about engaging the organisation's stakeholder communities in the co-creation of that future. It is the latter that is essential for achieving organisational congruence.

Discovering a shared purpose is concerned with finding a common answer, within each stakeholder community, to the question 'why do we exist (as an organisation)?'.

It is the most important collaborative learning exercise the organisation will undertake. A shared purpose is the foundation stone for building a congruent and sustainable organisation.

What is our ambition for the future?

Clarity of purpose provides the long-term rationale for an organisation's existence and a shared purpose underpins and encourages the cohesion of its stakeholder communities to manifest that purpose. The manifestation of a shared purpose is evident in an organisation's contributions over time. It is not evidenced by any single contribution, but rather the summary outcomes of the organisation's ongoing pursuit of its shared purpose.

Sustaining that pursuit is assisted by the establishment of 'markers' that map the journey and keep the organisation on-purpose as its contributions change to reflect shifts in stakeholder and environmental pressures. These markers are the goals that best define the organisation's medium-term expectations for success – the outcomes which reflect the progressive manifestation of its purpose.

The **ambition** of an organisation articulates a qualitative future state that is a manifestation of its core purpose. It reveals the future potential of a journey in pursuit of its shared purpose.

For an ambition statement to engage the total organisational community, it must be shared by that community and purpose aligned (authentic).

It must also be reasonably achievable (credible), have the potential to add equitable value for all stakeholders (beneficial) and be easy to remember and articulate (elegant).

Ambition defined as a medium-term goal is akin to the way vision (and often mission) is used in many organisations. But ambition is subtly different from vision (and/or mission) because of its connection to purpose. Ambition is not equivalent to the organisation's ultimate stretch goal, it is a journey marker or 'bright light' to focus contributions that manifest the organisation's purpose. The organisation does not derive its meaning from its ambition, but from its purpose. This typically contrasts with vision-mission models where the vision (strategic goal) is often proposed as the rationale for the organisation's existence.

Is our leadership enabling?

Enabling leadership is about contribution through service. It fosters organisational cohesion around a shared purpose; creates a positive and ethical organisational climate; builds meaningful relationships within its stakeholder communities. Enabling leadership encourages participation and collaboration to discover, co-create and deliver relevant and valuable outcomes for all stakeholders; and always acknowledges the potential of the organisation's people.

For an organisational community to discover and embrace its shared purpose, it must enjoy leadership that is committed to enabling and sustaining the pursuit of that purpose. Leadership which believes the manifestation of that purpose will generate outcomes that benefit the whole organisational community.

This is shared leadership, which is unselfish and focused on helping others to succeed and enabling the pursuit of a shared purpose that will result in equitable contributions to its collective stakeholder community.

Enabling leadership is about selfless service to others. It is not about demanding outcomes, but about encouraging outcomes through conversation and dialogue. It is not about 'commanding and controlling' the production of organisational outcomes, but about 'enabling and empowering' an organisational community to co-create its own future together. It encourages initiative and innovation, supports transparent and participative decision making, and promotes shared responsibility and accountability for delivering shared-value outcomes.

Enabling leadership is collaborative, values difference and diversity and fosters organisational cohesion around a shared purpose. It respects individual contribution and consistently advocates for the benefit of its total stakeholder community. Enabling leadership is a shared leadership construct and, therefore, it will be part of the organisational culture, the 'way we do things around here'. It will be evident in the way the organisational community interacts with each other. Because it is not a leader-follower construct, we cannot look to certain people for leadership. We must look to ourselves and our community colleagues and friends to behave as enabling leaders.

Leadership is not to be confused with management, the structures and disciplines we need to implement the strategies that achieve our ambition for the future. Enabling leadership enables and supports the open, flexible and adaptive networks, systems and processes that we need to sustain the ongoing manifestation of our shared purpose, but it is not a system or a structure. Enabling leadership is an attitude; a way of thinking and behaving.

Enabling leadership finds its power in the credibility of its voice: it does not need to shout authority; it can speak softly because it enjoys the respect and loyalty of a listening community.

A shared enabling leadership is essential for the development and sustenance of congruent organisations.

Can our organisation tell its story?

Reflecting on context is concerned with establishing the organisation's current reality, creating a summary view of the current challenges and opportunities facing the organisation. It is the creative tension between this current reality and the organisation's ambition for the future that will identify the opportunities for change and generate the ideas and strategies that are necessary to realise that ambition.

Reflecting on context is a total community activity, and a great opportunity to build community engagement. The collective knowledge of our organisational communities is a vital source of current and historical contextual information. Including these communities in the reflection process not only better informs the contextual analyses, it reinforces their sense of value and belonging, and informs their understanding of what needs to change and why. An organisation cannot expect the commitment of their communities without this understanding. Nor can the organisation claim to understand the change required or the strategies that can deliver that change without having listened to its collective stakeholder community.

As well as completing the normal contextual analyses (SWOT, PESTLE etc.), it is important to appreciate the organisation's story, its history and evolution. For many organisations, an examination of their 'roots' will uncover why they were created and this, together with an understanding of their evolution, can provide a valuable insight into their real purpose.

For most of us, a big part of who we are is a reflection of where we have come from, the life journey that has contributed to our presence in the world. Understanding that journey is often critical for creating our future. This is also true for organisations. Seeing the current reality within the context of the organisation's history is important for many reasons.

Firstly, it <u>celebrates the journey</u>, it acknowledges the past contributors and contributions. It remembers organisational achievements and disappointments and reminds people of the living nature of the organisation and the importance of community.

Secondly it <u>inducts newcomers</u>, reflecting on organisational history to ensure that individuals, groups and communities who have recently engaged with the organisation appreciate its origins and achievements.

Thirdly, it is an <u>instructive exercise</u>. It is not simply about what has been learnt and avoiding the mistakes of the past. It is also about seeing that history in the context of the present and creating the opportunity for new and relevant observations that can inform thinking about the way forward.

And finally, it is <u>sense making</u>. It creates a picture of the past that creates a platform for the future. It makes sense of what has been and what is now.

It gives the organisational community a sense of who they are and hopefully why they are important. For purposeful organisations, that picture is also confirmatory: it is an updated manifestation of their purpose.

An organisation that cannot tell its story, does not understand who it is. It is also unlikely to be convincing about where it is going next.

How do we respond to change?

Renewing strategy is concerned with developing the change pathways or strategies that enable the organisation to focus forward and transform its current reality to realise its ambition for the future. Renewing strategy is a dynamic process, continually re-tensioning the planning model to adjust the gap between the organisation's current reality and its ambition. It enables the organisation to regularly assess the opportunities for change and current organisational potential to close the gap.

To be useful tools in a rapidly changing environment, planning models must enable and encourage organisational agility by providing the capability to constantly refresh strategy and realign organisational activities. The rapid realignment of an organisation's activities also requires an adaptive management and organisational model that can accommodate and implement changes in strategic focus. Dynamic planning models allow the organisation to: maintain and communicate a current high-level strategic blueprint; reassign broad authorities for responsible and accountable community-based action; and reconfigure feedback loops (performance, risk and new intelligence) to continually inform and update the strategic blueprint.

Adaptive management models rely on collaborative organisational networks and alliances to provide a flexible organisational structure that can be quickly reconfigured to respond to shifts in its strategic focus. These networks and alliances provide a flexible framework for decentralising management, providing effective access to community knowledge and devolving organisational decision making. They enable the organisation to assemble and reassemble groups of well-connected, self-organising and self-regulating organisational units that can assume responsibility for implementing an evolving strategic agenda.

Dynamic planning and adaptive management models need a very engaged and congruent organisation to enable the adaptation responses to be rapid, aligned and always consistent with the purpose and ambition. Otherwise, we are likely to witness the imposition of relatively inflexible bureaucratic control and assurance systems to 'push and pull' the organisation towards its objectives. These control systems have the potential to defeat the organisational agility and flexibility an organisation is seeking to enable.

Contextual reflection and strategy renewal processes also provide the opportunity to identify stakeholder behaviours that are considered both desirable and necessary to achieve the organisation's ambition. These behaviours, typically referenced as organisational values (or guiding principles), must be capable of being shared by the organisation's stakeholder communities and, therefore, will be purpose aligned and usually ambition focused. They must also support the organisation's ability to respond to change by reinforcing behaviours that enable the flexible, agile and collaborative action that enables an effective response to change.

We do not need to emphasise those desirable behaviours that are already shared and operative within our communities. Rather, we need to identify and focus on the behaviours that need to change.

This includes those behaviours which, unless altered, impede community engagement and organisational congruence.

Organisational values are best expressed as action words or phrases which sit comfortably within the organisation's vernacular. To be effective, these action values need to be public and in everyday use throughout the organisation. They should present a constant and simple reminder of the shared organisational behaviours that are important for success. Skilfully composed action values provide an important mechanism for influencing behaviour changes across and within the organisational community.

Conversation starters

What is the purpose of our organisation or community?

- What is our raison d'être? Why do we exist?
- Is that purpose shared and embraced by our collective stakeholder community?
    - Or could it be? How do we know? How was it discovered?
- Does our purpose have the potential to generate 'equitable-shared value' for our collective stakeholder community?
    - How do we know? How do we define value?

What is our ambition for the future?

- Does this ambition manifest our purpose?
    - Is it authentic?
- Does this ambition represent an equitable-shared value contribution to our collective stakeholder community?

- o Is it (mutually) beneficial? Or does it preference certain stakeholders?
- Is our ambition shared and understood by our collective stakeholder community?
  - o Is it credible and elegant? How was it crafted?

Is our leadership enabling?

- Does our organisation or community enjoy shared leadership?
  - o Do we enjoy participative and collaborative leadership?
  - o Or do we have a leader-follower or hierarchal management control system?
- Do we enjoy a 'culture of community' where the contributions of all individuals are welcome, enabled and acknowledged?
  - o Is it a positive, open and ethical community where difference and diversity are embraced and dissenting views and opinions are welcome?
  - o Or is it a closed or partitioned community where participation and interaction is limited by rules, boundaries and managed interfaces?

Can our organisation tell its story?

- Do we understand and value our heritage?
  - o Is our organisation or community familiar with our history, the achievements and disappointments that contributed to our current reality?

- o Does our organisation or community acknowledge the contributions (and the contributors) that created the possibility of its future?
- Are we proud of our story?
    - o Does the history of the organisation or community create a positive platform for going forward?
    - o Does our story confirm the consistent manifestation of a shared purpose that is still relevant in the present?

How do we respond to change?

- Is our organisation or community 'change ready' or 'change averse'?
    - o Do we have the dynamic planning systems that enable us to anticipate and readily adapt to change?
    - o Do we have effective planning feedback loops that continually engage the collective knowledge and intelligence of our organisational community?
    - o Do we have the adaptive management systems which enable a rapid response to changes in strategic focus or direction?
- Do we champion the attitudes and behaviours that make us change ready?
    - o Do our organisational or community values (or guiding principles) encourage agile, flexible and collaborative ways of working?
    - o How do we know these values are embraced by our collective stakeholder community?

Acknowledgements

I am indebted to John Kay[36], Jerry Porras and Jim Collins[37], for their writings about organisational purpose.

9 | Our People

Organisations that engage all of their stakeholder communities are connected to the full potential of their collective knowledge and capability.

Figure 22: Organisational people

To create better health in a living system, connect it to more of itself.

Margaret Wheatley

People is one of the Congruence Framework's five factors. An organisational focus on people includes the total organisational **community** and emphasises the importance of successful conversations for strengthening the interpersonal relationships that enable engagement, facilitate collaborative learning and encourage congruence.

Who are our people? Who is our community?

Building organisational congruence requires a continuing focus on increasing engagement across and within the organisation's collective stakeholder community. That community is typically partitioned by organisations into a mix of internal and external groups. The organisation's internal community comprising its governance (board), management, staff and contractors is usually partitioned into committees, staff groupings (e.g. production, sales, marketing, customer services, corporate services) and projects etc.

The external community is usually divided into groups of investors, partners, suppliers, customers etc., and further partitioned by customer, partner, supplier and funder segmentations. Whilst acknowledging the operational rationale for this partitioning, there is an inclination to also treat these groups as distinct and somewhat isolated when developing and implementing organisational engagement strategies. Often these strategies view the engagement as a bilateral activity between groups that have direct operational or strategic connections (e.g. marketing, customer services and customers).

This partitioning limits the potential for organisational engagement and constrains the opportunities for organisational learning and development.

For example, encouraging an organisation's staff to be more customer-centred must be more than a corporate motivational mantra supported by customer focus training. It should be concerned with creating real opportunities for all of the organisation's staff to interact with its customers. Strengthening customer relationships is not just a role for marketing and customer services. Creating opportunities for the total staff community to participate within the customer interfaces expands the opportunities for organisational learning and increases the potential for strengthening both staff and customer engagement.

Likewise, the development of internal staff relationships and networks should not be constrained by operational partitioning. We need to find practical and productive (real) mechanisms to develop and sustain increasing connections across and within the organisation's staff communities. This is critical for increasing the level of engagement, knowledge sharing and collaborative learning that strengthens organisational cohesion and encourages congruence.

The organisation's **staff** are an integral part of the organisational community and play a vital role in the development of inter- and intra-community relationships. They are not a resource or (human) capital to be used up in delivering value to other stakeholders. This is why staff belong within the people and community focus of the Congruence Framework.

Figure 23: Organisational community

Most organisational communities have the potential to extend their positive influence beyond their stakeholder communities to a range of 'other external communities'. The people who comprise the organisational community have a wealth of connections to personal (extra-stakeholder) communities that could be productively shared with the organisation (e.g. community service, social, educational, religious and familial communities etc.). Often these personal community connections are important to enable the wellbeing, capability and, therefore, effective contribution of the organisation's people.

Thus increasing the productive engagement of an organisation's communities (staff, business partners and customers etc.) also means recognising and supporting their connections to their personal (extra-stakeholder) communities.

For example, supporting staff involvement in community service, enabling our customers to add value for their customers, or assisting supplier and partners to engage with their supply or value chains, sends a powerful message of acknowledgment to the organisation's current and potential (extra) stakeholder communities.

By acknowledging the importance of these personal communities we are extending a welcoming invitation for further engagement. These communities are full of potential connections (e.g. business partners and customers) that offer a rich opportunity for organisational development and growth. Congruent organisations are better placed to pursue this development opportunity because their people are more likely to represent them to their personal communities as organisations that are authentic, trustworthy and worthy of engagement.

Increasing positive engagement within and across an organisation's stakeholder communities requires the recognition of the collective and interconnected nature of those communities. The potential for strengthening organisational engagement should not be constrained by the boundaries that are typically imposed by operational partitioning of the organisational community. Nor by the formal organisational interfaces that interconnect that community. Organisational engagement strategies should deliberately link and integrate the relationship development opportunities across and within its different stakeholder communities.

Conversations that explore and develop inter- and intra-community relationships not only strengthen community engagement.

They also enable collaborative learning by increasing access to the collective knowledge and capabilities of the total organisational community.

How do we engage our stakeholder communities?

People connect and engage through conversation. Organisational engagement is encouraged and developed by hosting the successful conversations that enable and sustain meaningful relationships across and within the organisation's stakeholder communities. Successful conversations and the relationships they develop are enabled by a strong sense of shared purpose and mutual benefit, and supported by an organisational culture that is caring, trusting and collaborative.

Organisations that pursue congruence engage their communities in conversations about co-creating their future; conversations about their shared purpose and ambition and the potential for enabling leadership. Conversations about collaborative learning, embracing difference and diversity and creating outcomes that add value to their communities. These are the conversations that engage an organisation's stakeholder communities in manifesting their shared purpose. They foster individual inclusion and encourage organisational cohesion. How an organisation chooses to host these conversations will obviously vary according to its particular circumstances. However there are some common factors that are important for success.

Hosting successful conversations requires the creation of an enabling context, issuing a welcoming invitation with a possibility agenda and the creation of feedback loops which encourage dialogue and communicate and validate the conversation outcomes.

The conversation must invite the 'right' people, to discuss an agenda of mutual interest, within a context that encourages and enables their voice, about future possibilities they can genuinely influence. The conversation will be deemed successful if the participants have derived mutual (shared) value (as they define it) from the outcome.

Perhaps the most critical conversation for encouraging organisational engagement is the conversation that many organisations seem to find most difficult to host. This is the conversation about why they exist, about their shared purpose and ambition for the future. Participation in this conversation, which is a fundamental building block for organisational congruence, is often limited to a small group within the organisation's internal community. Typically, the organisation's governance, management and strategy groups take ownership of its strategic blueprint for the future. The involvement of a wider internal and external stakeholder group (where it takes place) is usually limited to consultation about situational and operational factors within their communities (the current realities). They are rarely invited to participate in the more serious conversations about future direction, key strategies and intended long-range outcomes.

Where planning continues to focus on maximising profit or shareholder wealth it is hardly surprising that the voices of those stakeholders with a focus on shared purpose and mutual benefit are also usually not heard. But where organisational planning is genuinely concerned about building congruence, the organisation must enable its total stakeholder community to be engaged in its conversations about why the organisation exists, its current presence in the society within which it operates, and its intentions for the future.

There are obvious logistical challenges in hosting a community conversation about the organisation's future. Extending the purpose and ambition conversation to include consideration of the organisation's participation and contribution strategies is likely to present similar logistical challenges for many organisations. These are challenges that can be overcome and should not be presented as excuses for avoiding important conversations. There are numerous community conversation methodologies that could be adapted and deployed to facilitate these important conversations (e.g. The techniques discussed by Juanita Brown and David Isaacs in *The World Café: Shaping Our Future Through Conversations*). However, only learning organisations that have clarity of purpose, enjoy enabling leadership, and foster a collaborative culture are likely to host the conversations that will seriously engage their total organisational community in co-creating their long-term future.

Do we value difference in our organisation?

Congruence is not conformity; it is about commonality and mutuality. A shared purpose provides a basis for organisational (and community) congruence, but without enabling leadership, meaningful relationships and collaborative learning that congruence will not be developed or sustained. These four essential factors for organisational congruence have a common theme. They all expect engagement with a shared purpose or common interest and the pursuit of mutual benefit or a shared-value outcome. It is this persistent and consistent focus on what the organisational community has in common (commonality) and what is mutually engaging and beneficial (mutuality) that enables the congruent organisation to positively engage difference and diversity within its stakeholder communities.

Difference does not become the particular focus of a community conversation or collaboration. The focus remains on the common interest and the creation of a shared-value outcome for the participants. Difference is viewed as an opportunity for adding value to that outcome. The presence of difference and diversity is, therefore, welcome and is non-threatening for both the difference presenter and the community.

Congruent organisations are focused forward on the possibilities and opportunities, they are not looking backwards and immobilised by problems. They are always open to different ideas and perspectives. They value the inclusion of different cultural, political and economic perspectives as essential learning inputs that contribute to the vitality and wellbeing of the community. Congruent communities integrate difference. They do not seek to moderate, absorb or otherwise eliminate difference. Difference is celebrated for its potential to make a positive contribution to the community. Difference can also reflect dissonance and dissent within a community. Differing perspectives that present as points of disagreement, objection, or concern can also be leveraged for mutual benefit, provided there is an underlying and unifying commitment to a shared purpose.

Leveraging difference is enabled and encouraged by the characteristics of a congruent organisation. The alignment between leveraging difference and building congruence is evident in Figure 24 below. Nevertheless, it requires a deliberate organisational focus to ensure that the potential difference opportunities are easily discovered, confidently presented and properly evaluated by the organisational community. Welcoming, embracing, exploring and integrating difference are the four processes that leverage the difference within an organisational community.

Welcoming difference means more than just being open to the opportunity that difference presents. It means being aware of the difference potential within the organisation's internal and external communities and actively encouraging and facilitating the discovery and presentation of difference. This requires an organisational attitude that frames the immediate challenges and problems that difference may present as positive longer-term opportunities.

Congruent organisations are able to do this because they have confidence in their future. Because of their long-term commitment to a shared purpose and ambition, they have the capacity to 'endure short-term pain for long-term gain'. Congruent organisations are also more likely to be aware of their difference potential. Their collaborative culture creates an environment where the voluntary disclosure of difference, and the presence of diversity, is both welcome and expected.

Embracing difference requires the organisation to acknowledge the potential of its difference (and diversity) to add value to the organisational community. In congruent organisations it is the strong (meaningful) interpersonal relationships that facilitate the positive accommodation of difference. The possibility conversations that develop and sustain these trust-based relationships are focused on common interest and the generation of mutual benefit. They are not focused on difference or diversity for its own sake. To the extent that difference is in play within these conversations it will be engaged for its real potential to add personal and collective value for the participants. The meaningful relationships that sustain congruent organisations provide a positive, non-discriminatory and purposeful context for embracing difference and diversity.

Exploring difference is concerned with providing a positive context for difference and diversity to be properly considered, for its potential value add to be unwrapped and assessed. The collaborative culture of congruent organisations provides such a context. It welcomes difference as a learning opportunity and acknowledges its potential value as a source of the collective knowledge that is vital for the long-term sustainability of the organisation. Collaborative learning also provides the mechanism to engage that difference and evaluate its potential to add value, to enhance the organisation's ability to create shared value for its stakeholder community.

Integrating difference is concerned with the application of the learning that results from welcoming, embracing and exploring that difference. The positive engagement of difference and diversity by an organisation is evidenced by the outcomes that actually result from leveraging that difference for the benefit of the organisation.

While collaborative learning provides the integration pathway, the effective integration of difference as applied learning is also dependent on having effective learning leadership. The enabling leadership and collaborative learning culture of congruent organisations provide an environment where the importance of difference and diversity is acknowledged and its exploration and integration for mutual benefit is encouraged.

While the diagram below presents leveraging difference as a set of sequential activities (welcome, embrace, explore and integrate), it is a dynamic process that should function continuously as part of an organisation's normal learning and development processes. Leveraging difference is essentially an attitude. It will be most successful where it is promoted and reinforced as a cultural norm.

The factors that build congruence in organisations do exactly that. They promote the leadership and cultural behaviours that welcome and embrace difference and the collaborative practices that explore and integrate its potential value.

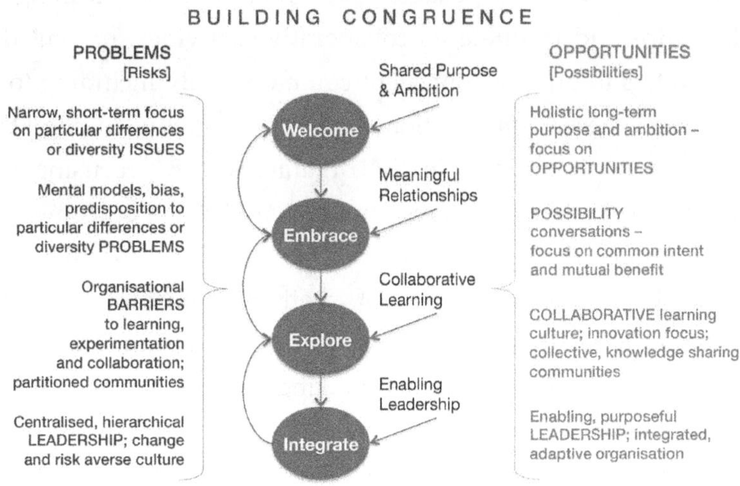

Figure 24: Congruence and difference

Do we care about our people?

Caring about the people in an organisation is concerned with helping them to build and be part of a congruent organisational community.

It is about creating the opportunity for them to participate in a meaningful way in the development of that community and acknowledging the value of their individual contribution. It is more than developing and sustaining their productive engagement with the organisation and its stakeholder communities.

Caring about 'our people' is concerned with personalising that engagement such that they feel they belong with the organisation; they feel included and 'at home' within 'their' organisational community.

The conversations that enable the organisation's meaningful relationships and facilitate its collaborative activities, present the opportunities to build a congruent community. By including 'our people' in these conversations we are acknowledging the importance of their voice in the organisation. By focusing the conversation on mutual interest and a shared-value outcome, we are reinforcing the validity of their personal perspective and acknowledging the mutuality of their relationship with the organisation. It is this acknowledgment that communicates their inclusion and creates a sense of belonging. It sends a message that the organisation recognises and respects the individual's place within their organisational community.

The feedback loops which enable and support collaborative activities also have the potential to confirm people's sense of belonging. The feedback that flows to individuals about their participation in organisational activities acknowledges their contribution. Constructive feedback confirms that not only is their voice welcome, so too is their contribution, the value they add to the organisation. This acknowledgement communicates the organisation's appreciation of the individual's role. It sends a clear message that they are welcome and their participation is valued by the community.

Enabling our people to be active participants within our organisational community also means caring about their individual wellbeing and their capacity to recognise and release their real potential to contribute.

In congruent organisations, the leadership focus on helping others to succeed makes caring for our people a community responsibility. And the collaborative culture offers the opportunity to make people development a collaborative community endeavour.

In a truly collaborative community, where personal difference and diversity is valued, people have a real opportunity to openly explore their potential with the help and support of their friends and colleagues. Collaborative learning not only provides a way of leveraging the collective potential of a community. It also provides the individual with a learning platform where they can access and engage the guidance and mentoring of their community. In this environment, personal development and occupational training can become more than a process to increase the operational efficiency and effectiveness of the organisational community. It becomes a collaborative endeavour focused on mutual benefit. There is an expectation that the learning is shared and that the community and the individual have a shared responsibility to help each other 'succeed'.

The shared leadership ethic which congruent organisations enjoy enables people to bypass the traditional hierarchical structures that usually 'control' personal development and occupational learning. In a congruent organisational community, these processes can be less structured, enabling individuals to access the people and the conversations (projects, discussion forums and community groups etc.) they need to help themselves and others discover and release their full potential.

The motivation and the responsibility to learn is not imposed by an organisational directive or a performance obligation.

It is derived from a voluntary personal commitment to the organisation's shared purpose and a genuine desire to help the organisational community, of which they are a valued member, to succeed – to manifest their shared purpose.

A caring organisational community will ensure that its people can initiate and participate in the learning conversations that enable them to be proud and capable members of their community. They will host or facilitate the community conversations that enable their people to be a vital participant in the co-creation of the organisation's future. And they will encourage and support a culture of enabling leadership and a collaborative learning environment to ensure that these conversations can be successful in creating shared-value outcomes for their participants and their community.

Congruent organisations and communities care about their people. Such caring is evident in the way they treat their people and engage with them to co-create a future together.

To continue this conversation about caring for our people: *refer to* **Part Three** *and consider the question* '**Do I love my people?**'.

Conversation starters

Who is our community?

- Who are our stakeholders (the individuals or groups that have a genuine interest in our organisation or community)?
    - What is the nature of their 'interest(s)' in our community? How do we know about their interest(s)?
    - To what degree are those interests shared by different stakeholders? Do we understand the complementary or conflicting nature of these interests?

- Do we recognise the collective potential of our stakeholder community?
    - How do the current partitioning and segmenting of our organisational community help to realise our collective potential?
    - Do we encourage the development of relationships and networks that span our organisational (community) boundaries and interfaces?
    - Does our organisation engage with the 'personal communities' of our organisational stakeholders?

How do we engage our stakeholder communities?

- Do we host the successful community conversations that encourage and enable stakeholder engagement?
    - Do we host conversations about our purpose and ambition and the potential for enabling leadership?
    - Do we host the conversations that facilitate meaningful relationships and explore the potential for collaborative learning?
    - Do we encourage our community to treat organisational meetings, discussions, forums and projects as community conversations?
- How do we enable the collective stakeholder community to participate in these conversations?
    - Do we create a context that encourages and enables the participation of the 'right people'? How do we decide who should participate?
    - What do we mean by participation?

Do we value difference in our organisation?

- Do we welcome and embrace the difference and diversity within our organisational community?
    - How do we discover and acknowledge that difference?
- Do we explore and integrate that difference and diversity?
    - How do we create a positive context to explore difference, diversity and dissent? How do we capture and apply our difference potential?

Do we care about our people?

- Who are 'our people'?
    - Who do we care about and why?
- How do we care for them?
    - What do we mean by caring?

Acknowledgements

I am indebted to Martin N. Davidson et al[38] for their writings about diversity and difference.

10 | Our Potential

Organisations that have a strong focus on learning will anticipate and embrace change in ways that continually develop their capacity to maintain relevance within their communities.

Figure 25: Organisational potential

The intuitive mind is a sacred gift and the rational mind is a faithful servant. We have created a society that honours the servant and has forgotten the gift.

Albert Einstein

Potential is one of the Congruence Framework's five factors. Organisational potential is released through collaborative **learning** which enables the organisational community to integrate difference and engage its collective knowledge, intelligence and know-how to pursue innovation and create positive pathways for change.

Do we have a learning centre?

The longer-term sustainability of any organisation is primarily dependent on its ability to remain relevant to its stakeholder communities. To maintain this relevance the organisation must be able to adapt to change in a way that continues its positive participation with and within those communities. The opportunity is to engage the organisational community in co-creating a response to change that generates shared value and sustains the pursuit of its shared purpose. It is to engage the potential (the collective knowledge and capabilities) of the organisational community, and adapt to change in a way that ensures the longer-term growth, stability and wellbeing of the organisation and the communities it serves.

The typical organisational life cycle tracks development from inception through growth to maturity and then eventual decline. Maintaining sustainability requires the constant extension and regeneration of this life cycle by continually reshaping and reinventing the way the organisation adds value within its stakeholder communities. The ability of an organisation to extend its life cycle will not only depend on its capacity to discover positive (value-adding) opportunities for change.

It will also depend on its ability to realise those opportunities. Some of those change opportunities will involve the modification or refinement of an existing product or service offer, often derived from a quality or continuous improvement program (derivative change). Others may involve new ideas that result in an entirely new way of adding stakeholder value – the sort of disruptive innovation that may even challenge the current business or organisational model (disruptive change).

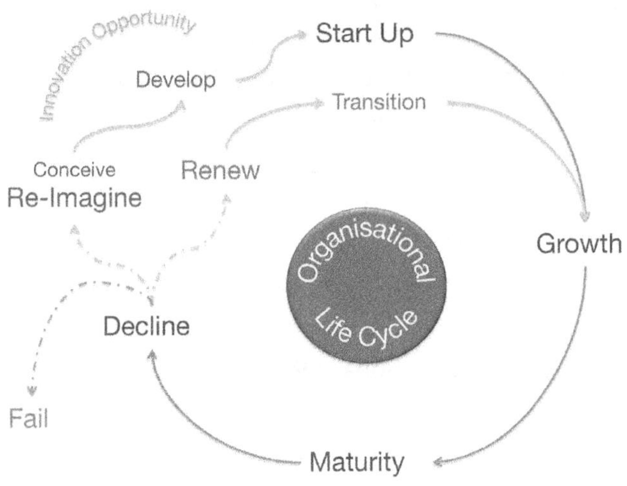

Figure 26: The organisational life cycle

To maintain its longer-term sustainability, the organisation must have the capability to positively navigate both derivative and disruptive change opportunities. Derivative change may continue to extend the growth of an existing (product or service, business, organisational) development cycle. However, it is the more substantial disruptive change that usually offers the opportunities to renew, refresh, and regenerate the organisational life cycle, and thus ensure longer-term organisational sustainability.

But only organisations that enjoy a strong collective commitment to their shared purpose will have the necessary courage to confidently embrace disruptive change, and to prefer the uncertainty of an unknown future over the apparent safety of a continuing program of derivative change.

Recognising and realising the positive opportunities for change is the role of the organisation's 'learning centre'. It is the learning centre that recognises the opportunities for organisational change and signals that a change response is necessary. It is the learning centre that ensures the organisation has a relentless focus on learning and renewal, and can engage the collective capabilities and knowledge of the organisation to embrace change as an exciting learning opportunity.

A **learning centre** in this context is a concept, construct, or force within the organisation which continually energises its community learning program. It may be realised differently in each organisation, but the expected outcome is energised leadership of the organisational learning agenda. The role of the learning centre is to engage the collective knowledge and innovation potential of the organisational community in the design and implementation of proactive and positive responses to derivative and disruptive change opportunities.

Many organisations aspire to be learning organisations, but how often is this aspiration visible as a tangible commitment to an active learning strategy? How many organisations really support a learning orientation by creating an awareness of the importance of learning and resourcing the time and space necessary to identify and implement learning opportunities? How often do organisations provide the opportunities for collective engagement in learning, creating the feedback loops and knowledge sharing mechanisms that inform collaborative learning? And how often are learning outcomes, successes and failures recognised and celebrated to reinforce and sustain a learning culture?

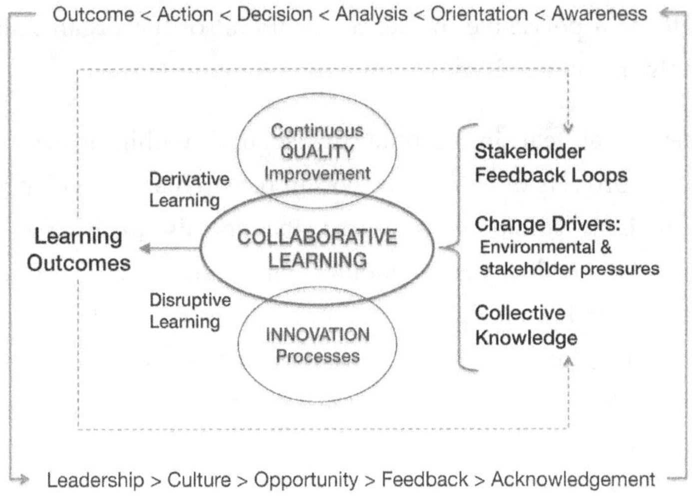

Figure 27: Organisational learning

Successful learning organisations embed (and resource) a culture of innovation and creativity; they value organisational knowledge, intelligence and intellectual capital; they actively pursue a learning strategy, founded in excellence or quality and continuous improvement and stimulated by new ideas. And they create networks of feedback loops, which identify and communicate learning opportunities, and acknowledge and reinforce learning outcomes. Successful learning organisations are not change reactive; they are proactive in seeking out relevant change opportunities and determined in the pursuit and implementation of positive adaptation strategies.

The challenge for learning organisations is to 'pick the winners'; to choose those change opportunities which best enable them to remain continually relevant to their communities. The obvious arbiters of what would constitute a good choice are the communities themselves. This is why the pursuit of learning needs to be a pervasive influence within all of the organisation's stakeholder communities.

Organisational learning cannot be isolated within learning or excellence projects or centres, or within research and development units: it is a collaborative effort that needs to involve the organisation's collective stakeholder community. This is because organisational knowledge is distributed throughout the internal and external stakeholder communities, and innovative thinking can originate wherever change impacts upon and within these communities. It is also because the real opportunities for learning will often occur at the edges and interfaces of the organisational community, and effective learning responses will require the collaborative engagement of people from different stakeholder communities.

How do we know what we know?

Knowledge is a fluid mix of framed experience, contextual information, values and expert insight that provides a framework for evaluating and incorporating new experiences and information.

Davenport and Prusak

Organisational knowledge is the collective knowledge of its stakeholder communities. It includes organisational intelligence (environmental, market, customer, business, process and product or service etc.) and intellectual capital (cumulative individual and group knowledge and experience).

It is a collective asset that includes both the codified and tacit knowledge (know-how) and experience of the individuals and groups that comprise the organisational community. Leveraging this knowledge for the advantage of the organisation requires a knowledge management strategy that recognises and explores its collective nature.

Sharing organisational knowledge is critical for enabling the organisation to be adaptive to change. Without timely and comprehensive access to its collective knowledge, the organisation's learning and innovation activities are unlikely to be adequately informed. The organisation will be less proactive in determining the nature and timing of its change responses, and it will tend to become change reactive rather than the assertive co-creator of its own future. The collective nature of this organisational knowledge, and its distributed ownership throughout the organisation's stakeholder communities, presents a real challenge for timely and comprehensive access.

To the extent that collective knowledge has been codified and stored by an organisation it has become collected knowledge that can, by various means, be made readily available to the stakeholder communities. The tacit knowledge that cannot be easily codified resides with the individuals, groups and communities that own it. Sharing collective knowledge requires access to both codified and tacit knowledge and that means it requires the collaborative participation of the tacit knowledge owners.

We not only need the participation of the organisation's collective knowledge custodians (individuals, groups and communities) to ensure we have access to the total organisational knowledge.

We also need these knowledge custodians to assist in making sense (understanding and interpreting the meaning) of that knowledge. It is this collaborative sense-making that releases the potential value of knowledge by sharing understandings that foster the creation and development of new collective knowledge. Sharing organisational knowledge is an essential part of any collaborative learning process.

Managing organisational knowledge requires more than efficient and effective systems and processes that collect, present and distribute that knowledge. It requires an organisational (enabling) leadership style and a learning culture that encourages the creation, development and sharing of collective knowledge. Leadership that is committed to sharing collective knowledge encourages and enables collaborative practices and prioritises the human and physical resources to effect open and efficient knowledge sharing.

An organisation or community only knows what it could know when it successfully engages its total organisational community in sharing their collective knowledge. It is the collaborative exploration of this collective knowledge that reveals what the organisation knows and releases the potential of that knowledge to inform its innovation and learning activities. It is through collaborative learning that an organisation can access its collective 'knowledge banks' and enable a proactive adaptation to change, which ensures its longer-term sustainability.

How do we generate new ideas?

Fostering innovation within an organisation requires a determined focus on developing innovation leadership, fostering a culture or philosophy of innovation and developing and resourcing processes that support innovation discovery and realisation. Innovative organisations position innovation as a cultural norm. They foster a learning culture which expects and enables people to generate new ideas. Such a culture encourages and supports people to challenge the status quo and take sensible risks to pursue new ideas.

These learning cultures require enabling leadership, which fosters trust-based relationships and encourages participation and collaboration across the organisation's stakeholder communities. Without such leadership, and the culture it engenders, it is unlikely that the organisational community (individuals, teams and groups) will have the necessary courage to face the important questions that challenge its existing organisational models. Only courageous communities will endorse new thinking and ideas that can radically alter their current situations. It is obviously simpler and safer to endorse the progressive change that comes from the continuous improvement systems. However, organisations that are constrained to operate 'inside the box' and focus on refining their existing business models are unlikely to deliver the disruptive innovation (innovation resulting from disruptive change) that can secure long-term sustainability.

Innovative organisations are typically led by innovative people who ensure that their organisations are populated at all levels with people like themselves (innovators). At the same time, these leaders recognise that achieving innovation outcomes requires two complementary capabilities: the capability to discover the innovation opportunity and the capability to deliver (operationalise) that opportunity. Both must be fostered by a supportive culture and enabling processes.

Some may argue that discovery skills are more important for strategic, marketing and development roles, and delivery skills are more essential for operational roles. Or that organisational leadership must be discovery focused rather than delivery focused for innovation to be effective. Or that the need for discovery skills is more important during the embryonic stage of the organisational lifecycle, with delivery skills assuming more importance as growth to maturity takes place.

However, the potential for new ideas to sustain organisational growth and development is not limited to particular stages of the organisational lifecycle or to particular people or units within the organisation. It is, therefore, important that an appropriate mix of discovery and delivery skills is present wherever and whenever innovation opportunities can arise. Thus, organisations should ensure that these skills exist and are balanced within all of their organisational communities or teams.

Figure 28: Balancing the innovation skills mix

Achieving that balance requires the organisation to recognise where the skill gaps exist and to ensure that compensating and complementary skills are made available.

If an organisation is serious about innovation it will ensure that its governance, management and operational teams are comprised of people who can demonstrate they have the necessary discovery-delivery skill mix. Innovative organisations actively engage in recruitment and development processes that identify and develop people who can engage with disruptive innovation. The organisational leadership ensures that these people are enabled at all levels in the organisational community to continually seek, recognise, evaluate and implement new ideas.

For many organisations it seems to be a challenge to properly enable and integrate the quality (continuous improvement) processes that drip feed derivative innovation (the innovation resulting from derivative change). Enabling the processes that engage with disruptive innovation is likely to be an even greater challenge. For derivative and disruptive innovation to become part of the organisation's normal way of operating it not only needs the 'right' people to be involved; it also needs to make a substantial investment in the learning facilities and processes that enable innovation and in providing the time for its people to participate in learning opportunities.

If the organisation supports a culture of collaborative learning then it has the necessary learning processes to accommodate innovation discovery and delivery behaviours. The existence of trust-based (meaningful) relationships which value difference and diversity will support the necessary questioning and networking behaviours that identify, challenge and qualify new ideas. The collaborative nature of the collective learning process will support the associating (solution investigation or brainstorming) activities and enable the experimentation (prototyping) necessary to assess and refine the new ideas.

Collaborative learning is also delivery focused. It supports adaptive learning processes, which enable the learning participants to successfully navigate change, and co-create shared-value outcomes. Provided the collaborative learning conversations are hosted in a way that promotes an innovation agenda, and encourages participation of people with the appropriate discovery and delivery skills, collaborative learning can enable and support innovation discovery and delivery processes.

To continue this conversation about innovation and creativity: *refer to* **Part Three** *and consider the question* '**Where is my creative space?**'

Do we create opportunities for learning?

Providing the opportunity for collaborative learning is about creating an environment where the organisational culture and leadership support the required knowledge sharing, innovation and collaborative processes. It is also about creating the time and space for those collaborative learning processes to occur, facilitating the opportunities for the necessary learning conversations to take place. These are the conversations which enable participants to question and challenge their current environment; to openly share their knowledge and experiences; to experiment with new ideas; and to reflect on and learn from their successes and failures.

Creating the opportunity for organisational learning is enabling these conversations to be a normal part of everyday organisational life.

It means encouraging and supporting learning conversations to be the 'way we do things around here' and fundamental to the way all stakeholders interact with each other. This means viewing all community interactions and encounters (meetings, forums, discussion groups etc.) as possibility conversations with the potential for learning – conversations with the opportunity for genuine (reflective and generative) dialogue about the possibilities for co-creating a better future for the collective stakeholder community.

Creating opportunities for collaborative learning is, therefore, about creating the time and space for these community conversations to take place. How often are organisational meetings and discussions constrained by their architecture and timing? How many conversations are significantly influenced by the presence of positional power and politics and the incessant urgency for immediately meaningful and implementable outcomes?

How often do organisational efficiency requirements constrain participation, space and time, and inadequate meeting agendas limit the frames of reference and the potential for discursive dialogue? Therefore, the first challenge is to allow the time for these conversations to take place. Not just time for interaction but time for preparation, action and reflection.

This means preferencing the important conversations – those that offer the opportunity for co-creating outcomes that connect to purpose. How often is the time for conversations about the future (strategy and planning) limited in favour of conversations about the present (operational, problem solving etc.)? For example, how often do conversations about purpose and ambition become discussions about budgets and resources?

The challenge is to set an agenda that demands a linkage to purpose; that frames all organisational conversations within a broader purpose-ambition agenda; and that makes the potential importance of the conversation apparent to all participants.

Figure 29: Enabling learning conversations

The next challenge is to find a way to include relevant participation in the learning conversations from across and within the organisation's stakeholder communities. This is not just a question of who is invited, but why and how they are selected. The invitation and context for the learning conversations should make it obvious to the participants why they were chosen and how the learning connects to, and is expected to contribute to, the life (purpose and ambition) of the organisation. It is important that the invitation to participate is seen as endorsing learning and reinforcing its importance as a central and expected organisational activity.

Organisational learning is also an important and effective stakeholder engagement tool. The serious inclusion of an organisation's stakeholders (individuals, groups and communities) in collaborative learning opportunities, and related knowledge sense-making activities, not only acknowledges their potential learning contribution. It also increases their engagement with the outcome, creating an increased sense of collective ownership of their organisational future.

Engaging the organisational community in learning conversations also activates important feedback loops. The traditional feedback loops (e.g. customer feedback systems and quality systems), which focus on well-defined community interfaces (e.g. the customer or supplier interfaces), provide a relatively limited source of new knowledge and learning opportunities. The wider opportunity for feedback comes from engaging the organisational community in learning conversations. This engagement opens up a broader network of feedback loops that can operate across all community interfaces (internal and external) and span stakeholder communities via collaborative projects and other conversations. In this way, the feedback can be contributed directly and in a timely manner by participants who are equipped to make sense of the new information.

Activating these feedback loops requires inviting the right people to join the learning conversations and providing the time and space for their active involvement.

Another challenge is to ensure that organisational learning has a tangible (visible and measurable) outcome. Applying organisational learning is not only concerned with ensuring an appropriate return on the investment in knowledge sharing and collaborative learning processes.

It is also vital for the development and reinforcement of a learning culture. Learning needs to be an organisational attitude, the continual pursuit of better ways to identify and harness the opportunities for positive change. Reinforcing that attitude and energising the learning processes requires the timely, visible and effective implementation of our learning outcomes. In simple terms, people need to see the fruits of their labour.

Organisational potential is released by engaging the total organisational community in a collaborative and proactive learning and development strategy. Exactly how this is achieved will vary in each organisation. What is important is to ensure that a serious learning focus exists, that it has effective and energetic leadership and its constituent elements (systems and practices) promote the necessary collaborative engagement with the organisation's collective stakeholder community.

Conversation starters

Do we have a learning centre?

- Are we a learning organisation (or community)?
  - Do we understand our current positioning within our organisation or community life cycle and how to extend or regenerate that life cycle?
  - Do we have a force within the organisation which continually energises our community learning program? Do we have a learning culture?
  - How do we focus and prioritise our learning agenda?
- Do we have the capacity to deal with significant change?
  - Do we have a capacity for learning that enables us to anticipate and deal with disruptive change?

- o Or, is our learning focused on dealing with derivative change and/or occupational training that is motivated by improving the 'bottom line'?
    - o What is our track record in successfully navigating disruptive change?
- Does our organisation or community facilitate collaborative learning?
    - o Does our leadership demonstrably endorse and enable collaborative learning across and within the organisation or community?
    - o Do we engage the whole organisational community in learning? Or, is our learning focus centred within special groups, teams or projects?
    - o Do we adequately resource the time and space for collaborative learning?
    - o Do we have the necessary organisational or community practices and systems to enable and support collaborative learning?

How do we know what we know?

- How does our organisation or community share its collective (tacit and codified) knowledge?
    - o How do we understand the nature and scope of our organisational or community knowledge and know-how?
    - o How do we accumulate and store that collective knowledge?
    - o How do we provide our community with timely access to our collective stored knowledge and know-how?

- How do we enable our organisation or community to make sense of its shared knowledge?
    - o How do we enable our organisation or community to understand and unlock the potential of its shared knowledge?
    - o Does our collective stakeholder community participate in creating and implementing our knowledge management strategies and systems?
    - o How do we focus and prioritise our knowledge management agenda?

How do we generate new ideas?

- Are we an innovative organisation or community?
    - o Do we have a learning culture and leadership that encourages and enables innovation?
    - o Is innovation a shared learning responsibility within the organisational community or is it the preserve of special groups, teams or initiatives?
    - o Is the organisational community actively encouraged and supported to challenge the status quo and take reasonable risks to pursue new ideas?
    - o Do we seriously invest in the learning systems and processes and make the time for innovation discovery?
- Do we have the capacity to engage in innovation?
    - o Do we have the necessary innovation discovery and delivery skills to achieve innovation outcomes? Are these skills distributed throughout the organisational community?
    - o Does our organisation or community have the courage and coherence to embrace disruptive innovation?

o What is our organisational or community track record in discovering and delivering both derivative and disruptive innovation outcomes?

o Do our organisational learning practices and programs enable and encourage the integration of new thinking and new ideas?

Do we create opportunities for learning?

- Do we create the time and space for learning?

    o Do we view our community interactions and encounters (meetings, forums, discussions, projects etc.) as conversations with the potential for collaborative learning?

    o Are these interactions and encounters positioned as collective learning opportunities?

    o Do we adequately resource these interactions and encounters (with time, space and systems) to enable the participation and knowledge sharing that creates a learning opportunity?

- Do we provide effective learning feedback loops?

    o How do we capture and share feedback from our organisational and community interfaces, projects, interactions and conversations?

    o Are our learning feedback systems focused on specific interfaces and/or interactions or are they an integral part of our collective learning processes?

    o How do we ensure that learning outcomes are successfully implemented and shared with our collective stakeholder community?

I am indebted to Yasar F. Jarrar and Mohamed Zairi [39] for their research about organisational knowledge; Jeff Dyer and Hal Gregersen[40] for their writings about innovation; Michael H. Hugos[41] for his thoughts on business agility; and Amy C. Edmondson[25] for her contribution to organisational learning.

11 | Our Participation

Only organisations that collaborate with their stakeholder communities to co-create their future will create the contributions that sustain the long-term engagement of those communities.

Figure 30: Organisational participation

The co-creative enterprise is not about 'build it and they will come'. Rather, it is about 'build it with them and they're already there'.

Venkat Ramaswamy and Francis Gouillart

How do we add value within our communities?

How an organisation decides to participate with and within its stakeholder communities to co-create the equitable shared-value outcomes that manifest its shared purpose, will determine the quality and relevance and, therefore, value, of its contribution to those communities. That participation is influenced by the structure of its operating model. The operating model influences how the organisation interacts with each community, how it determines an appropriate contribution for each community, and how it creates and delivers that contribution to each of those communities.

An organisation's contribution to its stakeholder communities can be described as its value proposition; the articulation of the proposed value exchange between the organisation and its communities of interest. The term 'value proposition' is traditionally focused on an organisation's customer or user community. But for congruent organisations, all stakeholder communities share in the value created by the organisation, and therefore the organisation's value proposition is for all of its communities.

Value in this context is a relative and multifaceted concept, defined from the perspective of each party to the proposed exchange. It includes both tangible and intangible elements.

Within the last decade there has been a significant shift from a traditional focus on the more tangible aspects of value (e.g. the features and benefits of the product or service) to the intangible aspects related to the human factors associated with the value exchange (e.g. the interaction of the customer or the product or service user experience), and other consequential benefits (e.g. inclusion and belonging). By way of example, an organisation's tangible value proposition to its customers is typically represented by the format of its product and service offers (design, quality, availability, pricing etc.). For its business partners and suppliers the tangible value proposition is the offer to purchase their products and services. And for the organisation's staff, the tangible value proposition is usually the provision of employee benefits (remuneration, development etc.) in exchange for their services.

However, there are many intangible attributes of value that are important in determining an organisation's value proposition. Many organisations and their communities value acknowledgement, association (recognition, representation), and inter-connectedness (membership, inclusion, belonging). The importance of these attributes is clear, for example, in the value attached to co-branding and sponsorship (community and individual) and loyalty programs. Organisations, communities and individuals can also value co-alignment, which underpins concepts like connectedness and association, and is often ideologically based on a common or shared purpose, culture and/or values.

The value of alignment can be associated with market positioning and validation (both individual and community) or perhaps the opportunity to highlight and support organisational attributes that add value for the wider community.

Communities and individuals also value the nature and quality of their interactions with the organisation, their inter- and intra-community engagement experience. This is not just about the customer or user experience but the experience of all organisational stakeholders who participate in the creation and execution of the value exchange.

There are obviously many ways in which an organisation can add value (make contributions) to their communities. Unfortunately many organisations' value propositions are still shaped by a profit or wealth creation maxim applied by their ownership communities (shareholders, investors and funders). Often the effect of applying that maxim is to foster a win-lose proposition where the value exchange usually favours one organisational group (its ownership and/or investor community) at the expense (value deprivation) of one or more of its other communities.

Congruent organisations endeavour to create a mix of tangible and intangible value that maximises and balances the value exchange across and within their stakeholder communities. They seek to continually create organisational value propositions that offer a win-win outcome for all their stakeholder communities. They do this by focusing on co-creating outcomes that manifest their shared purpose and represent equitable-shared value for their whole organisational community.

While it is the clear intention of congruent organisations to balance the value exchange within their stakeholder communities, evidencing the equity of that exchange remains a challenge, especially where it involves intangible elements. In order to achieve this equitable sharing of value, the organisational community needs a way of assessing the tangible and intangible value associated with the organisational contribution to each of its communities. Perhaps this is a challenge best resolved by the organisational community? If we involve the whole organisational community in setting its strategic agenda, they will be engaged in a collaborative process to agree how the organisation intends to participate with and within each of its stakeholder communities. They will be involved in framing the organisation's future contributions to its stakeholder communities and therefore agreeing the nature of the value to be exchanged.

We should not underestimate the potential of a genuine community of purpose, guided by enabling leadership, to frame a contribution agenda that meets the expectations of its community. In other words, we should expect a congruent organisation to positively engage its stakeholder communities in the co-creation of a shared future.

How do we know our contributions are relevant?

Relevant in this context means value, both tangible and intangible. The assumption is that the more valuable an organisational contribution is to an individual or community, the more relevant it will be. Perhaps the simplest way to understand and confirm the relevance of an organisation's contributions to their stakeholder communities is for those communities to be involved in co-creating those contributions. Co-creating contribution engages the organisational community in a collaborative process where they are co-arbiters of the value generated for both their own stakeholder community and the organisation.

And where the organisation is focused on generating equitable-shared value, it is in the best interests of the collaborant communities to find ways to maximise the collective value to be shared. A singular and selfish focus on a particular community or group of stakeholders is simply not in play. The focus is on the collective future of the organisational community, on co-creating the best outcome for all participants.

By genuinely engaging its stakeholder communities to co-create a shared future, the organisation expands its interaction opportunities within its own communities, and through those communities can extend its reach into other connected (extra) communities. This intra-extra community collaboration expands the organisation's capacity to learn from and with its stakeholder community. It increases the organisation's access to its collective knowledge and the fresh thinking and new ideas, which can shape the value creation process and discover innovative ways to create and deliver more valuable outcomes.

Genuine collaborative endeavour that spans boundaries within the organisational community, can also uncover, explore and secure opportunities for achieving resource, supply chain, distribution channel and other operational efficiencies. And where co-creative endeavour engages the collective capability of the organisation, it can also reduce the risks of realising other value creation opportunities. Engaging the diverse perspectives and capabilities of the collective stakeholder community helps the organisation to identify, qualify and assess these risks. And the involvement of this community with the value creation processes assists both risk monitoring and management processes. Because these communities have a collective interest in maximising the shared-value outcome, they become motivated risk managers.

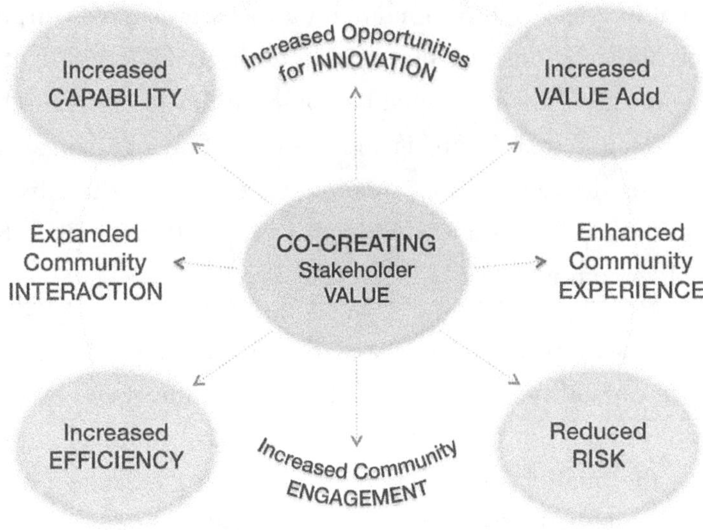

Figure 31: Impacts of organisational co-creativity

When an organisation increases the opportunities for its stakeholder communities, and their people, to participate in activities that create shared-value outcomes, they are also increasing the level of engagement of those communities. Where those outcomes manifest the shared purpose of the organisational community, it confirms the value of 'belonging' to that community. Therefore, organisations that genuinely involve their stakeholder communities in co-creating a shared future are also adding value by building community. They are strengthening the connectedness of the organisational community, and creating a sense of belonging, which is a critical part of the value exchange in developing congruent organisations

Win-win value propositions have the potential to engage the collective capability of the organisational community to maximise the opportunity for creating shared value by finding ways to increase the quality and efficiency of the value creation process and reduce the delivery risk. For an organisation to maximise the relevance and, therefore, value of its contributions to its stakeholder communities, it should engage those communities in co-creating its contributions.

Are we a connected community?

The co-creation of shared stakeholder value within an organisation requires the positive collaboration of its stakeholder communities. Effective collaboration is enabled by meaningful relationships, which enable the organisation to engage and organise its collective capability, and to shape value-creating networks and alliances. This is how the organisation participates effectively within its stakeholder communities to co-create outcomes that manifest its shared purpose.

By way of example, the organisation's value chain, including its supply and distribution channels, is effectively a group of value-creating networks and/or alliances, sets of community connections that enable the pursuit of their shared purpose.

These networks and alliances, which provide the pathways for organisational learning and a platform for collaborative endeavours, allow the organisation to remain agile and adaptive in pursuit of its purpose. For the organisation to be able to rapidly reform and realign these networks and alliances, to address new or changing value-creation opportunities, this web of organisational, community and individual connections must be **flexible, open, secure** and **enabling**.

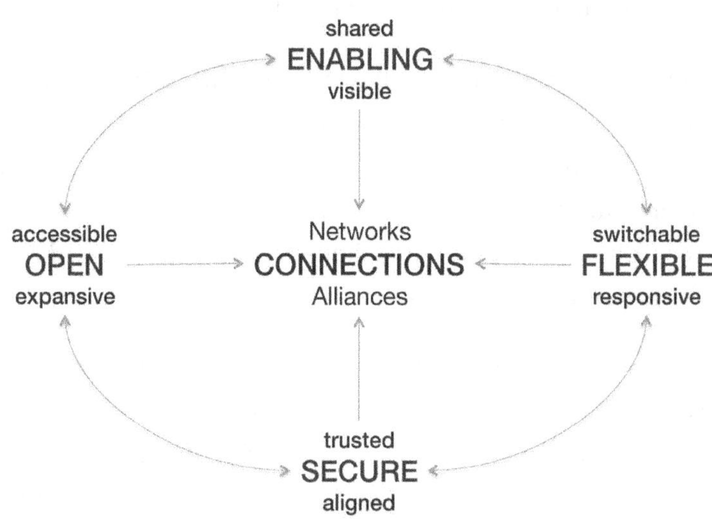

Figure 32: Community connections

Flexible: To be a responsive and adaptive organisation (i.e. to be sustainable) the organisation needs to be able to realign its people and resources to take advantage of both planned and unexpected value-creation opportunities. The organisation needs the capability to flex (disconnect and reconnect) its organisational structures to reshape and support the networks and alliances that can maximise the value created.

Therefore it needs its inter- and intra-community connections to be flexible – **responsive and switchable**.

Open: Value-creation opportunities can occur within and between any of the organisational communities and involve the complete range of organisational activities. These opportunities may involve the creation of new or hybrid activities and require the involvement of other external organisations, communities or individuals. This means that all of the organisation's communities must have the capacity to adapt their internal and external relationship structures (groups, projects, partnerships etc.) to enable a particular opportunity to be realised.

Not only does this require flexible inter- and intra-community connections, but also that those connections are accessible to 'outsiders' and have an outward (non-insular) focus, a capacity for extra-community engagement. This means that the connections between the organisation's stakeholder communities need to be open – **accessible and expansive**.

Secure: Change can present an opportunity for the creation of substantial stakeholder value. For organisations to have the courage to embrace change, particularly disruptive change, as a positive learning opportunity, they need to be confident that their community networks and alliances have the capacity to sustain the impacts of that change. They need to know that those networks and alliances have the resilience to embrace, explore and extract value from these change opportunities.

The inter- and intra-community connections, which enable these networks and alliances, are created through relationships. Where those relationships are built on mutual trust and respect, and aligned with the organisation's shared purpose, they make

connections within the organisational community that are secure –
trusted and aligned.

These meaningful relationships enable the organisational
community to be confident about its ability to reshape and realign
its networks and alliances to respond to change; to reconfigure its
operating model as necessary to take advantage of new value-
creation opportunities. Because the connections that enable these
networks and alliances are secured by a shared purpose and trust-
based relationships, they accommodate the openness and
flexibility that is essential for creating their resilience.

Enabling: The creation and reshaping of effective and efficient
organisational networks and alliances is enabled by open, flexible
and secure (intra, inter and extra) connections within the
organisational community. The opportunity for the organisational
community to create stakeholder value by sharing the potential of
those connections is dependent on the community knowing about
that potential. This means that the organisation needs to find a
way of communicating how its operational and transitional (e.g.
project) networks and alliances are currently organised. And to
convey the potential of those networks and alliances by
communicating the nature of the connecting relationships and the
capabilities (knowledge, skills etc) of the relationship participants.

How an organisation decides to make the potential of its
community visible to its community will obviously depend on its
operating context. But sharing that information with all its
stakeholder communities is how the organisation enables those
communities to assess the potential of existing connections, and to
explore the opportunities for creating new connections and thus
forming new networks and alliances.

Congruent organisations are connected communities. They encourage the development of open, flexible, secure and enabling connections across and within their stakeholder communities. They build meaningful relationships that underpin those connections and provide the enabling leadership that can facilitate the continual reshaping of their community networks and alliances. Congruent organisations can rapidly reform and realign their collective capabilities to realise the potential of value-creation opportunities that manifest their shared purpose.

Expanding and enhancing the connectivity within an organisational community means increasing the quantum and quality of the connections across and within the organisation's current and potential stakeholder communities. It is about growing the organisation's influence within its current communities and extending its reach into new communities of interest.

For many organisations the marketing effort is primarily focused on building relationships with its customer community. For the congruent organisation expanding connectivity is concerned with building the relationships with and within all of its stakeholder communities. The marketing focus of a congruent organisation seeks to expand and enhance all of its (inter-, intra- and extra-) community connection possibilities.

Does our brand resonate within our communities?

An organisation's brand is intended to express the intrinsic value of the organisation (who the organisation is and what it stands for) to all its stakeholder communities, not just to its customer community.

It is a construct designed to facilitate an emotional and functional connection with the organisation's primary value proposition. In the context of this discussion about congruent organisations, that value proposition expresses the nature of the organisation's contribution to its stakeholder communities, the shared-value outcomes that will manifest the organisation's shared purpose. Therefore, an authentic and sustainable brand will connect the stakeholder community with the organisation's special or unique character. It will connect the community with its shared purpose and its ambition for the future.

'Branding' an organisation is essentially concerned with increasing its presence within the hearts and minds of its stakeholder communities. Organisations develop a positive presence within their stakeholder communities by engaging those communities with their value proposition. But it is not enough to persuade those communities about the potential benefits of engaging with the organisation's shared purpose and ambition for the future. They must also demonstrate their genuine interest in each community by co-creating outcomes that manifest that purpose and add value for that community. And they must do that in a way that appreciates the community's participation in the value creation process. Their community interactions must be consistent with their shared purpose and encourage and acknowledge the community's contributions. In essence, the organisation must behave authentically within its stakeholder communities.

For an organisation's brand to resonate within its stakeholder communities, the organisation must have an authentic presence within those communities. It must participate within those communities in a way that confirms its alignment with its shared purpose and ambition.

The visible, transparent and consistent alignment of the organisation's voice and actions with its purpose and ambition, and a strong track record of co-creating shared value, demonstrate the organisation's integrity and strengthen its authentic presence within its stakeholder communities.

The challenge for most organisations is to create an authentic presence within all of their stakeholder communities. Obviously, this will not be possible without a shared purpose. But even the existence of a genuinely shared purpose does not lessen the organisation's challenge to achieve the strategic and operational balance that results in the creation of equitable-shared value for each of its stakeholder communities. The organisation cannot prefer the owner community and the generation of shareholder wealth over the creation of economic and social value for its employee community. Nor can the organisation preference the value it creates for the customer community at the expense of an inequitable distribution of value to its supply chain communities.

Unfortunately, we see many examples of organisations and communities where this wealth distribution is inequitable, where the collective organisational community is dysfunctional, and power (usually economic and sometimes political) is used to disenfranchise some stakeholder communities. The organisational brand is far from resonant in these communities and the organisation will be perceived as unauthentic by some of its stakeholder communities.

The authenticity of an organisation's presence within their stakeholder communities can also be influenced by the way they communicate with those communities. Effective communication is simply sharing the right information with the right people in the right way.

The right information must include what the community wants to know, not just what the organisation wants to tell it. The right people are all the members of the community that have an information need. And the right way is successfully connecting the right people in the community with the information they need.

To understand what an organisational community wants to know, requires a deep understanding of their concerns, intentions and ambitions. Developing this empathetic awareness comes from genuine dialogue with a community that feels it is an active and welcome participant in the life of the organisation, and knows that its participation and contribution are valued. To enable such dialogue, and the careful listening that it involves, the organisation should engage its organisational community in conversations about its value proposition. These conversations have the potential to be successful because they are focussed on the manifestation of a shared purpose and therefore the co-creation of shared-equitable value for all of the participants.

Successful community conversations strengthen the organisation's presence within their stakeholder communities by demonstrating the organisation's genuine concern for the wellbeing of those communities. Successful conversations enable the authentic presence of all of the conversational participants.

They create the opportunity for generative dialogue that results in the co-creation of shared-value outcomes for the participant community. These shared-value outcomes demonstrate the authenticity of the organisation's engagement with its stakeholder communities. They strengthen the organisation's presence and, therefore, the resonance of its brand within its stakeholder communities.

Congruent organisations have a vibrant presence within their stakeholder communities that reflects their genuine interest in the future wellbeing of those communities. They create that presence by hosting successful conversations with their stakeholder communities about a shared future and the co-creation of mutual value outcomes. And they demonstrate the authenticity of their presence by interacting with those communities to create shared-value outcomes that benefit the whole organisational community. The brand of congruent organisations resonates strongly within their stakeholder communities.

Conversation starters

How do we add value within our communities?

- Does our organisational value proposition expect to create equitable-shared value for our stakeholder communities?
    - o Does our value proposition express the manifestation of our core purpose?
    - o Does our value proposition include all of our stakeholder communities?
- How do we measure the value we add (our contributions) to our stakeholder communities?
    - o What are the key tangible and intangible attributes of the value we add to our stakeholder communities?
    - o How do these attributes align with the expectations of our stakeholder communities? How do we know?

How do we know our contributions are relevant?

- Do we collaborate with our stakeholder communities to co-create our contributions?

- How do we engage with our stakeholder communities
  to determine the nature and value (the relevance) of
  our contribution to their community?

Are we a connected community?

- Do we have effective networks and alliances with and within
  our stakeholder communities?
  - How do we choose who to network and form alliance
    with?
  - How do we create and sustain these networks and
    alliances?
  - How do we measure the effectiveness of these
    connections?
- Are our community connections (relationships) flexible, open,
  secure and enabling?
  - Can we easily switch connections to respond to new
    opportunities?
  - Are these connections open and available for the wider
    community to access and utilise?
  - Are these connections resilient? Will they sustain
    disruptive change?
  - Are these connections visible and open to all
    stakeholders? Are they open to potential (new)
    stakeholders?

Does our brand resonate within our communities?

- Do we enjoy an authentic and vibrant presence within all of
  our stakeholder communities?
  - How engaged are our stakeholder communities with
    our organisational purpose and ambition for the
    future? How do we know?

- o Is the nature of our organisational interactions with our stakeholder communities always consistent with who we claim to be – our shared purpose and ambition for the future? How do we know?

- o How do we communicate with, and within, our stakeholder communities? Do we host successful conversations with our communities?

Acknowledgements

I am indebted to Venkat Ramaswamy and Francis Gouillart[42] for their writings about co-creation; to Rob Cross and Robert J. Thomas[43] for their writings about social networks; and to Peter Senge et al[44] for their thoughts on presence.

12 | Our Wellbeing

Sustainable organisations genuinely care about the collective wellbeing of their stakeholder communities.

Figure 33: Organisational wellbeing

Goodness is the only investment that never fails.

Henry David Thoreau

> **Wellbeing** is one of the Congruency Framework's five factors. The longer-term **sustainability** of an organisation is dependent on its ability to act as a capable, resilient and responsible citizen, and to secure the long-term wellbeing of its stakeholder communities.

How sustainable is our organisational community?

A **sustainable organisation** is one that is equipped to maintain the longer-term engagement of its stakeholder communities in the pursuit of its shared purpose, and to continually manifest that purpose by co-creating equitable-shared value for those communities. The sustainable organisation engages its collective capability to sustain that pursuit for the longer term. It has the capacity to successfully negotiate ongoing and disruptive change, and the ability to continually co-create shared-value outcomes that address the social, cultural, economic and environmental needs (the wellbeing) of its stakeholder communities. Organisational sustainability is, therefore, inextricably linked with the wellbeing of those communities.

Community wellbeing is dependent on the collective 'health, wealth and happiness' of the community. It reflects the degree to which the social (health, welfare, education etc.), cultural (identity, diversity, values etc.), economic (prosperity, employment, sustenance etc.), and the environmental (physical and natural environment) needs of the community are being met.

Sustainability in this context is, therefore, not just concerned with the organisation's interaction with its physical environment (its 'green' agenda), but also its interaction with the social, cultural and economic environments of the communities that participate in its ecosystem. The long-term survival of an organisation depends on its ability to continually adapt to changes within that ecosystem; reshaping and realigning its participation to ensure that it continues to co-create equitable-shared value for the participant communities. This effort includes continually rebalancing its social, cultural, economic and environmental agendas to ensure the organisation's contribution remains relevant to those communities.

Sustainable organisations assume a collaborative responsibility for the wellbeing of their stakeholder communities. They pay responsible attention to the social, cultural, economic and environmental needs of those communities to ensure that they continue to co-create contributions that enhance the overall wellbeing and sustainability of the entire organisational community.

Sustainable organisations must be able to rapidly adapt to changes in their operating environment. They must possess the capability to adjust their operating frameworks and resourcing strategies to address positive (value-creating) opportunities for change. These organisations must have agile strategic, governance and management systems that enable the effective, localised and collaborative ownership of change (value creation) opportunities. They also need flexible resourcing, which enables their collective monetary, infrastructural and intellectual assets to be readily deployed to enable the effective realisation of change opportunities.

Sustainable organisations need the 'inner strength' to deal with continuing change as an inevitable 'business as usual' phenomenon. They must have a capacity for change that is energetic (enabled and supported) optimistic (possibility focused), aware (informed and knowledgeable) and confident (experienced and assured). They need to feel confident about their ability to explore and successfully negotiate and derive shared value from change opportunities. This requires leadership that is change oriented; a collaborative culture that willingly engages collective knowledge and capability; and resourceful management that can find a way to make the change happen. Sustainable organisations must be **resilient** organisations.

> **Congruent organisations are sustainable organisations with a strong focus on the wellbeing of their stakeholder communities.** They are confident, change-oriented and resilient organisations anchored by their long-term commitment to a shared purpose. They are enabled by their collaborative learning culture to facilitate the productive sharing of their collective knowledge and capability. They enjoy an adaptive and agile operating style which is supported by their enabling leadership and facilitated by their flexible community networks and alliances. Those networks are secured by meaningful relationships built on a shared commitment to the long-term co-creation of mutual benefit and the wellbeing of the whole organisational community.

Is our organisation fit for purpose?

An organisation (or community) is 'fit for purpose' when it has the capability to develop and utilise its resources to pursue and manifest its purpose – to create equitable-shared value for its stakeholder communities. These capabilities include the collective skills and experience of their people (people competencies) and the organisational governance, management and operational systems (framework competencies) that enable its people to create, manage and deploy the organisation's resources (or assets) for the benefit of the organisational community.

The organisation's core capabilities also include its organisational culture, the practices and behaviours that influence how the people and framework competencies will be engaged and applied. A fit organisation will have timely access to the core competencies that are relevant to its particular context (the strategic and operating environments and the change opportunities those environments present). And it will possess an organisational culture that enables it to apply those competencies to maximise the creation of stakeholder value.

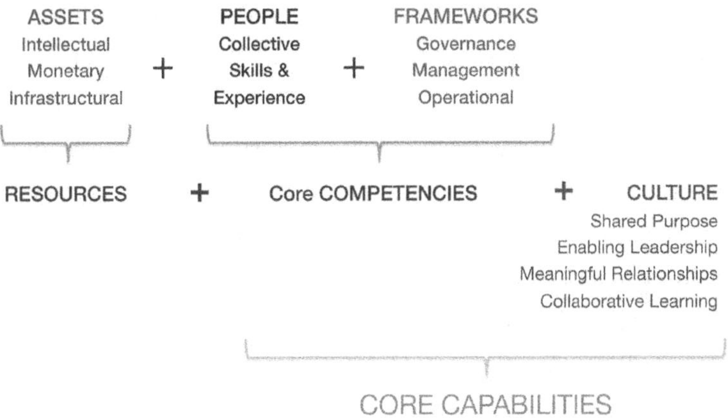

Figure 34: Competencies, culture and capabilities

The term resources refers to the organisation's **assets** and includes all of the monetary, intellectual and infrastructural assets which are owned, controlled or managed by the organisational community and available for deployment in pursuit of their shared purpose.

The organisation's core competencies refer to the combination of the organisation's people competencies and what we have termed **framework** competencies (governance, management and operational systems).

Congruent organisations do not refer to their **people** as human capital or human resources. Their people are considered to be members of the organisational community and participants within its ecosystem. People perform a critical role in the development and utilisation of organisational resources. Their skills and experience (competencies) form part of the organisation's collective capability.

Usually people in this context will refer to the organisation's management and staff, which include their contractors and consultants – the 'employed' community who can be directly influenced by the organisation. In congruent organisations the people who are engaged with its shared purpose, and for mutual benefit, extend beyond its employed community to include all of its communities of interest (e.g. suppliers, customers etc) many of whom cannot be directly influenced by the organisation. However, they form an important part of the organisation's collective skills and experience and their productive engagement is usually essential for the effective operation of the organisation.

Therefore, developing an organisation's people competency is not just concerned with hiring and training its employed community. The organisation must also be concerned with finding ways to engage the relevant competencies of its non-employed community. An organisation can develop its people competencies by hiring and training the right people – staff, contractors and consultants.

And it can expand those competencies by contracting and collaborating with appropriate business partners, suppliers and customers to access the external skills and experience it needs to manage and deploy its resources. But it may not be able to productively engage those competencies, especially the competencies of its non-employed community, without the leadership, organisational culture and framework competencies that enable its people to feel and act like an integral part of the organisational community.

An organisation can also hire consultants and advisors to help its employed community to build excellent governance, management and operating frameworks. But those frameworks may not be successfully deployed if they are not designed to reflect the way the organisation prefers to operate and they are not embraced by the whole organisational community. Excellent people and framework competencies only create excellent organisational capability when the organisational leadership and culture enables the collaborative engagement and productive application of those competencies in manifesting the organisation's purpose.

Thus, assuming an organisation has the capacity to access the appropriate people competencies it needs to pursue its purpose, its fitness becomes dependent on having the right leadership and culture to engage and apply those competencies. It is the enabling leadership and collaborative learning culture of congruent organisations that provides the opportunity to engage both their employed and non-employed communities in the development of the people and framework competencies that will benefit the whole organisational community.

Because of their commitment to a shared purpose, congruent organisations are naturally motivated to prioritise the creation of equitable-shared value for their stakeholder communities. Therefore, they naturally focus their attention on building the people and framework competencies that enable them to be fit for purpose. Their commitment to a shared purpose enables them to access and engage the collective skills and experience of their whole organisational community. And their enabling leadership and collaborative learning culture means they will engage their people in developing and deploying the core competencies they need to be successful – to create the outcomes that manifest their shared purpose.

Is our organisation resilient?

Resilient organisations (and communities) have the capacity to anticipate and manage change in a way that enhances their ability to pursue their purpose. They are able to effect appropriate and timely adjustments to their strategies, operating models and organisational structures to successfully navigate change opportunities and challenges. Resilient organisations emerge from a change experience with an enhanced appetite for change. They learn from the change experience and become more resourceful as a result of that experience and better equipped to deal with future unexpected or disruptive change. Resilient organisations are continually learning how to become more resilient.

Building organisational resilience is about creating the organisational capacity to recognise and respond to change in a way that maintains the organisation's stability and enhances its performance – the successful manifestation of the organisation's purpose.

An organisation's resilience, which is evidenced by its capacity to successfully navigate change, is influenced by four key factors:

- **Responsiveness**: The change orientation of the organisation, its attitude to change which is influenced by its leadership and culture. Resilient organisations are open to change and view it as a potential value generating opportunity. They are responsive, not reactive or averse, to opportunities for change.

- **Knowledge**: The change awareness of the organisation, its capability to anticipate, recognise and understand the change opportunities and learn from its change experiences. Resilient organisations are learning organisations. They are knowledgeable about the potential for positive change that exists within their own stakeholder communities and their external environment.

- **Resourcefulness**: The change adaptation capability of the organisation, its ability to successfully negotiate the change opportunities in a way that adds value to the organisation. Resilient organisations adopt flexible planning and organisation structures and are resourceful in the way that they use innovation and collaboration to respond positively to change.

- **Confidence**: The change appetite of the organisation, the ability of the organisation (and its stakeholder communities) to continually energise and resource change initiatives and sustain the impacts of ongoing and disruptive change. Resilient organisations are confident about their ability to negotiate change in a purposeful way that adds value for their communities.

Figure 35: Drivers for organisational resilience

Congruent organisations are resilient organisations. They have a positive attitude to change and are confident about their ability to successfully negotiate change opportunities. They are learning organisations with a possibility focus and see change as an opportunity for the creation of shared value for their stakeholder community. Their collaborative learning culture facilitates the sharing of collective knowledge which enables them to identify advantageous change opportunities and define an appropriate response. That same culture enables the engagement of their collective capabilities to realise the value in the change opportunity.

Congruent organisations are strategically agile and operationally adaptive. Because they are always purpose focused and enjoy strong community engagement, they can accommodate substantial shifts in the strategies that are necessary to achieve their longer-term ambition.

They prefer flexible and dynamic planning processes, which enable them to rapidly refocus and realign their strategies, operating model, organisational structures and resources to take advantage of change opportunities. The pursuit of their shared purpose is guided by a high-level strategic blueprint, which is an open, flexible, transparent and outcome-focused mechanism designed to frame the collaborative projects that will deliver its change agenda and learning outcomes.

Congruent organisations support adaptive organisational and management models that can facilitate the delivery of their change responses. Unlike the bureaucratic, risk averse and highly partitioned organisational models that result from command and control leadership, enabling leadership fosters the creation of adaptive management models that enable self-organising and self-regulating communities, interconnected by relationships that support a web of collaborative networks and alliances. These networks and alliances (between individuals, groups and communities) provide the basis for an adaptive organisational structure which can flex to accommodate the organisation's change agenda. They can be created, reconfigured or disassembled as required to enable the implementation of the collaborative endeavours that will deliver the required change responses.

Adaptive management models are typically characterised by highly devolved (decentralised), transparent and flexible management-decision frameworks supported by open access to the organisation's collective knowledge banks. They expect constituent groups and communities (agents) to have considerable autonomy and accountability to create and execute the projects and initiatives that will achieve the organisation's ambitions.

Enabling the distributed autonomy of groups and communities will inevitably result in some duplication of people and resources. However this is often beneficial as it creates a level of redundant capability that strengthens the resilience of the organisation.

In sharp contrast typical command and control management models rely on centralised regulation by plans, budgets, rules, hierarchal decision structures and control and compliance systems. The centralised rigidity of these models typically creates change-averse or reactive organisations that are slow to recognise and respond to change opportunities.

Some organisations adopt a hybrid management model where there is a mix of centralised and distributed functionality. They use the adaptive models to increase their responsiveness in change-sensitive areas (e.g. customer management) and centralised models to increase control where change represents a serious risk (e.g. regulatory compliance management). However, the resilience of these organisations remains reliant on the adaptive model for value creation. They need to be aware of the potential for the control model, which is focused on value protection, to encourage a protective, risk-averse focus which can constrain its appetite for positive change.

Congruent organisations are collaborative learning communities that are connected by meaningful relationships, which are secured by a shared purpose and sustained by the creation of shared value. They are resilient organisations, strategically agile and operationally adaptive, and confident in their collective capability to continually identify and integrate positive opportunities for change.

Does our organisation behave responsibly?

The notion of 'organisational responsibility' has been widely discussed since the 1950s with reference to various concepts including, but not limited to, ethical and sustainable business practices, corporate citizenship, triple bottom line (people, planet, profit) and corporate social responsibility (CSR). CSR is perhaps the most widely-referenced concept. Broadly speaking, all of these concepts define or frame organisational responsibility by referencing the societal responsibilities of the organisation, its accountability for the impacts of its behaviour and practices on the health and welfare (social aspects) of society, and the environment within which it operates. The organisation has a responsibility to balance its social, cultural, economic and environmental (or ecological) impacts in delivering to the collective expectations of its community. Balancing these impacts is important for the sustainability of both the organisation (which is an accountability to its stakeholder communities) and the wider community and its operating environment (which is an accountability to its societal community).

An international standard guideline for developing organisational social responsibility (ISO 26000:2010) was released in 2010. This standard, which presents a potential conceptual framework for organisational social responsibility (OSR), summarises 37 social responsibility issues under seven subject headings and attempts to incorporate relevant aspects of other international standards and agreements. It is not an elegant framework, which perhaps reflects its negotiated development path and the need to integrate existing standards and practices. Also, it is an issues-based rather than principle-based framework, which may mean it is not flexible enough, even as a guideline, to allow organisations to adapt it to reflect their particular circumstances.

However, the standard does create an important opportunity for an ongoing international conversation about OSR and the expectation is that it will be further developed to reflect emerging best practice.

Figure 36: Organisational social responsibility

The release of ISO 26000:2010 is a welcome development, but its real impact remains to be seen. In the interim, the dialogue and debate about definitional, application and measurement issues associated with OSR is ongoing and organisations continue to adopt different approaches according to their own priorities and circumstances. In the absence of a generally accepted, elegant (simple) and useful concept of organisational responsibility, there will continue to be confusion about how an organisation is expected to discharge its social, cultural, economic and environmental (ecological) obligations to its stakeholder and societal communities.

Two factors contributing to this confusion are the different motivations of organisations who adopt an OSR approach and the preferences of the dominant stakeholders who influence that motivation. Motivations include a mix of compliance, profitability, ecological and sustainability drivers and frequently it is the owner stakeholder (e.g. shareholder or investor) who is the dominant influence in which OSR approach is adopted. This means that ownership value generation (frequently profit motivation) is often the dominant driver which may bias the choice of OSR approach adopted. Using a more holistic approach, which embraces all of the stakeholder communities (e.g. consumers, partners, society etc.), would balance the motivations and influence of individual stakeholders. This would ensure that the OSR practices adopted respond to the preferences and concerns of all stakeholder communities, including the societal community within which the organisation operates.

Another challenge in defining an OSR framework is to ensure that it is conceptually robust, but also flexible and adaptive. It needs to enable organisations to recognise their particular environmental situations and make an appropriate response to their diverse stakeholder and societal communities. This means a useful framework must be built on a set of commonly acceptable core principles which allow organisations to create a response that is principle based and reflective of their particular operating environment. OSR issues may then be addressed by applying the principles in a way that is appropriate for the organisation.

Finally, the title OSR may also be problematic. Organisational social responsibility is used as a summary label for social, cultural, economic, ecological and good governance responsibilities of an organisation. While all of the issues to be addressed by OSR have a social aspect, it may be more helpful to refer to OSR simply as organisational responsibility.

I suggest **organisational responsibility** could be defined as four interrelated and interdependent accountabilities, which together provide a principle-based conceptual framework that can be applied by any organisation (or community) to reflect its particular circumstances.

- **Building sustainable communities**: Creating contributions that enhance the wellbeing of their stakeholder communities. Improving the social, cultural and economic viability of those communities and the sustainability of the physical and natural environments within which they operate. The *responsibility* to create a sustainable organisation by working to ensure the sustainability of its stakeholder communities. This recognises the organisation's *requirement* to contribute to building a sustainable society.

- **Making societal contributions**: Pursuing and manifesting a shared purpose that is concerned with creating value for the society within which it operates. The *responsibility* to have an overarching moral purpose that is beyond profit and concerned with improving some aspect of that society. This recognises the organisation's *requirement* to be a positive force for good within its own society.

- **Co-creating equitable-shared value**: Ensuring that the organisation's stakeholders have an equitable share in the value they co-create with the organisation. The *responsibility* to collaborate with its collective stakeholder community to generate win-win outcomes that create shared value and manifest their shared purpose. This recognises the organisation's *requirement* to care for its people by behaving as a community of purpose.

- **Enabling good governance**: Establishing and maintaining organisational governance frameworks that ensure that its leadership, management and decision-making processes are authentic, ethical, open and transparent, and enable the co-creation of purposeful and equitable shared-value outcomes. The *responsibility* to ensure that it operates in a way that it can achieve the first three accountabilities. This recognises the organisation's *requirement* to act as a responsible member of its own stakeholder community.

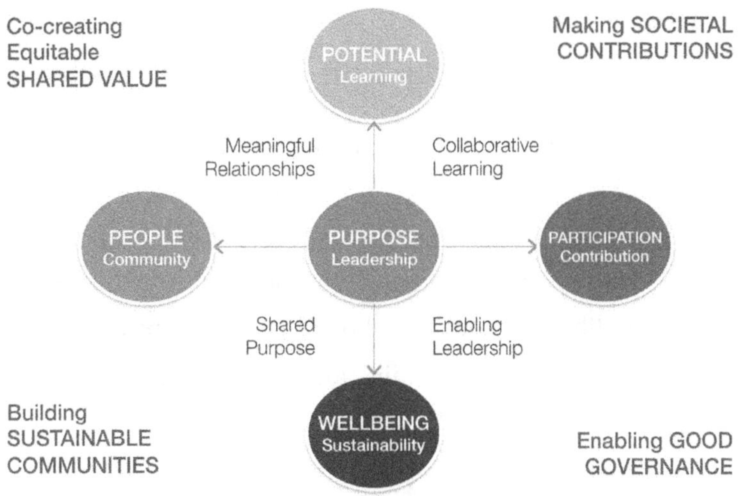

Figure 37: Factors in organisational responsibility

Congruent organisations are communities of purpose, which engage their stakeholder communities in the pursuit of a shared purpose, which is beyond profit and instead is concerned with the creation of purposeful mutual value for those communities. They assume a collaborative responsibility for the wellbeing of their stakeholder communities.

They accept accountability for co-creating contributions (mutual value outcomes) that address the social, cultural, economic and environmental priorities and concerns of those communities. In this way, they ensure that their own sustainability is underpinned by the sustainability of their stakeholder communities.

Congruent organisations are responsible organisations. They behave as responsible members of their own stakeholder community and as responsible citizens within the society in which they operate.

Conversation starters

How sustainable is our organisational community?

- How does our organisation continue to assure the social, cultural, economic and environmental wellbeing of its stakeholder communities?
    - How does our organisation contribute to the economic wellbeing of our stakeholder communities?
    - How does our organisation recognise and support the social and cultural needs of our stakeholder communities?
    - Does our organisation have an agenda to sustain and/or enhance the physical and natural environments of our stakeholder communities?

Is our organisation fit for purpose?

- How does our organisation engage the skills and experience of the people in its collective stakeholder community?
    - Who are our people? How do we recognise and engage their collective competencies?

- How does our organisational culture encourage and support our people to participate and contribute to their full potential?

- Do we have governance, management and operating frameworks that enable us to develop and utilise our collective capability?

  - How do we define the nature and relevance of the core capabilities of our organisational community?

  - Do our governance, management and operating frameworks allow us to engage and apply these core capabilities in a timely manner?

Is our organisation resilient?

- Do we have the capacity to successfully navigate disruptive change?

  - Is our organisational culture change receptive or change averse?

  - Are we change oriented (responsive), change aware (knowledgeable) and change adaptive (resourceful)?

  - Are we confident about our ability to negotiate significant change?

- How do our organisational systems facilitate our positive response to change?

  - Are we an agile organisation?

  - Do we have the planning and management systems that enable our organisation to adapt to unexpected change?

  - Do those systems enable an appropriate, collective and rapid response to change?

Does our organisation behave responsibly?

- How does our organisation deal with its social, cultural, economic and environmental (ecological) responsibilities to its organisational and societal communities?

  - Does our organisation have an 'organisational responsibility' agenda? How does it prioritise and action that agenda?

  - Does our organisational purpose have a societal focus? Is that focus evident in our organisational activities and the outcomes we create?

  - Is our organisation a community of purpose? Do we really care about our people?

  - How do we ensure the sustainability of our stakeholder communities?

- Does our organisation enjoy responsible governance?

  - Do our organisational governance frameworks ensure authentic, ethical, open and transparent leadership and management?

Acknowledgements

I am indebted to Liisa Valikangas[45], and Timothy Vogus and Kathleen Sutcliffe[46] for their writings about resilient organisations; to Jeremy Hope, Peter Bunce and Franz Roosli[47] for their writings about adaptive organisations; to Adam Werbach[48] for his writing about organisational sustainability; to Constance Helfat et al[49] for their writings about organisational capabilities; and to Christine Arena[15], Wayne Visser[50] and Marcel van Marrewijk[51] for their thoughts on responsible organisations.

Part Three – Thinking about Congruent Individuals

A congruent individual is a person who lives their life on purpose. They seek to co-create an authentic presence with and within their communities that integrates and aligns who they are with what they do. They have a learning orientation that welcomes difference and diversity, and continually seeks opportunities for personal development and renewal. And they develop and sustain their communities of interest by building meaningful relationships that are based on selfless service and the generation of mutual value.

13 |My Purpose

People who know and live their life purpose have the capacity to co-create communities that will transform the world we live in.

Figure 38: Individual purpose

There are certain things that are fundamental to human fulfillment. The essence of these needs is captured in the phrase 'to live, to love, to learn, to leave a legacy'. The need to have a legacy is our spiritual need to have a sense of meaning, purpose, personal congruence, and contribution.

Stephen R. Covey

What is my unique purpose?

To begin, let us reflect on what we mean by purpose.

Purpose is about contribution. Our purpose gives meaning to our existence on this planet. It defines our unique personal role in the society in which we live, what is expected of us by the Universe of which we are part. Our purpose is about how we as individuals will enrich our own lives and the lives of others. It defines how we will participate as individuals within our personal communities. It prescribes the nature of the contribution that we will make to our families, our friends, our colleagues, associates and the wider community.

Our purpose may be expressed in words that are similar to the purpose of others, but it is unique in the sense that only we can manifest our purpose. The nature of the contribution we make to our communities will be uniquely personal, an expression of the talents and gifts that are ours alone to share for the benefit of others.

Purpose is beyond profit. It is not focused on personal wealth as defined in economic or physical terms. Purpose is not selfish.

It has a selfless focus on others and prioritises the wellbeing of the societal community in which we live. The manifestation of our purpose or 'how we show up in the world' is concerned with building the wellbeing of our community, the collective health, wealth and happiness of the people we care about. Wealth in this context includes the social and material (economic and physical) capital we need to sustain our own lives and the lives of our community. But the creation and utilisation of this capital is not for its own sake or to preference the few at the expense of the many. Purposeful wealth creation has a total community focus. It is the creation of the social and material capital required to enable our shared purpose. It is a means to an end (individual and community wellbeing) and not an end in itself.

Purpose lives in the present; it is not a future state. Purpose is not our vision for the future, some aspirational future state that we will create over time. Our purpose is the inner driving force or imperative that sustains and guides our life on a daily basis; that deeply held conviction about who we are that is timeless, always present and always relevant in 'the now'. Our intention or ambition for the future is our best description of what we believe the manifestation of our purpose will look like in the medium term. It can be a useful marker to light an unfolding pathway for the manifestation of our purpose. But don't be surprised if it changes over time as your purpose unveils new and more presently relevant ways to manifest itself in your life and in the lives of your community.

Purpose is enabling and inspiring; it is not a constraint. As we have already noted, our purpose is not a destination, it is a core, selfless and ever-present proposition that sustains our life journey. It inspires and energises that journey.

The enduring presence of our purpose means that it cannot be constrained by our personal frameworks or mental models. Our purpose is, in essence, the free and true spirit within us, an expression of our inner being, our unique connection with the Universe.

Our purpose will often reflect a deeply held moral conviction or proposition about our place in the world. It defines who we are and why we are here in terms of the contribution we will make to the community we are part of. That definition may be informed by our religious convictions, our personal ethics and/or other personal frameworks that guide our thinking and our behaviour. But our true purpose will not be constrained or blunted by these frameworks. Such frameworks may provide helpful parameters for our life journey but, at the extreme, they can also misrepresent or distort our true purpose.

Purpose is usually discovered with difficulty; it is not easily chosen. It is not a choice between rational alternatives. It cannot be 'worked out' by manufacturing a set of possible options (or strategic alternatives) and fitting them together like a word puzzle. Purpose is not crafted, it has to be discovered. Our purpose will not be easily discovered. We are often very attached to who we currently are and perhaps less interested in the risks of exploring who we might actually be. Our mental models, our way of thinking about ourselves and the world we live in, can build a strong attachment to learned views of ourselves and others that are not conducive to change. To break free from a current reality that is defined by our past, to suspend our view of the present and see our world differently, we need to engage our intuitive self. We need to access the potential of our inner being, that inner source of knowledge about who we are.

The discovery of our unique purpose is a very personal and evolutionary journey which typically involves periods of deep reflection. Our life story, with its record of challenges and achievements, successes and failures, celebrations and disappointments, provides an important opportunity to reflect on and learn from (and let go of) our past. Each of our memorable life encounters holds a clue to our real purpose, each significant life event whether viewed historically as positive or negative, presents a positive learning opportunity. Reflecting carefully and positively on our life experience not only clarifies what we care about, what we value and the truths we hold dear, it also helps to create a future perspective that can embrace the events of our past as a series of 'life gifts' for the future.

Our deeply held values and our convictions and beliefs also provide useful clues as to the nature of our purpose. Provided we can separate and clarify our values and beliefs from the prejudices and distortions often embedded in our inherited and learned mental models, then we have another valuable set of purpose indicators. But the unfolding of our true purpose will not be guided solely by our life story or our values analysis. It will be guided by our intuition, that sense of 'knowing' through which we can access the greater wisdom of the Universe. It is this knowing that helps us to make sense of our life, to strip away the 'noise' from our life story and values analysis and to come to 'know' our true purpose.

Our purpose quest can be a lonely journey or one we undertake in the company of others. We can share insights and seek other wisdoms to clarify and confirm an emerging truth, a thrilling and enlightening sense of who we are and what we 'know' to be true for us.

However, once we have made the decision to discover and live our life purpose, we should expect that decision to be challenged. Our rational mind will challenge the logic of our intuitive wisdom and test our resolve to continue. If we overcome these mindblocks, if our decision to begin the journey represents a genuine commitment, then the pathway forward and the resources and assistance we need to follow it will emerge. We simply need to be alert to what shows up to guide, encourage and support us on our way.

As Johann van Goethe once said:

> *Until one is committed, there is hesitancy, the chance to draw back. Concerning all acts of initiative (and creation), there is one elementary truth that ignorance of which kills countless ideas and splendid plans: that the moment one definitely commits oneself, then Providence moves too. All sorts of things occur to help one that would never otherwise have occurred. A whole stream of events issues from the decision, raising in one's favour all manner of unforeseen incidents and meetings and material assistance, which no man could have dreamed would have come his way.*

Then, as our journey progresses and our purpose gradually unfolds and becomes clear, its authenticity, its unique truth for us, will be evident in its nature:

- our purpose will express our unique **potential**
- our purpose will concern **selfless service** to others
- our purpose will be about a **contribution** that is beyond profit
- our purpose will embrace the **truth** of us
- our purpose will express our **presence** in the world
- our purpose will feel enabling and **inspiring**
- our purpose will **energise** us and engage others

- our purpose will **enlighten** our life journey and **sustain change**
- our purpose will be **discovered** not crafted

Individual purpose concerns our long term contribution to our individual stakeholder communities. An authentic individual purpose is not focussed on maximising personal wealth; it has a selfless focus on others and prioritises the overall wellbeing of our societal community. A strong individual purpose guides our life journey and sustains us through periods of turmoil and change. It is difficult to discover and often challenging to manifest in our daily lives.

What is my ambition for the future?

Our purpose is the quintessential statement about who we are, not who we will be in the future. It is an articulation of our unique connection to the Universe of which we are part, an expression of the potential for our presence in the world. It anchors and guides what we will do, the possibilities that exist for us to live in a way that aligns who we are with what we do. But it does not prescribe or dictate our future options. Our hopes and plans for the future are energised and enabled by our purpose, by our connection to the Universe. But creating our possible future, living our life on purpose is up to us. This is where we exercise our free will in choosing what we will do to express who we are, how we will manifest our purpose during our life on earth.

Making the life choices that connect with our purpose and align our being with our doing requires our constant attention. Charting our life journey in a way that guides the choices we make requires thoughtful planning.

We need a life plan that frames the possibilities that our life could present in a way that guides the choices we will make. We also need a dynamic planning model that can accommodate a changing view of what our future could look like – a flexible pathway forward that can respond to shifts in our focus as we encounter and embrace, or discount, new possibilities; a life plan that points the way forward and reminds us of what is important, what we need to care about and take care of. To create that life plan we need to have a view of the future we intend to create for ourselves by living our life on purpose. We need to understand our ambition for the future.

Our ambition for the future is essentially a glimpse of our purpose manifested, a future view of our presence in the world as an expression of our life on purpose. This means that it will have similar characteristics to our true purpose. Therefore, an authentic ambition for the future cannot be selfish; it will be concerned with our contribution to others. It will not be focused on expanding our personal wealth, importance, status or reputation, except as these things may be necessary to secure our wellbeing and enable our purposeful contributions to our communities. It is not a certain and measurable future goal expressed as a firm statement of what we will achieve in our life. It is, rather, a beacon, a soft guiding light that illuminates a possible future, a potential manifestation of our purpose.

Our ambition for the future is not about what we want to do; it is about who we wish to be. It is our clearest view of what success would look like if we were to live our life on purpose.

In writing about individual ambition, I have encountered some difficulty in clearly separating the concepts of purpose and ambition.

This is because ambition, portrayed as the future manifestation of our purpose, is challenged by the notion of a purpose that is always relevant in the now. It is almost as though ambition is a redundant concept for a life plan where the ultimate goal is to live 'on purpose'. Where in a sense our future ambition is fused with our ever-present purpose; where our ambition is essentially the pursuit of a life on purpose; and where we continually strive to be present (living in the now) in a purposeful way. Thus, you could argue that all we need to do is centre or ground ourselves in our purpose and allow our life to emerge or unfold through our relationships, roles and communities. In other words, to focus on *being*, and let the doing unfold.

We have talked about our purpose being our unique connection to the Universe, an expression of our unique life presence, the essence of who we are. That essence is ever present, it is timeless. Our quest is to discover (access), understand (know) and live (be) our purpose, to make it fully present within our life on earth; like an expedition, an evolutionary journey into the unknown. We may have a compass that points towards our 'true north' (our purpose), and we may also have a map of our potential life space (our roles, relationships and communities). But, in order to set our course for the future we need a view of our ultimate destination. We need that glimpse of our future created by living our life on purpose. We need an ambition for our future.

Because we can be who we need to be in many different spaces, the manifestation of our purpose can take many forms. The challenge is to identify an overarching ambition that includes the many life contributions that will express our purpose. One way to identify our ambition for the future is to consider how our purpose may be manifested within each of our communities of interest.

How our particular talents, gifts and capabilities could be applied to create a purposeful contribution to each of these communities.

This means identifying each of the communities with whom we share a common interest (e.g. immediate family, extended family, social, sporting, community, religious, educational, philanthropic, work etc.), and considering the nature of the role we play or would like to play within those communities. For each role we could then define the contribution we would hope to make if our role focus and activities were always consistent with living our life on purpose.

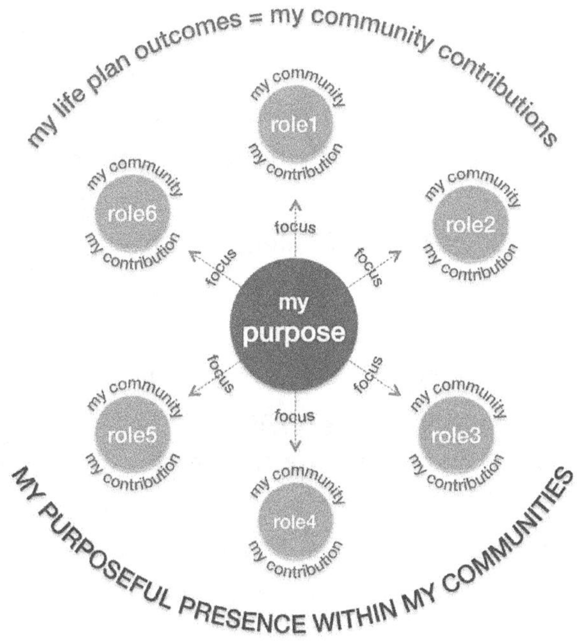

Figure 39: Ambition and contribution

By considering our intended contributions to our various communities of interest, we may begin to see the overall character of the person we expect or hope to be within those communities. We may be able to see the potential for an overarching contribution to all of our communities, which builds a picture of what living our life on purpose could or should look like. That common or overarching contribution, the real value we could and should add to our communities, is likely to be the best current view of our ambition for the future – a contribution that discloses an exciting and energising view of our possible future and purposeful presence within our communities of interest.

This role-focus approach to personal life planning is not new thinking. I first encountered it many years ago as a CEO facilitator of Stephen Covey's Seven Habits program, which I introduced as an integral part of an organisational and cultural change program. All of the organisation's managers and staff were invited to participate in the program which included an integrated work-life planning process. It is a testament to the impact of the Covey program that 70% of the staff volunteered to participate in and commit personal time. The program language and principles became embedded in the organisation's thinking and processes. And it survived well beyond my time with the organisation even without the participation or support of a new CEO. Although vision-led rather than purpose-driven, and now over 20 years old, I believe there is still much to commend the Covey approach as a basis for planning, integrating, living and balancing how we should 'be' in the 'doing' of our many life roles.

Whether we need to see ambition as a separate and interim future view of our life purpose will depend on where we are in our life journey and how we choose to create our life plan.

Those of us who are well-travelled and clear about our life roles may be content to unfold our purpose within each of our communities – to see our ambitions for the future within each of our roles. Those of us less travelled or less well-travelled may be less certain about our future life roles. We may need that beacon, that guiding light that sharpens our focus. We may need to know our overarching ambition for the future.

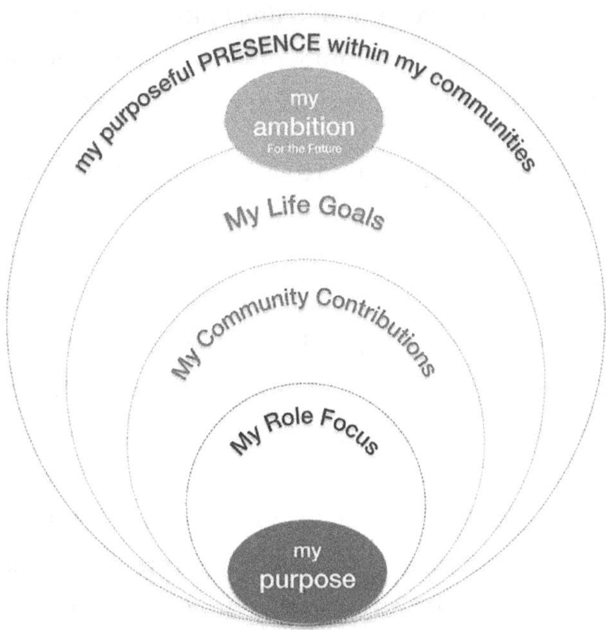

Figure 40: Ambition and presence

What will be my legacy?

I also have to thank Stephen Covey for showing me the power in this question. It is a question that places our present within a future frame and has the potential to inform our thinking and our conversations about our purpose and ambition.

It is a question openly and honestly explored from the heart, which tests the authenticity of our purpose and ambition statements. It challenges the nature of our current presence in the world, how we are living our life, and provides important insights and understandings to focus our future life planning.

To frame the question we simply need to identify our communities of interest (family, educational, social, work etc.), the roles we perform in those communities and the people (or groups of people) who matter most to us in each of those communities. Depending on our age and circumstances, we may need to envisage some future communities we expect to belong to and roles we would like to occupy in those communities.

Next we need to envisage a future and significant event in our life, a significant anniversary or birthday, or perhaps the time of our departing. Imagine that the group of people that matter most to us are all present at this significant event and each is invited to present their tribute to our life. Finally, assuming that you have lived your life on purpose, write down what you know or hope that these people who matter to you would say, as they reflect on your role and time in their community. For example, how would your life partner remember you? How would your children reflect on your life as their parent? What would your best friends recall about your social roles? How would your colleagues remember your contribution in your work roles?

Reflecting on your written record of these imaginary tributes to your life should enable you to:

- check the validity of your purpose focus and intent by comparing some of your expected life outcomes (the manifestation of your purpose) with the intent of your purpose and ambition statements

- identify some important gaps between the way you are currently living your life and your expectations of living your life on purpose

- understand what needs to change in the way you are currently performing your key life roles in order for your intended outcomes (your contributions to your communities) to align with your purposeful life

Although this exercise will inform and enable our life planning, its real value is to challenge the authenticity of our purpose and ambition statements within a community context. It is a way of checking that our intended contributions, which will manifest our purpose, have the potential to add real value in our communities. We are imagining our future, envisaging the potential for a life lived on purpose.

However you choose to explore this question, it will open a thought-provoking conversation about your life. This is a conversation you can choose to have with yourself or with others, people from the communities in which you play a role. If you have the courage to invite others into this discussion, to check how you actually show up in your communities, you will have engaged in a learning conversation that has the potential to make a real difference for all involved. If you enter the conversation 'on purpose', in a spirit of 'selfless service' and expect a 'collaborative learning' experience, then you will build community with the participants. You will bring new meaning to your relationships and you will have taken a significant step towards living your life on purpose.

How authentic am I?

Much is written about authenticity as being the key to living a happy, meaningful and fulfilling life – the simple idea that being who you really are provides the best, perhaps the only, opportunity for a joyous and rewarding life. In principle, I can agree with this view, but only if we are clear about what we mean by authenticity. What we mean by being who we really are.

The dictionary defines authentic as not false or copied, genuine, real. Being authentic therefore is about showing up as who we are, presenting the real and genuine us. In the context of our discussion about individual congruence and living on purpose, who we are is defined by our purpose. Being authentic in this context, therefore, simply means being true to our purpose – creating a presence in our life that is a genuine reflection of our core purpose, a presence where our actions (our doing) are consistent with who we are (our being). In contrast, being unauthentic, being 'off purpose', is where our doing doesn't match our being – where our actions are out of synch with who we really are. In this space, we have become detached from our core purpose. Our minds are probably in control and our mental models (both positive and negative) are in charge of expressing who we are. In these situations we are most likely stressed and our individual wellbeing is either corrupted or seriously at risk.

For many of us, our authenticity is distorted by the persona we create to fit with the expectations of our roles within our communities of interest. These 'masks' as I prefer to call them are often carefully manufactured by our past and present, learned and inherited, life and community influences, to present what we expect our role presence demands or requires.

Most of us will acknowledge that the person who shows up at work is often not the same person who shows up at home, and can be different again from the person who shows up at our local club or church meeting. We can even mask the roles within a single community. At work, the person who shows up at the senior management table may be different from the person managing their work team, and different again from the person who enjoys a collegial drink after work.

Whether we consciously create these multiple personas or they are masks that we have just grown up with, I believe at some level we will be aware of their existence. That awareness may simply be a feeling of discomfort, a sense that something is wrong or a more obvious dysfunction in our relationships with others. Whatever the origin or nature of our masks, the effort required to continually mask our life, the negative energy we deploy in creating and maintaining these masks is draining. The stress that continual masking generates, as we deal with a life of conscious or unconscious inconsistency, can be very disabling. As we continue to bury our frustrations and fears, as we continue to present the unauthentic us, we are blocking the path of purpose, the flow of energy that can enable our wellbeing.

Imagine if we could eliminate these energy blockages, if we could dissolve our masks and simply be who we are. Imagine if we could become more authentic. Being authentic requires us to develop two capacities:

- the capacity to know who we are, to be constantly aware of our purpose, our true self

- the capacity to monitor our actions to ensure that we only act in ways that express our purpose and create a presence that is consistent with that purpose

For the sake of this discussion, I will assume that we do know who we are, that we can articulate our core purpose. However, that does not mean that we have developed a way of being constantly aware of our purpose or the capacity to monitor the alignment of our behaviours with that purpose.

Asking the question 'how authentic am I?' is a good place to start developing the self awareness we need to become more authentic. Exploring the answers to that question will also challenge and clarify our understanding of our purpose and ambition for the future. If we ask the question of ourselves, the usefulness of the answer will be depend on our own self awareness and the degree to which we can be objective and measured in our own self criticism. If we pose the question to people within our communities, we begin a conversation that has the potential to change the nature of our relationships and the way we present in those communities. If we have the confidence to engage other people in our authenticity conversation we have taken an important step towards becoming more authentic. Those conversations will not only increase our awareness and understanding of our real presence in each community, they will present opportunities to change the way we engage with those communities.

Community conversations that constantly reference our purpose will also sharpen our understanding of who we are. And as we become more authentic, as our community participation aligns with our purpose, as our doing becomes the manifestation of our being, we will see the potential of living a life on purpose.

Am I joyful?

This apparently simple question is one of the more searching questions we can ask. Like the previous questions it can begin a conversation that will challenge and refine our sense of purpose and ambition. But it also has the potential to deepen our understanding of why a strong connection to our purpose is essential to lead a joyful life.

Being **joyful** (full of joy) is a state where we experience a heartfelt sense of elation, jubilance and delight; an overwhelming sense of gladness and happiness; and a deep feeling of satisfaction and contentment. While an abiding sense of **happiness** is at the core of being joyful, actually being joyful is more than just being happy. It is also about feeling deeply content, that sense of restful satisfaction with our life, a sense of pervasive tranquillity within our world which we could describe as being peaceful.

Being joyful is also about being at **peace** with ourselves and our world, having a deep sense of quiet and still oneness with the Universe. And yet being joyful is still more than feeling happy and peaceful. The overwhelming sense of gladness and heartfelt delight that accompanies a joyful experience speaks clearly of **love**, the feeling of loving and being loved simultaneously. Not a fleeting or selfish love, but an intimate, enduring and unconditional feeling of love for all of which we are part.

And so I suggest that being joyful is about living a life that is an outward expression of our deeply felt inner sense of our tranquil peacefulness, abiding happiness and unconditional love.

Being joyful is a wonderful entanglement of peacefulness, happiness and love. It is about revealing who we really are – the truth of us. It is about being our authentic self. Being joyful is the expression of a deep inner sense of wellbeing that flows through us when we are truly present, when we are living our life on purpose.

If I had to choose between these entangled concepts of peace, happiness and love, I would probably choose love as the energy which enables the other two. It seems to me that both peace and happiness flow from love. On the other hand, I know that where you find true inner peace there will also be love; where you find true inner happiness, peace will also be there. And where love abides, there will be both peace and happiness.

Of course, we know that our happiness is not found within our material or external worlds. True happiness is not derived from accumulating possessions or satisfying our emotional or physical needs. Enduring happiness comes from within. Likewise, the tranquillity and peace that reflects a deep sense of contentment with our life cannot be created from our external world. The lasting peace we seek does not flow into us from our outside world; it can only flow from us. It is a peace that emanates from our core being.

In a similar way, our capacity for unconditional love, our capacity to love ourselves and others without limitation, is only possible if who we are at the deepest level is an expression of that love. To borrow the Ghandi expression, 'we must be the love we expect to see in the world'.

Figure 41: Joyful congruence

What is clear is that we cannot think our way into joyfulness. We cannot construct a joyful life; we can't 'do joyful', we can only 'be joyful'. As Rupert Spira observes in his book *Presence, the art of peace and happiness*:

> *Your self, aware presence, knows no resistance to any appearance and, as such, is happiness itself; like the empty space of a room it cannot be disturbed and is, therefore, peace itself; like this page, it is intimately one with whatever appears on it and is thus love itself; and like water that is not affected by the shape of a wave, it is pure freedom. Causeless joy, imperturbable peace, love that knows no opposite and freedom at the heart of all experience...this is your ever-present nature under all circumstances.*

It is relevant to note that love underpins much of our congruence framework. The enabling (self) leadership ethic of selfless service to others, the principles of commonality and mutuality that are critical for the development of meaningful relationships, and a learning orientation that welcomes difference and diversity, are all enabled by a core purpose that embraces unconditional love.

If our purpose is the expression of who we truly are – our real presence or authentic being in the world – then it must reflect the love, peace and happiness that it embraces. A life on purpose must, therefore, be joyful. This assertion raises the following questions:

- Are our purpose and ambition statements joyful? Do they embrace the peace, happiness and love that reflect a joyful presence?
- Are we at peace with our world? Do we have an enduring sense of inner peace and tranquillity? Is that peacefulness reflected in our presence?
- Are we happy? Do we feel a deep and abiding sense of gladness and contentment in our life?
- Do we have the capacity for unconditional love? Can we reference that love in action in our relationships with ourselves and others?

The answers to these questions, or our conversations around the topics they suggest, can take us another step towards living our life on purpose. Such conversations have the potential to help us assess our current presence in the world. They can enable us to reflect on our previous conversations and integrate our discoveries. And they offer the opportunity to refine and focus our purpose and ambition for the future.

Imagine if...

Imagine if we all had the opportunity to know and live our true purpose?

Our purpose embraces the truth of us and expresses our unique potential for selfless service to others. Our purpose feels enabling and inspiring.

It energises our presence in the world and enlightens and sustains our life journey. If we know our purpose we have discovered who we are. We understand how to give our life real meaning. By choosing to live our life on purpose we are choosing to be joyful. We are opting to reveal the truth of who we are, to align our inner being with our outward presence in the world.

This alignment will create a deep inner sense of wellbeing, a sense of inner peace and happiness, which flows from knowing that the way we are living our life is the true expression of our authentic self. We will know that our authentic presence in the world is the difference we can make.

If we all could live our purpose we would exist in a world where selfless service was pervasive; where building and sustaining community was a way of life; and where co-creating equitable-shared value for all was the norm. Wouldn't that be different?

Imagine if we had a purposeful presence in our communities?

Within the communities with whom we share a common interest or purpose, we have the opportunity to build meaningful relationships. Those relationships enable us to co-create outcomes that manifest our shared purpose and generate equitable-shared value for our ourselves and our communities. By collaborating with our communities to co-create these outcomes, which are beyond profit and represent selfless service to others, we are using our purposeful presence to co-create a shared future that values community.

We are helping to build communities of purpose that enable the positive integration of difference and diversity. Such communities can change the way our world works!

Acknowledgements

I am ever grateful to the late Stephen R. Covey[52] for his timeless contribution to vision led and integrated life planning; I am also indebted to Eckhart Tolle[53] for his teachings about living in the now; to Wayne Dwyer[54] for his discussions about intention, ambition and meaning; to Charles Guignon[55] for his writing on being authentic; to Mike Robbins[56] for sharing his learning and experiences about authenticity; and to Rupert Spira[57] and Jan Frazier[58] for reminding me about the importance of presence.

14 | My People

A life on purpose within a community of purpose has the potential to change everything.

Figure 42: Individual community

Go to the People
Live with them,
Learn from them,
Love them.

Start with what they know,
Build with what they have.

Lao Tsu

People is one of the Congruence Framework's five factors. Our individual congruence is enabled by developing meaningful interpersonal relationships with the people in our **communities**. These relationships facilitate our collaborative learning, which enables us to embrace the difference and diversity we encounter, and deal positively with change. Our community relationships expand our capacity for knowing and offer the opportunity to co-create a future with people that we trust and care about.

Is this my community?

During our lifetime, we will participate in many different communities, interacting with groups of individuals with whom we may, for a time, share a common interest. These communities will include our personal communities, our immediate and extended families, our close friends and mentors, and perhaps our religious communities. We will also participate in local communities such as our schools and universities, clubs and social networks, and our workplaces. And whether we recognise it or not, we also belong to a universal community, our 'super community' that recognises our presence on earth as an integral part of the wider Universe that we all inhabit.

Our time in some of these communities may be fleeting (e.g. our educational communities) and in some we may spend a lifetime (e.g. our family community). We may choose to join some of these communities (e.g. our friends and other social and sporting communities); some of our communities may have been chosen for us by other people (e.g. our religious community); and some communities may choose us (e.g. followers and fan groups, professional peer groups).

In some of these communities we may have been actively engaged and very happy and in others we may have been disengaged, distressed and very sad. Whether our participation in these communities is or was mostly circumstantial or completely voluntary, reviewing our participation, both in the present moment and with the wisdom of hindsight, can help us appreciate the difference that true community could make to the way we live our life.

For each community (or organisation) we are or have been involved with, consider the following questions:

- Was my time with the community generally productive?
    - o Was it a positive and engaging experience which enabled me to grow and develop 'knowing' that I value today?
    - o Was it a largely negative or disabling experience which limited my potential growth and development?
- During my time with the community, did I make a significant contribution to the life of the community?
    - o Or did I remain relatively distant from the community and only participate in what was required of me or the things that interested me?
    - o And, how was my participation acknowledged by others in the community – positively, negatively or not at all?
- Did I feel relaxed and comfortable within the community?
    - o Or was there always a feeling of uncertainty or disquiet from tensions surrounding my involvement with or within the community?

- Did I develop productive relationships within the community, the friends, colleagues and mentors that I still value today?
    - Or was there an absence of significant relationships and/or those that I experienced were often unproductive and sometimes destructive?
- And finally, did the community seem to be coherent? Was it a mainly harmonious group of people committed to a common interest?
    - Or was it a dysfunctional group, splintered, siloed or confused about its direction and raison d'être?

If your response to these questions is generally positive, then you have probably been privileged to participate in communities where you had genuine interests in common and within which you have experienced positive relationships. These are probably communities that enabled and assisted you to be relatively authentic, to align who you are (your being) with much of what you were enabled to achieve (your doing).

If your community experience has been more negative than positive, then it is very likely that you had no real interest in common with most of the members of the communities you have been interacting with. Possibly, your participation was in some way forced or involuntary. Or perhaps you just made a bad connection and/or selected the wrong community. If you had no shared reason or purpose for belonging to these 'negative' communities, then the basis for developing productive relationships and engaging in collaborative learning would be severely constrained. Your access to the enabling collective energy and capacity of the community would be very limited. And if your individual purpose was not aligned with the collective intent of the community, your ability to contribute by being your authentic self would also be very limited.

If you reflect on your experience within these negative communities, you will probably agree that it was, or still is, a struggle (perhaps an impossibility?) to live your life purposefully – to 'be' in a community to which you do, or did not, belong.

In spite of having no real interest in common with the majority of the community, you may have developed some productive relationships with individuals in these communities. However, these relationships were not really enabled by the community, but rather by an interest in common with specific people within the community. In fact, you probably created another personal community within the local community. Perhaps this is how many of us cope with our existence, and possibly waste our real potential, in dysfunctional communities.

The essential element of community is the common interest that binds the community together. This commonality of interest also provides the catalyst for the development of meaningful relationships within the community, relationships that are built on trust and respect. It is these relationships that enable collaborative learning, the positive integration of diversity and difference, and the co-creation of shared futures.

These meaningful relationships can make a significant contribution to our individual congruence by expanding our capacity for knowing. They are essential conduits for learning, presenting different perspectives and providing the opportunity for honest feedback that enables us to 'see differently'. They can also provide a source of confidence and support, giving us the courage to try new things, to 'act differently'. Most importantly, true community, through the meaningful relationships it enables, allows and encourages us to be who we are, to be authentically present as congruent individuals.

In contrast, communities that don't work, that are perhaps not communities at all, can disrupt and destroy our individual congruence. These communities lack the coherence that a true commonality of interest enables. They typically have disparate stakeholder-specific and/or confused collective objectives. They often defeat the potential for community by discouraging interdependent relationships and obstructing collaborative endeavour.

People who need (or rather decide) to stay connected with these dysfunctional communities are forced to make their own way, creating linkages that work predominantly for them alone. This inevitably leads to disconnected sub-communities and the organisational siloing that adds to the community (or organisation) dysfunction. The opportunity to engage the full collaborative capacity of the community to expand collective learning and individual knowing is lost. Our ability to contribute, to be fully present in the community, to be who we are, is severely limited.

Worse still are those communities where we participate without having any real interest in common with the members of the community. In these communities, we are loners and there is little opportunity or encouragement for us to be authentically present. We are required to continually manage our presence, to mask our participation so that we fit in; to be who we are supposed to be and to do only what is expected of us. These situations can be very destructive as they obstruct the release of our real potential. They sap the energy that should be directed towards living purposefully. They can infect our other communities by reducing our physical and emotional capacity to participate and therefore limit our potential contribution to those communities.

And they deny us the time-opportunity for being who we can be, to have a joyful life.

I suspect that many of us have participated at one time or another in these dysfunctional communities. Often the level of dysfunction is substantial and pervasive and usually presents as the antithesis of a congruent community. There is no real common intent (or shared purpose); leadership is disabling; collaborative learning is not enabled or encouraged; difference and dissent are not really tolerated; and the potential for productive (meaningful) relationships is defeated by a paucity of trust and respect within the community.

Once we have clarity of purpose and are committed to live our life on purpose, it becomes more difficult for us to participate in communities with which we have no common interest (or no shared purpose). To live purposefully, we need our communities to be places where we can be authentically present – places where our interaction with other community members can nourish our life by enabling us to manifest our true purpose and 'be all that we can be' within that community. For that to happen we need our communities to have an engaging collective common interest; to embrace a leadership style that encourages productive (meaningful) relationships based on trust and mutual benefit; and a culture that fosters collaborative learning and the positive integration of difference and diversity. We need our communities to be congruent communities.

If we are committed to living purposefully, and we find ourselves for whatever reason in an incongruent community with which we have no real (purpose-based) interest in common, we have three choices:

Leave the community – choosing to focus our attention on an alternative future.

Where there is a fundamental misalignment of our individual purpose with the perceived interests of the community, then our continuing participation may not be beneficial for us or for the community. This misalignment could reflect the fact that we have simply outgrown the community, that the manifestation of our purpose requires new knowing that is not available within this community. Or it may reflect an overwhelming sense of incompatibility with the values and actions of the community, a realisation that we can no longer be authentically present within this community.

Failure to resolve a fundamental misalignment with any of our communities can have serious life consequences. If our level of incompatibility with the community requires us to continually manage our presence within the community, to maintain a constructed existence that continually masks our real presence, then the related anxiety and stress of maintaining our community involvement can threaten our individual wellbeing. The consequences of remaining in this highly stressful situation has the potential to make us mentally and physically ill.

We are not talking here about the normal stresses and strains of community life, the personal challenges associated with integrating difference and diversity or dealing with negative community feedback etc. We are talking about a fundamental misalignment between the way the community operates and the way we need to live our life – a level of incompatibility that results in feelings and behaviours that disrupt our life on a daily basis and reduce our capacity to live a purposeful life.

Only by breaking free of these communities can we release our true potential and fulfill our life purpose.

But what if we are prevented by physical and/or emotional constraints from leaving the community? In these circumstances, hibernating or changing our communities become the only options.

Hibernate within the community – choosing to hide out and await the influence of alternative factors to hopefully bring about positive change.

Rather than leave the community, we may choose to remain and withdraw, to live 'under the radar'. We may seek to control our level of community interaction and minimise the opportunities for stressful or anxious engagement with community members. Perhaps we believe that the problem lies with us and that by taking time out we can reshape our interactions to create positive relationships and a longer-term positive future within the community. Or perhaps we expect that given time, external factors (for example a change in community leadership) will significantly change the community landscape for the better.

These may be plausible resolution strategies, but only if they are realistic and offer genuine opportunities for our purposeful and timely realignment with the community. And we will know the truth of these expectations. We will know whether they represent real options for the future or whether they are simply ways of avoiding the changes we need to initiate for our own sake. If our hibernation is in essence avoidance, then we have increased the risk of harming our wellbeing. The energy and focus required to cocoon our community experience, to continually wrap and distance the ongoing negative influence of a community we are still part of, will severely deplete our emotional and physical reserves. We will be too exhausted by 'doing' to create time for 'being' the person we were intended to be.

Change the community – choosing to make a difference by being an influence for positive change within the community.

There will be times in all of our communities when we experience periods of incompatibility, times when we find ourselves in conflict with the community or with some of its membership. Understanding the nature of that incompatibility will provide the necessary insight to choose the best way forward. Where that incompatibility simply reflects a learning opportunity for ourselves and/or our community, we should have an opportunity for positive resolution, perhaps through collaborative engagement with our community. On the other hand, where the incompatibility reflects a fundamental conflict between our individual purpose and the actual common interest of the community it is unlikely to be easily resolved. In this situation, if we are committed to our purpose, and the community is generally aligned with its expressed intention, we are most probably faced with the leave or hibernate options discussed above.

However if the incompatibility is due to a lack of clarity of community intention, or a way of operating that is in conflict with the community's stated intention, then perhaps we have a third alternative. Perhaps we have the opportunity to be an agent for change. Maybe by living purposefully within the community we can become a powerful force for positive change. Perhaps we can reform or even re-create the community by being 'the change we want to see'. To know the truth of this possibility, we should access our spiritual knowing, the universal wisdom which can guide us on our pathway forward.

'Is this my community?' is a question that we should ask of all of our personal and local communities. Provided we are clear about our purpose, we can pose the question fearlessly in the knowledge that the pursuit of our true purpose is in the mutual best interests of both ourselves and our communities. If, for any of the reasons discussed above, we do not belong in a community then our ability to contribute is compromised as is the potential of the community to enable and support our life journey.

The options of leaving our communities can be painful considerations, but if the conflict of interest is real and serious, then remaining in these communities can be much more harmful for everyone concerned. Who knows, leaving our closest communities may be the most positive contribution to change (for ourselves and the community) that we can make.

Are my relationships meaningful?

Meaningful relationships continually acknowledge the value of their participants. They find their meaning in a strong mutual interest or shared purpose. These relationships are nurtured within an atmosphere of mutual trust and goodwill, by welcoming conversations that embrace difference, promote understanding, and encourage learning and collaborative engagement to co-create outcomes that generate equitable value for all participants.

Meaningful relationships are one of the four essential building blocks for creating both individual and community congruence. They are win-win relationships which acknowledge the mutual interests of the participants. Meaningful relationships are based on commonality of purpose and the generation of mutual (equitable-shared) value outcomes.

They create connections between individuals that are characterised by trust, co-operation, open communication and acknowledgement. These connections enable the collaborative learning that helps both individuals and organisations to discover and live their true purpose.

At an individual level the health and vitality of our interpersonal relationships is an important factor in developing and sustaining our overall wellbeing. Meaningful relationships provide an essential source of nourishment for our human spirit, a source of love, affection and affirmation of who we are and what we stand for. They also provide an important source of our learning and development, the opportunity for community and the potential to co-create our future with other like-minded individuals.

Meaningful relationships enable and assist us to live our life on purpose. If these relationships are devoid of meaning, if they lack the vital elements of common interest (or shared purpose) and the potential for mutual benefit, then they are likely to be dysfunctional at some level. That dysfunction can contaminate our authentic presence within our communities and constrain our opportunities to pursue a life on purpose.

At a community level, our interpersonal relationships form the social ties that bind our communities together. Meaningful relationships provide the cohesive force which connects individual community members and enables the community to effectively function as a collective. They also enable the collaborative learning that is essential for the longer-term development of the community and its individual members. It is the strength of these relationships (their level of meaningfulness) that determines both the effectiveness and longer-term viability of the community.

Based on our definition of meaningful relationships, the answer to the question 'are my relationships meaningful?' will depend on answers to a number of related questions. For each of your important relationships within your personal (e.g. family, friends) and local (e.g. workplace) communities, consider the following questions:

- What is the truth of your relationship connection?
    - Is it based on a deeply held shared purpose or common interest?
    - What is the vital sense of commonality that interconnects you? Is it strong and focused or weak and nebulous?
- What is the benefit that you derive from the relationship?
    - Does the relationship create valuable outcomes that enable and sustain your authentic presence in the community?
    - Does it make a positive contribution to your overall wellbeing?
    - Or does the relationship sap your energy and goodwill for little or no significant personal or overall community benefit?
- Is the relationship enabling and acknowledging?
    - Is the relationship characterised by a deep sense of trust and respect?
    - Is the relationship open and welcoming? Does it enable conversations that acknowledge and support your purpose?
    - Is the relationship collaborative? Does it engage you in opportunities to co-create outcomes for the benefit of yourself and others?

o   Or is this relationship 'all take and no give'? Does it feel one-sided, unsupportive and enervating?

These are searching questions and the answers may not be immediately obvious. However, if we are clear about our own life purpose, then we will know the real truth of these relationships without needing to perform a detailed examination. By focusing our attention on each of the relationships, our spiritual knowing will reveal its true nature. We will be enabled to understand both the current reality and the future potential of the relationship. We will just know if this relationship has the potential to add value to our authentic presence within the community.

If we cannot somehow define the engaging commonality and mutuality that underpins any of our important community relationships, then it is unlikely that they can be meaningful relationships for us or the other participants. It is, therefore, questionable whether these relationships can enable our positive presence within our community, or contribute to either our individual congruence or the congruence of our community.

And, if these relationships are critical to our effective membership of the community, the answers to these questions of commonality and mutuality may again raise the issue of whether this personal or local community is indeed our community. We may again be faced with the decision to consider leaving, hibernating within or endeavouring to change the community.

If this is a community that we have confirmed is our community, a community where we have a strong attachment to its common intent or shared purpose, then choosing to leave may not be a sensible or even a viable option. If we have a relationship that is not working for us within a community we are committed to, then

I suggest that we have three go-forward options: we can choose to leave, hibernate, or change the relationship.

Here again, our spiritual knowing is available to guide our decision process. If we focus our attention on the relationship, we will know if it has the potential to be productively reformed, or whether it should be distanced or entirely exited. We will understand the relative importance of the relationship, its potential to contribute to our authentic presence in the community and to enable our individual congruence. We will also understand whether we can (and should) still achieve the presence and congruence we seek by pursuing the relationship or by closing it down, either temporarily (by hibernating) or permanently (by leaving).

We know from our previous discussions that conversation creates the opportunity for relationship and that successful conversations enable and sustain meaningful relationships. Therefore, if we choose to reform any of our relationships, to make them more meaningful, we need to create the opportunity for successful conversations between the relationship parties.

We already know that we can encourage and enable such conversations by:

- Creating (or co-creating) a safe and enabling (physical and emotional) space for the conversation to take place and issuing a welcoming invitation to participate.

- Suggesting (or co-creating) an open (possibility) agenda for the conversation that provides the opportunity to explore topics of mutual interest; an agenda that allows for both parties to explore the potential for investing in a shared purpose and the co-creation of mutual benefit.

- Building a climate of trust and respect, participating in the conversation in a way that increases the potential for genuine dialogue, by:

    o **listening**: remaining attuned, attentive and fully aware of all participant inputs, not only listening carefully to what they say, but trying to really understand what they think and appreciate how they feel

    o **respecting**: openly encouraging and valuing the active participation of all relationship parties, respecting difference and dissent as opportunities for learning

    o **suspending**: remaining open to new ideas, new ways of thinking and the possibility of different outcomes, suspending judgements based on existing mental models

    o **voicing**: being an active and authentic voice in the discussion, making a thoughtful, deliberate and purposeful contribution to co-creating a cohesive outcome, to releasing the potential for a meaningful relationship

- Ensuring that we establish the open feedback loops which enable the conversations to continue and develop through ongoing discussion and reflection.

By establishing a positive (safe and welcoming) context for the conversation to take place, we have created the opportunity for a discussion that can negotiate difference and dissent in a positive way. We have created the potential for the conversation to move through confrontational argument into a more reflective open dialogue which can enable and encourage the free exchange of ideas. Once in this space, with an agenda which includes a focus on shared purpose and mutual value outcomes, we can begin the generative dialogue that can create new meaning for the relationship. We have created the opportunity to transform meaningless relationships into meaningful relationships.

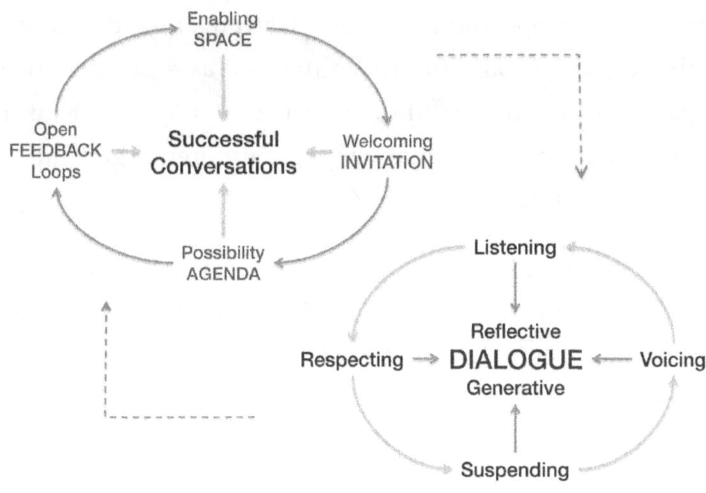

Figure 43: Enabling successful conversations

How do I deal with difference?

For most people, the many faces of difference are a constant presence in their life. We encounter difference on a regular basis as we interact with the numerous communities that are part of our life context.

Our experiences with different ideas and opinions, people, languages and beliefs etc. are part of normal life experience. How we interact with such differences can reveal much about our personal authenticity, who we really are and the truth of our presence within our communities.

We can choose to manage or mitigate the difference we encounter in a way that avoids any disruptive impact on our life. We can choose to ignore, discount or deliberately avoid difference as an unhelpful distraction or diversion. Or we can choose to welcome and positively negotiate and/or integrate the difference that life presents as an opportunity for our learning and development. Basically, we can choose to view difference as a positive, neutral or negative aspect of our life experience. It's all about attitude, confidence and approach, how we view difference generally and how we deal with it.

If we are clear about our purpose and we are genuinely trying to live our life on purpose, then I suggest we will have the capability, confidence, and the wisdom to positively integrate the difference we encounter in our life. We will be able to see difference for what it really is. We will recognise immediately when difference in its many forms presents as an unhelpful distraction from our purpose and needs to be carefully negotiated. And we will know when difference presents as an opportunity for learning, as a positive challenge with the potential to enhance our understanding of our life purpose. In these situations we will welcome difference as having the potential to renew and refresh our life journey. And we will integrate positive difference in a way that creates valuable outcomes for ourselves and our community.

If we are unclear about our purpose, or our presence within our communities is not authentic, then the opportunity to engage positively with difference will be obscured. Our lack of clarity about who we are will prevent us from seeing the truth of the difference we encounter. We may not see its real relevance and potential as a learning opportunity for us. We are likely to ignore or reject difference or attempt to moderate it in a negative way that is unhelpful to ourselves and our community.

And, if our presence within the community is masked or managed it will lessen our engagement with the community and thus our ability to positively integrate the difference we encounter. We are unlikely to have the full support of the community to either engage with the difference opportunity or to carefully negotiate its influence. Our encounter with difference is more likely to be singular, possibly confrontational and unhelpful to anyone.

To reflect on how we typically deal with difference in our life we could ponder the following questions:

- When I encounter difference, in any of its forms, what is my typical reaction?
    - Am I cautious, uncertain or perhaps even fearful?
    - Am I curious, interested and perhaps even excited?
    - Do I feel ruffled, destabilised, unable to cope or sometimes angry?
    - Do I feel reasonably calm, open and quietly confident?
- How do I typically deal with the difference I encounter?
    - Do I try to ignore difference, to minimise its potential impact on my life?
    - Do I mostly welcome difference and look for ways to capture the positive opportunities for change?
    - Do I try to avoid engaging with difference, to protect myself from the potential impacts of change?
    - Do I seek difference out, am I constantly looking for opportunities to refresh and renew who I am and what I do?
- What are the usual consequences of my encounters with difference, diversity or dissent?

- o Are there often unresolved issues and negative impacts on myself and/or others?
- o Are the outcomes generally mixed and sometimes not helpful for anyone? At other times do good things happen?
- o Is there always a positive in the mix? Is it never a clear picture and not everyone (including me) benefits?
- o Can I usually see the positive side even in those outcomes which were unexpected and/or seen by some as unhelpful?

By reflecting honestly on these questions, we may be able to form a picture of our attitudes and responses to the difference, diversity or dissent that we encounter. That picture will typically challenge our purpose. The way we feel about difference and how we choose to deal with it are significantly influenced by the confidence we have in ourselves and our life journey. That confidence is related to our understanding of our life purpose and our level of commitment to living our life on purpose.

If we know who we are and are committed to living our life purposefully then difference in all of its forms will be the 'spice of our life'. It will be a normal but very exciting part of our life journey. We will be constantly, perhaps not always consciously, on the lookout for the signals that difference presents. We will embrace these signals as opportunities to reconfirm, refresh and renew our life presence. And most probably we will be somewhat curious if these differences are missing from our life. This attitude to difference (and diversity) will permeate our interaction with our communities. It will signal to those that present difference that their participation is welcome and their contribution is valued. We will welcome and embrace the presence of difference (and diversity) in all of our communities.

Do I love my people?

Do you know your people, and do you love them?

The above quote was the keynote address by Mother Teresa to a conference of HR professionals. Apparently, it stunned the audience, but after a brief period of silence, she received a standing ovation.

I once attended a master class in Florida which was facilitated by the CEO of a successful US telecommunications company. I have never forgotten his succinct definition of what he considered to be the role of a CEO in a 21st century organisation. He said:

Your job as CEO is simply to point the way forward and love your people. If you do that, your people will make it happen, they will look after you, each other and the company.

By 'pointing the way forward' he meant setting a collective vision for the future and holding that vision focus as the core strategic idea for the company. By 'your people' he meant the whole company including its owners, customers, business partners and suppliers, the total organisational community. And by 'loving your people' he meant having a deep sense of affection, respect and genuine concern for the collective welfare of that community (the company). I also remember his observation that using the phrase 'caring about your people' would probably be more acceptable within the corporate community, but for him it was a weak alternative. He felt that it did not express the same leadership intention or commitment. It did not express the courage and integrity of being able to say openly and honestly that 'I love my people'.

Clearly, the answer to the question 'Do I love my people?' depends on who we consider to be 'my people' and how we define 'love'.

Within the context of this discussion about our people and our community it seems reasonable to define my people as all of those people who constitute your communities of interest. This includes all of the people with whom you enjoy, or have the potential to enjoy, a meaningful relationship based on a shared purpose and the generation of mutual benefit. My people may reference a small personal community (myself and my life partner) or a larger local community (my workplace or social communities) or both.

To define what we mean by love in this context, perhaps we could begin with a biblical definition (1 Corinthians 13:4-8):

> *Love is patient, love is kind. It does not envy, it does not boast, it is not proud. It is not rude, it is not self-seeking, it is not easily angered, it keeps no record of wrongs. Love does not delight in evil but rejoices with the truth. It always protects, always trusts, always hopes, always perseveres.*

This definition of love is very demanding. It is unconditional and seemingly unlimited by the constructs of community and purpose that are an important focus in our current discussion. But, it is a very relevant definition for our discussion about individual congruence. It expresses the concepts of authenticity (truth and trust), purposefulness (hope, patience and perseverance) and selflessness (kind, not self-seeking or proud), all of which are key attributes of enabling leadership. And so it seems we may infer that people who have the capacity to 'love their people' are probably also enabling leaders.

Enabling leaders are people who share an authentic (and therefore purposeful) presence within their communities that is focused on selfless service to others. They are likely to enjoy a deeply shared affection within their communities which derives from the leadership culture they enable within those communities. A culture based on the truth and hope of a truly shared community purpose; the trust and respect of meaningful community relationships; and the positive experience of genuine community through collaborative learning and the co-creation of shared-value outcomes.

Therefore, by reflecting on our personal leadership style, and the culture that it engenders within our communities, we may understand our capacity to love our people.

Consider your response to the following questions:

- Am I an authentic member of my communities?
    - Do I show up as who I really am (purposefully present and unmasked) in my personal and local communities of interest?
    - Are my community relationships truly meaningful, based on commonality of purpose and mutual benefit?
    - Do I enjoy the trust and respect of my communities?
- Am I honestly focused on selfless service to others?
    - Do I place the interests of others above my own?
    - Am I really focused on creating win-win outcomes for the longer-term benefit of all my community stakeholders?
- Do I collaborate with my communities?
    - Do I honestly see the future as co-created with my communities?

-     o   Do I constantly seek to learn from my communities?
-     o   Do I embrace difference and diversity; openly share what I know: and seek to understand and enable the contribution of others in my communities?
- Do I acknowledge the contributions of other people?
  - o   Do I openly and freely acknowledge the potential of other people within my communities?
  - o   How do I acknowledge the individual and collective achievements of my communities?
- Do I love my people?
- Am I an enabling leader?

Our capacity to love ourselves and to love the people within our communities is fundamental to our capacity for the self leadership from spirit that is important for our individual congruence; and also for the shared leadership that fosters congruence within our communities. The question 'Do I love my people?' is a relevant and enlightening question to ask about how we interact with each and all of our communities.

Imagine if...

Imagine if we were not welcome in our communities.

By definition, our communities are those people with whom we share a common interest or purpose and a commitment to co-create a shared future. If our authentic presence is unwelcome in any of these communities then we must consider the possibility that they are not our communities. Perhaps we do not really share the purpose or intent of the community. Or perhaps we believe that the behaviours of the community, and/or the outcomes it is creating, are in conflict with its stated purpose or intention.

Whatever the reason for the disconnect, if our relationships within the community are seriously broken, we should consider our options to leave the community. If we genuinely believe that the disconnect can be resolved, we could elect to hibernate within the community while resolution is effected.

Or we may decide that we can make the change that is necessary to rebuild our positive relationships within the community.

If we decide to remain in a community where we are not welcome we put our physical and mental wellbeing at risk. The stress and anxiety of continually managing an unwelcome presence can have serious physical and mental health consequences. If we cannot be authentically present within our communities, then they are not our communities. We will know the truth of whether they could be in the future or not. But masking our participation to appear to belong or fit in is not a long-term option. Continuing our participation in an unwelcoming community not only compromises our opportunity for achieving individual congruence, it also distracts us from the contribution we could be making to our other communities.

And it denies us the time-opportunity for a joyful life.

Imagine if all of our communities were purposeful and collaborative.

Purposeful communities are committed to the pursuit of their shared purpose. Collaborative communities are enabled by positive trust based relationships, which create the social ties that bind the community and facilitate its effective collective action. These meaningful relationships, which are secured by a shared purpose and sustained by the generation of equitable-shared value for their participants, create the opportunity for building collaborative communities of purpose.

Meaningful relationships are developed by community conversations, which enable genuine dialogue about shared purpose and the opportunities to create shared-value outcomes.

If we are prepared to host these conversations we can create the opportunity for collaborative community. If we are an authentic participant in these conversations, we will influence the co-creation of purposeful outcomes. Thus, we can choose to encourage the development of meaningful relationships and, therefore, the co-creation of collaborative communities.

If all of our communities were purposeful and collaborative, they would enable and support us to live our life on purpose. They would help us to be congruent individuals and we would help them to be congruent communities. What a difference we could choose to make!

Imagine if enabling leadership was a pervasive influence within our communities.

Enabling leaders are people who share a purposeful presence within their communities. They are focused on selfless service to others which creates a collaborative and generous culture of community based on the truth and hope of a truly shared purpose. They have meaningful community relationships which foster a climate of mutual trust and respect. And they encourage and enable a sense of genuine community through collaborative learning and the co-creation of shared-value outcomes.

Enabling leadership is a shared leadership ethic which has the wellbeing of its total community at heart. It encourages and supports a shared culture of collaborative community which acknowledges the potential, participation and contribution of its individual membership. If enabling leadership was a pervasive influence within our communities, we could experience the joy of belonging to a caring community that encourages and enables us to live our life on purpose.

Enabling leadership can make all the difference in the world!

15 | My Potential

My presence has the potential to make the world a better place. Who I am makes a difference!

Figure 44: Individual potential

Look, it cannot be seen – it is beyond form. Listen, it cannot be heard – it is beyond sound. Grasp, it cannot be held – it is intangible. These three are indefinable; Therefore they are joined in one. From above it is not bright; From below it is not dark: An unbroken thread beyond description. It returns to nothingness. The form of the formless. The image of the imageless. It is called indefinable and beyond imagination.

Lao Tsu

How do I release my potential?

Our real potential, and our challenge as human beings, is to live our life on purpose. For those of us with the courage to take up that challenge, discovering and manifesting our purpose will be our life journey. Releasing our potential begins with the discovery of our unique purpose – that deep appreciation and clear understanding of who we are and why we are here.

If we are clear about our purpose and we genuinely seek to make it our life focus, to be all we can be in this world, then as we have already discussed, 'all sorts of things occur to help one that would never otherwise have occurred'. It is important to appreciate that we are not invited to be someone we cannot be. Our voyage of discovery will not reveal a purpose that we are incapable of manifesting. We are intended to live our life on purpose, that is our real potential.

That is not to say we cannot 'construct' a purpose (more likely a vision or mission) that will not be realisable. However, a constructed or crafted purpose is unlikely to reflect a presence that is the truth of us. Remember our observation that purpose is not crafted, it is discovered.

The Universe will not assist us to realise a construction of ourselves that misrepresents the truth of our presence. This is why we must endeavour to discover an authentic purpose, a purpose that reflects who we really are.

Releasing our potential is therefore firstly about deciding to lead a purposeful life, and then finding ways to utilise the gifts and talents we have been given to make that life our reality, to make us fully present in our world.

Inevitably, pursuing a life on purpose will require us to make changes in our life, probably major changes. Our decision to live purposefully will almost certainly be immediately challenged by a series of obstacles that are designed to test our resolve. We will encounter new ideas and opportunities that will seriously challenge some of our existing patterns of behaviour and ways of thinking. Embracing these new opportunities to live our life differently will require us to escape from the constraints of old mental models that are no longer relevant to our present. We will need to transform or let go of the things that don't work in our current life. We will need to develop and embrace new thinking and new behaviours that enable us to pursue our life on purpose and sustain an authentic presence within our communities of interest.

Being authentically present in our communities means continuing to make relevant contributions to those communities that are consistent with who we are. As the needs of our communities change over time, and as we join new communities, we need to change the way we participate in those communities for our contributions to remain relevant. To remain present in those communities we need to find new ways to contribute that are consistent with our life purpose.

We need to make changes in our life to ensure that how we participate within our communities remains consistent with who we are.

Making fundamental changes in our life requires courage, determination and confidence. We need to believe that we will make the right choices. That the changes we make continue to maintain our presence within our communities of interest and keep our life on purpose. Our capacity or appetite for positive change, to successfully negotiate those change opportunities that keep us on purpose, is sustained by our 'personal learning centre'. This is a concept or construct used to describe the capacity we have to utilise our knowledge, intelligence and our creativity to continually adapt to changes in our environment in a way that sustains our life on purpose.

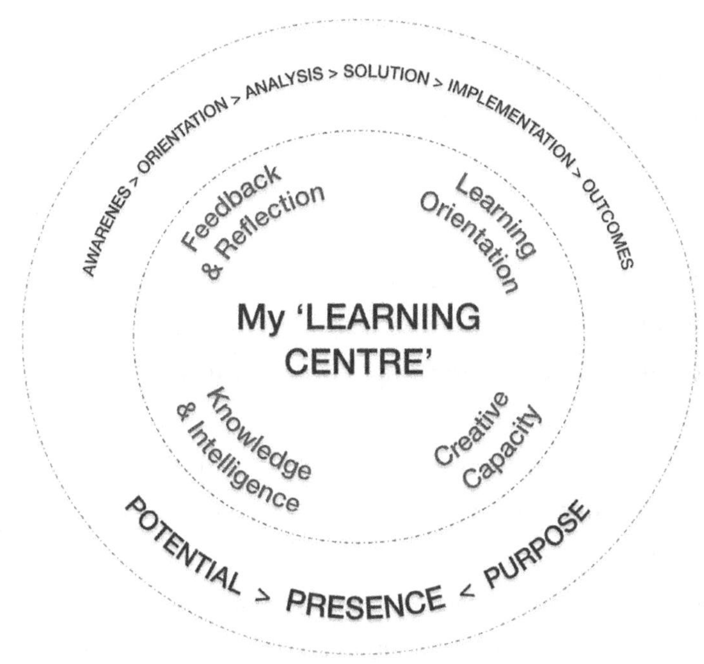

Figure 45: Individual learning

Our personal learning centre plays a critical role in enabling the release of our potential. It is the job of our personal learning centre to anticipate, identify and negotiate our opportunities for positive change. It is our long-range warning system that uses our personal reflective and community feedback loops to detect when a change response may be necessary or desirable. It is also our knowledge and intelligence centre that understands the nature of the change opportunity and the response required for a positive outcome. Our personal learning centre is also our resident change manager. It enables us to access and integrate our knowledge and creativity to design and implement an appropriate proactive and positive change response. It is our personal learning centre that keeps us present!

The effectiveness of our personal learning centre will be reflected in the way we deal with change in our life. If we generally have a positive attitude to change, then the chances are that we have an active learning centre which is sustaining our capacity to be change receptive. If that is true, then:

- we will be constantly seeking opportunities to make our life more purposeful
- we will welcome change as an exciting opportunity for personal growth and development
- we will embrace difference and diversity in all of their forms as learning opportunities
- we will view problems and challenges as presenting opportunities to explore new ideas and create innovative solutions
- we will possess a capacity to anticipate and manage change in a way that creates positive outcomes for ourselves and others

If, on the other hand, we have an aversion to change, then our personal learning centre is most likely in a state of disrepair and unable to assist us to negotiate change in a positive way. The following statements are likely to be more or less true:

- change usually presents challenging or threatening situations that are difficult to resolve and make us feel uncomfortable and/or insecure
- change seems to take us by surprise and often results in outcomes that seem to make our life worse
- we are sometimes confronted with change that we find overwhelming or even depressing
- we are often challenged by aspects of the difference, diversity, conflict and dissent we encounter within our communities
- we find it difficult to deal with risk and uncertainty and usually try to control and minimise the change in our life; and (therefore)
- we always prefer to use tried and trusted methods to resolve our life problems and challenges

If most of these statements hold a ring of truth for us, then we clearly lack the confidence to negotiate change in a way that results in good outcomes for us and for others. Almost certainly we don't know or don't trust our capacity to deal with change. Our personal learning centre needs a wake-up call!

Awakening our learning centre simply means increasing our focus on learning, creating more opportunities for learning to occur, and finding ways to develop our capacity to learn. It means acknowledging the importance of learning in pursuing a life on purpose, and committing to a learning strategy as an integrated element of our life plan.

Increasing our **opportunities for learning** is firstly about developing a learning orientation. This means making a commitment to learn, increasing our awareness of our learning opportunities, and making real time for learning and creating positive learning spaces. We can make a start by:

- being more aware of our natural and community environment; taking the time to pay more attention to what is happening and the learning opportunities in our immediate world

- placing ourselves more often in spaces, places and situations where we can observe and listen to our world; positive spaces that enable us to be really present and see and hear what needs to change in our life

- being open to change; seeing all of our life encounters (physical, intellectual, social, emotional and spiritual) as positive learning opportunities, purposeful signals for change

- creating and sustaining personal feedback loops; actively seeking feedback from our communities (our families, friends and colleagues) about the authenticity of our presence

- setting aside time on a regular basis to withdraw, relax and reflect on our observations and consider our responses to the learning (change) opportunities presented to us

- programming our life so that we have the time and the opportunities to do all of the above

Developing our **capacity to learn** means improving our analysis of our learning opportunities. It means improving the way we develop, access and utilise our knowledge and intelligence to appreciate our opportunities for change and increasing the engagement of our creative capacity to develop positive change solutions. It also means becoming better at implementing and developing more effective (internal and external) feedback loops to enable us to learn from our change outcomes.

Using our capacity to know (our knowledge and intelligence), accessing our creative capacity and enabling our feedback loops, is the focus of the discussion that follows. For now, it is sufficient to acknowledge the critical role of our personal learning centre in enabling our individual congruence by helping us to keep our life on purpose. It is our personal learning centre that identifies the opportunities for positive change. It guides our response to change in a way that sustains our community contributions and maintains our authentic presence within our communities.

What is my capacity for knowing?

Knowing can be loosely defined as possessing knowledge, information or understanding, the state of being aware or informed.

Our capacity for knowing, therefore, reflects our ability to acquire such knowledge and understanding. Our ability to acquire the facts, truths, principles and know-how that constitute our knowledge base includes our ability to modify that knowledge to create new knowledge. We have the ability to comprehend and make sense of our knowledge and information and in so doing, to continually make our knowledge contextually meaningful.

We do this by engaging our intelligence (defined simply as our ability to learn and understand) to access and make sense of what we know, and to create meaning relevant for our context. Thus, our capacity for knowing could be defined as our ability to integrate our knowledge and intelligence to create meaning.

But knowing something also implies that we understand the truth of what we know. It suggests that we have confidence in the integrity and relevance of what we know. That what we know is authentic and has meaning for us that is consistent with our understanding of who we are. To know the real truth about ourselves, the essence of who we are, implies that we have an understanding of our place in the Universe. To achieve this understanding our knowing requires a universal dimension which provides the insight we need to 'see' the truth of us, to know and understand our true purpose in life.

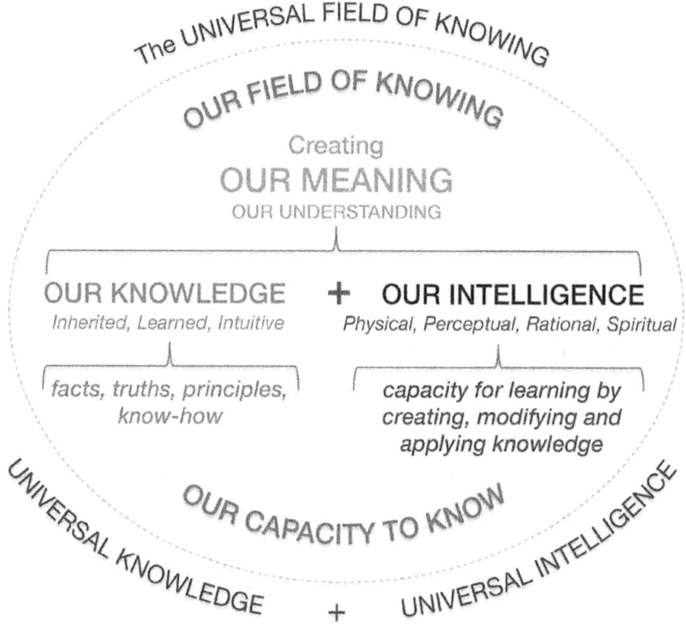

Figure 46: A model of knowing

Our knowing has two primary dimensions:

- **Vocational knowing**: which encompasses the knowledge and intelligence we need to live within and contribute to our community and to do our life's work.

- **Spiritual knowing**: the knowing we need for being truly present and to live a purposeful life. This is the knowing that reveals our true purpose; the knowing that unfolds and guides our life journey; the knowing that releases the real potential we have to live our life on purpose.

We need to engage and develop both of these dimensions of knowing to enable our authentic presence and release our full potential to live our life on purpose.

To develop our capacity for knowing, we need to attend to both the expansion of our knowledge; and to the development of the intelligence that we use to apply that knowledge to create meaning and expand our understanding of the world we live in. Because the development of our knowledge and intelligence is an interdependent activity, as we use our intelligence to create new understanding, we are also at the same time developing our intelligence.

Our knowledge base can be divided into four interrelated sets of knowledge, each of which can be broadly defined as follows:

- **Inherited knowledge** includes our innate or genetic knowledge that we acquire from our birth parents. There is much debate about what this knowledge set may include, but the possibility that we inherit significant knowledge, which is fundamental to our capacity to live our human life, seems entirely plausible to me.

- **Learned knowledge** includes both our rational and sensory knowledge, and the experiential knowledge that we have acquired by using our reasoning and perceptual abilities. We also derive important knowledge from what we term our 'common sense', which I consider to be knowledge that derives from the community from which we come or are part of (*sensus communis*). This knowledge is most probably a blend of our inherited and learned knowledge.

- **Intuitive knowledge** refers to the knowledge gained from our insights, the truths and facts that we apprehend directly and apparently independent of any process of sensing or reasoning. Perhaps some of our intuitive or 'unlearned' knowledge is simply part of our inherited knowledge, a sort of dormant knowledge that we access as we need it? Perhaps some of our intuitive knowledge is part of our sensory knowledge base, knowledge that we have perceived using our so-called 'sixth sense'? Or perhaps our intuitive insights reflect our capacity to access a wider field of universal knowledge that extends beyond the limits of our inherited and learned knowledge?

- **Universal knowledge** refers to our access to the dimension of knowledge that exists in the wider Universe of which we are part, and which I believe we have the capacity to know. This universal knowledge, together with the intelligence we use to access it, is available to us to increase our understanding of the Universe. It extends and informs our other knowledge sets to enhance our capacity for knowing, and thus expand our potential to create the meaning that enables us to live our life on purpose.

Some may consider our universal knowledge to be equivalent to our intuitive knowledge, or our intuitive knowledge to be a subset of our universal knowledge. Others may consider our inherited knowledge to be a subset of our learned knowledge, which we are somehow born with a 'blank knowledge slate'. The only real importance of the above categorisation is the distinction drawn between our inherited, learned and intuitive knowledge sets (which we could call our local knowledge set), and the existence of a universal knowledge set, whether or not it includes our intuitive knowledge as a subset.

The proposition that we have access to universal knowledge (however we define it) that extends our 'local' capacity to know and understand who we are is fundamental to this discussion.

I find it difficult to conceive of a situation where our acquisition and utilisation of knowledge does not involve our intelligence. We may consider that our inherited knowledge and some of our learned knowledge is simply acquired directly from its source. However, our intelligence is usually engaged to apply or make contextual sense of this knowledge and in so doing creates new understanding and expands our overall knowledge set. Our intelligence is, therefore, a key factor in developing our capacity for knowing.

I am aware that there are differing views about the categorisation of intelligence, but I am comfortable with a proposition that there are four basic kinds of intelligence:

- **Physical intelligence**: the innate or instinctive capacity of our physical human form to learn and adapt to complex changes in its operating environment.

- **Rational intelligence**: our ability to make meaning through reasoning which is often equated with our intellectual capacity (IQ).

- **Perceptual intelligence**: our ability to make meaning by using our senses; to make sense of our environment through what we see, hear, smell, taste and feel (PQ).

- **Spiritual intelligence**: our ability to find meaning and purpose in our lives, the ability to 'see' and understand our interconnectedness with the Universe (SQ).

This categorisation of intelligence does not differentiate emotional intelligence, which has received a lot of attention in recent years. That is because I consider emotional intelligence to be a hybrid of our rational and perceptual intelligence. I think that our ability to recognise, understand, use and manage our emotions and the emotions of others requires a combination of both our rational and perceptual abilities.

The primary usefulness of this four-part categorisation is that it enables us to differentiate between the intelligence associated with our vocational and spiritual knowing; in particular to propose that there is a different intelligence associated with our ability to access and utilise our spiritual knowing. I believe that we have a spiritual intelligence that enables us to utilise our universal knowledge to add value and meaning to our life. Our spiritual intelligence gives us the capacity to continually reframe our human experience by placing it within a larger universal context. It enables us to check the relevance and authenticity of our vocational knowing by referencing the truth of who we are.

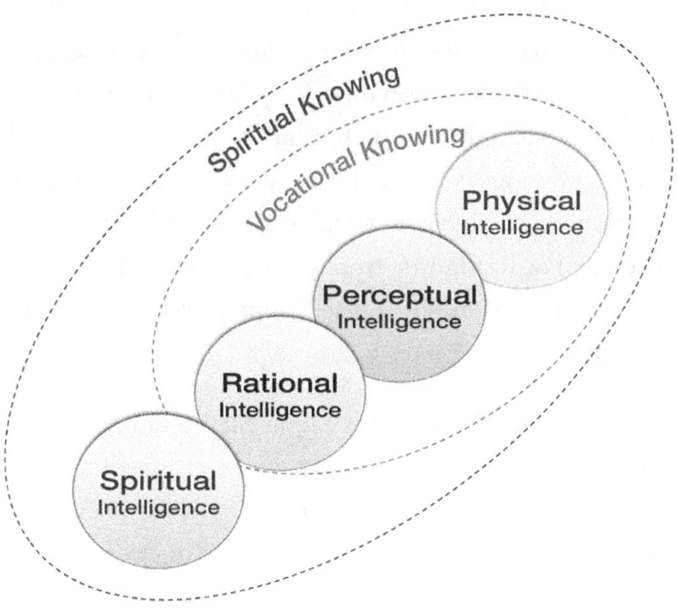

Figure 47: Intelligence and knowing

We need all of our intelligences to be really present in our life, but it is our spiritual intelligence that enables us to access the universal knowing that reveals our true potential and guides the creation of our authentic presence. Our spiritual intelligence enables us to transcend the limits of our vocational knowing and access a spiritual dimension of knowing through which we can see and create our life on purpose. We can activate our spiritual intelligence and access this universal field of knowing by focusing our attention on the source of this knowing, often referred to as our 'inner self'.

One way to focus our attention is to use meditation, a process of thinking, contemplation and reflection which can enable us to see life from our centre.

Meditation, in its many forms, enables us to achieve a stillness – a quiet presence where the focus on our inner world can open pathways to spiritual knowing. We can choose a receptive meditative focus where we quieten our mind to become still and open to the knowing of the wider universe. In this space, we are without intention, we have no specific agenda. We are not seeking any particular knowledge or to answer any particular questions, we are simply being quietly present, open and receptive to new understandings.

Or we can choose to concentrate our meditation, to focus our attention on a particular question or a subject for which we need new understanding; knowing that seems to be beyond our reach. In this space, we have intention and are seeking answers, but we must still remain open to the knowing we encounter, ever aware that our intention may be challenged, informed or reformed by the new understanding we seek. For example 'what is my true purpose?' or 'what is my ambition for the future?' We simply 'hold' the question and await the flow of knowing that will enlighten us with the meaning we need, not necessarily the meaning we expect. Sometimes that meaning we receive may cause us to reframe or abandon the question that we are holding. We are not looking for the 'right' answer, we are seeking enlightenment and so we must remain open and receptive to 'what turns up'. And if nothing turns up, we reflect on the real relevance of the subject to our purpose. It may be knowing that we do not need, or perhaps not at this time.

We can also focus our attention without engaging in formalised meditation. We can seek universal understanding about something by simply holding our intention (our question or request for understanding) within our presence.

We can do this in numerous different ways by focusing our thinking, contemplation and reflection, which is essence are another form of meditation.

One way to hold our intention is to make it a deliberate and particular (concentrated) focus within our presence. We can do this on a periodic basis by creating a particular time and space for contemplating our intention, perhaps by placing ourselves in a relaxing space and just reflecting on our intention, or by spending time writing about our intention, unfolding our understanding of why it is important to us.

Another way to hold our intention on a more constant basis is to place it in a 'pocket of our mind' and take it with us wherever we go, remaining alert for input of any kind. In this way, our intention becomes part of our everyday life – it is always there in the background, suspended and awaiting enlightenment. Our spiritual intelligence is ever present and ever active, and our meditation, in its various forms, becomes more than just a state we enter periodically, it becomes a way of life.

This discussion about our capacity for knowing is deliberately focused on our capacity for spiritual knowing because it is this capacity which defines our real potential for creating meaning in our life. There is much we can do to improve our physical, rational and perceptual intelligence and thus to better access the inherited and learned knowledge that comprises our vocational knowing. But if we recognise the natural capacity that we have to engage our spiritual intelligence and unlock our spiritual knowing, then we have admitted our capacity to know and manifest our true purpose in life.

Whatever process or pathway we choose to access this spiritual dimension of our knowing, we will be focusing our attention on our inner world. To achieve this focus usually requires time alone, enabling spaces and often quiet stillness, to create a receptive connection with our Universe. If we do not invest time in seeking this spiritual knowing, if we do not focus our attention to engage our spiritual intelligence, then our knowing will be limited to the vocational dimension. We will not come to know all that we could know. There is a good chance that our life will be more about doing than being and we will be less present than we could be.

Consider the following questions:

- When was the last time you took real time out for yourself, when you created quiet time and space for your own personal reflection and renewal?

- When was the last time you engaged in any form of meditation, when you reserved time for contemplation about your life in general or about particular aspects of your life?

- Do you often attempt to resolve your life challenges by seeking internal rather than external guidance, by trying to access your spiritual knowing rather than your vocational knowing?

- Have you ever invested time in discovering who you really are – the essence of your authentic self, your true purpose in life? Do you often spend time contemplating that purpose and what it means for you?

- To what extent are you at peace with yourself and your world? How connected are you to your inner self? Do you see the world from your centre?

If you are seeking a happy and joyful life, then you must recognise that the pathway to joyfulness is through your spiritual knowing. And the pathway to spiritual knowing is through the engagement and development of your spiritual intelligence.

Where is my creative space?

To develop and sustain a positive attitude to change, we need the capacity to view all of our life challenges and difficulties as learning opportunities and be able to convert those opportunities into positive (purposeful) learning outcomes. As our world becomes increasingly more complex and fast paced we cannot simply rely on what has worked in the past to resolve the challenges we encounter.

Nor will we be able to rely on what we currently know to successfully negotiate the web of change opportunities that will come our way. We need to create new and innovative solutions to take advantage of these opportunities to sustain our authentic presence in our communities and to live our life on purpose. To do that we will need to access and develop our **creative capacity**, the capacity that we all have to know and to imagine what could be, to create original and meaningful (productive) new ideas, and put these new ideas into practice.

Using our **imagination**, we can see our current reality through a different lens. We can break free from our existing mental models, the traditional ideas, rules, patterns and relationships that tie our present to our past. We can transcend what we currently know and create new and enlightening perspectives of our past and our present. Most importantly, our imagination enables us to envision a new future, new possibilities and new solutions to the problems and the challenges that we face. Our imagination is the cornerstone of our creative capacity.

Using our **creativity**, we can explore and evaluate the many possibilities that we have generated by our imagining, by seeing things differently.

We can create meaningful new ideas, processes, interpretations etc. by exploring our change opportunities (problems or challenges) from multiple perspectives, by using our creativity to reframe and rethink the possible solutions. Then we can evaluate our ideas by experimenting and testing to see what works and potentially discover more new possibilities from our apparent failures, learning to see failure as a valued correction or refinement within our creative process.

Finally, we can use our **innovation** to apply our new ideas to our life situation and create new outcomes, new ways of being present in our world. Innovation is essentially the applied result or realisation of the ideas generated by our imagination (our innovation discovery space) and explored by our creativity (our innovation evaluation space).

Some of our innovation may reflect original or breakthrough thinking that can result in the disruptive change, change that significantly alters our presence in our communities. However, much of our innovation is more likely to result in derivative change, which involves the adoption and application of existing 'community knowing', and results in outcomes that represent relatively minor changes in the way we live our life. As we will discuss later, this so-called derivative change (because it is derived from what we already know) is just as important as disruptive change for refreshing our presence and keeping us on purpose.

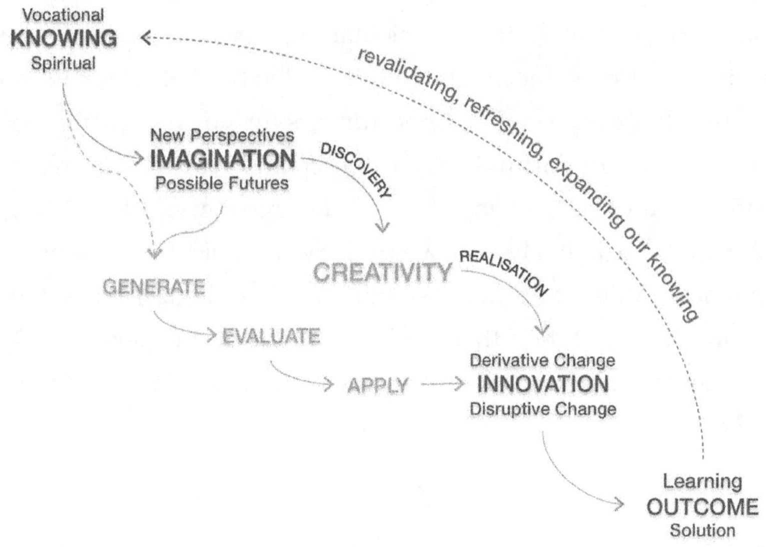

Figure 48: Our creative capacity

Creativity is not the preserve of special people or associated with particular occupations. We all have the capacity to be creative. We all have an imagination that can envision a different future. We can all have new ideas which we are capable of exploring and evaluating. And we can all choose to risk the application of those ideas to change the way we live. However, the extent to which we use our creative capacity to release our potential by negotiating positive change depends on three interlinked factors:

- our commitment to live our life on purpose, the clarity of purpose that guides our positive response to change in our life

- our learning orientation and change appetite, the degree to which we have a confident and positive attitude to change

- our creative capacity, the degree to which we have developed our capacity to imagine, create and innovate; our ability to discover and realise the new ideas that will refresh and sustain our authentic presence in our communities

Our learning orientation will influence our ability to recognise creative opportunity. If our orientation is weak (our personal learning centre is inactive) then it is likely that we will not recognise life's problems as opportunities for positive change. We will not see the opportunity to use our creative capacity to create a positive outcome. Even if we do recognise the change opportunity, it is likely that we will try to avoid the problem or apply our traditional problem-solving methodologies. We will try to reproduce a solution that works from our past experience. The opportunity for new thinking and the production of new solutions will be lost.

A strong learning orientation (an active personal learning centre) enables us to frame all of our problems and challenges as opportunities for change. It gives us the confidence to say 'yes' to these opportunities and the courage to take risks and experiment with new ways of negotiating change in our life. If we are determined to live our life on purpose, then we have adopted a life perspective which enables us to view problems as change opportunities. And we have the motivation to explore all of the possibilities to discover and realise life-affirming (purposeful) outcomes. If we do not have a clear and committed life purpose, then we will have difficulty framing life's problems and challenges as opportunities for positive change, as opportunities to enhance and sustain our authentic presence.

Clarity of purpose provides a critical benchmark for assessing life's problems and challenges and is a key driver for pursuing the best possible solutions. If we are purpose driven and view all change as an opportunity to manifest that purpose, then we need to negotiate change in a positive way.

We need to create outcomes that presence our life on purpose. Achieving this intention or ambition for our future will simply not be possible by reproducing solutions from our past experience. We will need to find new ways to negotiate change and sustain our authentic presence in our communities. We will need to be creative.

And so we return to the title question of 'where is our creative space?' In which of our life spaces do we currently exercise our creative capacity? How do we exercise our imagination? How do we generate new ideas? And how do we experiment with and apply our new ideas to create our future, to live our life on purpose?

Some of us may have a particular creative space. Perhaps our work is essentially creative or a place where we interact with people we would call 'creatives'. Or perhaps we have a creative pastime or hobby that we would call our creative space. Others may consider that they have no creative space, that creativity simply doesn't play any significant part in their life. And still others may see their whole life as a creative endeavour. They view their total presence on earth as their creative space.

I suggest that we all have a creative space, but the nature and scope of that space, the degree to which it really influences our life, will depend on how we exercise our creative capacity. At one extreme, our creative space is small, our creative capacity is rarely engaged and has little impact on most aspects of our life. At the other extreme, our creative space is large and our creative capacity is an essential and active influence in our life. Our creativity is pervasive in all aspects of our life. We are living a creative life, actively creating our own future, our authentic presence in our communities.

One way to develop our creative capacity is to locate its current space in our life and attempt to grow that space by expanding the application and influence of our creativity to more and more aspects of our life. Another way is to engage our creativity capacity as a constant and pervasive force in our life; to attempt to see our whole life as a creative endeavour.

If we intend to engage our creative capacity to create our life on purpose, to be the creative force in our own lives, we need to access our ability to **imagine** (to see the possibilities for different futures), to **create** (to explore the potential of new solutions), and to **innovate** (to risk new ways of being present).

Seeing – focusing our attention

In order to imagine the future as full of positive possibilities we need to increase our future focus and decrease our attachment to the present. We can do this by deciding to apply a creative focus to all of our life challenges and problems; by determining that we will create new and meaningful (purposeful) solutions in preference to applying our traditional problem-solving approaches.

By focusing our attention on future possibilities, we transcend our current reality and become more open to new possibilities. We increase our awareness of what could be. We empty our mind of the clutter of past experience and the influence of old mental models and create a fresh space for our imagination and creativity to flourish. If we focus our attention on purposeful solutions, we increase the likelihood that our imagination will preference ideas which are meaningful, ideas that have the potential to enhance our presence.

Exploring – creating a positive space

The productive exploration of ideas requires a positive attitude, an affirmative mindset that welcomes all ideas as potential opportunities for positive change. If we have a deficit mentality which constantly sees 'the glass as half empty', then we are likely to discount the full potential of our new ideas. We can help to create a positive mindset by exploring our ideas in a positive creative space; a space that enables us to be on purpose and encourages the contribution of other wisdom and knowing.

We also need to recognise that good ideas require a period of gestation; that filtering new ideas and allowing them to develop and mature takes time and cannot be pressured. Not all of our ideas will measure up. Some will need to be abandoned, some will change shape, and some will be integrated with other ideas to form new ideas. We should not be negative about this filtering process, which may seem to fail many of our bold new ideas. The failure, correction and refinement of ideas are a very important part of our creative process.

Risking – building confidence and courage

It is one thing to have good new ideas. It is quite another to implement them, to make them meaningful by producing a life-enhancing outcome. Being innovative in the way we respond to life's change opportunities means doing things differently, risking new ways of being present. Taking risks requires the courage to confront potential failure in its many guises. There can be unexpected outcomes that don't meet our expectations or the expectations of our communities; outcomes that need remedial action to recover our presence; or outcomes that confront us with new challenges and problems.

If our ideas are conceived on purpose then these outcomes are not failures, they are learning adjustments, signals that further change is necessary to renew or refresh our presence. Provided we have not forced the creative process to produce a predetermined solution, we should be confident that any of our creative outcomes will have the potential to be positive, even if that is not obvious at first sight. The 'catch 22' is that the only way to build the confidence to take risk is by taking risk.

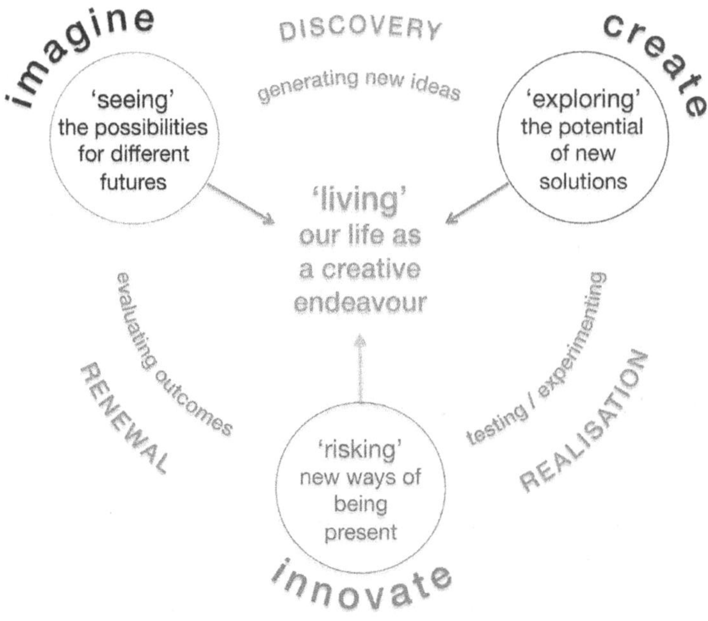

Figure 49: Our creative space

And finally, a word on **collaborative learning** and the benefits of engaging our communities to broaden and deepen our creative capacity. Not only do we not have all the good ideas, we may not be in the best position to evaluate those we do have.

Congruent individuals enjoy meaningful relationships with their communities that are built on trust, respect and mutual benefit. They share an enabling leadership ethic (selfless service to others) that allows them to engage their communities in the co-creation of their future. These communities can provide the source of new wisdom and knowing that assist our creative process.

By engaging with our communities we can share our knowing and wisdom and contribute to their creative process. Perhaps some of our new ideas are meant for other people, parts of their life jigsaw, and vice versa. Engaging in collaborative learning (co-creativity) can expand our creative capacity by helping us to see more change opportunities, explore more solution options, and mitigate our risks by learning from the experience of others that we know and trust.

How do I sharpen my life focus?

Broadly speaking, most of us will encounter two kinds of change during our life journey. Occasionally, we will encounter significant challenges that tend to 'stop us in our tracks' and cause us to seriously reconsider our life going forward. Examples might be the loss of a significant person in our life; the failure of an important relationship; the distancing or demise of a significant community of interest; or challenges associated with a significant illness.

These times of **disruptive change** in our life are usually highly stressful and often accompanied by feelings of great loss and uncertainty. While disruptive change can seriously challenge our purpose in life (our raison d'être), it often presents a significant opportunity for creating positive change outcomes.

We can often take advantage of these life changing events to rethink and redefine our future. In spite of the pain and sadness typically associated with disruptive change, it can also offer real opportunities for great joy. This is because disruptive change often contains the seeds of a new beginning, an opportunity to renew and refresh our life on purpose.

We often encounter times of disruptive change as a result of not addressing the less confronting change opportunities that come our way on a regular basis. The challenges and opportunities for learning that are an essential element of any life journey are there for a reason; they present the chance to make positive incremental changes in our life. These are the **derivative change** opportunities (so called because they derived from what we already know) that are designed to keep us on purpose.

Change opportunities are the prompts or signals that we need to make progressive change in our life, to continually fine tune our presence, and so avoid the confrontation of distressing disruptive change events. If we continually fail to notice or act on these 'signals', then we are almost certainly creating a disruptive change opportunity that will seriously interrupt our life at some point in the future. A confronting change that will demand that we alter the course of our life journey.

We can, of course, choose to ignore our derivative change opportunities and opt for a life of disruptive change. This is a choice to spend significant periods of time 'off purpose' and opt for major corrections that wrench our life back on course, usually for a brief time only. It is a choice to be less authentic and thus compromise our opportunity for real happiness and fulfillment.

We can also choose to ignore our disruptive change opportunities, but I suggest that we do this at our peril.

The stress and tension that will result from ignoring disruptive change, from deciding to remain off purpose and be continually inauthentic, has the potential to seriously impact our wellbeing. Trying to ignore disruptive change can shift our life pathway towards unhappiness, stress and potentially serious illness. The subliminal stress of continually masking our life, of continually suppressing our authentic self and maintaining a fabricated presence in multiple communities, will eventually show up as serious dysfunction and probably, ultimately as life threatening illness.

So we need to cultivate and harvest the flow of derivative change opportunities that keep us on purpose. We need to discover and action the incremental changes in our life than enable us to sustain our authentic presence in our communities. We can do this by monitoring our life on purpose, by continually checking our authenticity to discover and action opportunities to better align our 'doing' with our 'being'.

Effective monitoring requires effective feedback loops, personal, community and universal 'listening centres' that discover and communicate opportunities for change. Our personal feedback loops are activated and maintained by our reflective and meditative practices. By making time and space to focus on our purpose, to reflect on the authenticity of our life, and being alert for new knowing to emerge, we keep our personal (inner) feedback loops open and attentive.

As we have observed previously, all of our community encounters are potential learning opportunities that can present important feedback on the authenticity of our presence, and are thus, opportunities for positive change.

Maintaining active community feedback loops requires us to be proactive in creating the encounters that enable such learning to occur. It is not just about being open, positively receptive and listening to what our communities are saying. It is also about having processes for seeking specific feedback from those we know and trust – looking for advice and constructive criticism by hosting community conversations about our purpose and our presence in our communities. This is the realm of collaborative learning where we engage in the co-creativity that is so important in achieving both individual and community congruence. By engaging in reflective conversations with our community, we become part of the community feedback loops. We contribute to community learning and ultimately to the congruence of our communities of interest.

Our spiritual knowing, through which we can enjoy the energy, wisdom and guidance of our universal knowing, is also an important source of reflective feedback. When we exercise our spiritual intelligence to access this knowing, we are in effect activating our universal feedback loop. This 'super feedback' loop surrounds and supports our community and personal feedback loops by providing a universal context for our learning conversations. If you like, it is our ultimate quality assurance process that shapes our change opportunities to ensure they have the potential to enhance the authenticity of our presence. Feedback loops are essentially continuous learning loops. They are our continuous improvement or quality system that sharpens the focus of our doing and our being and keeps us on purpose.

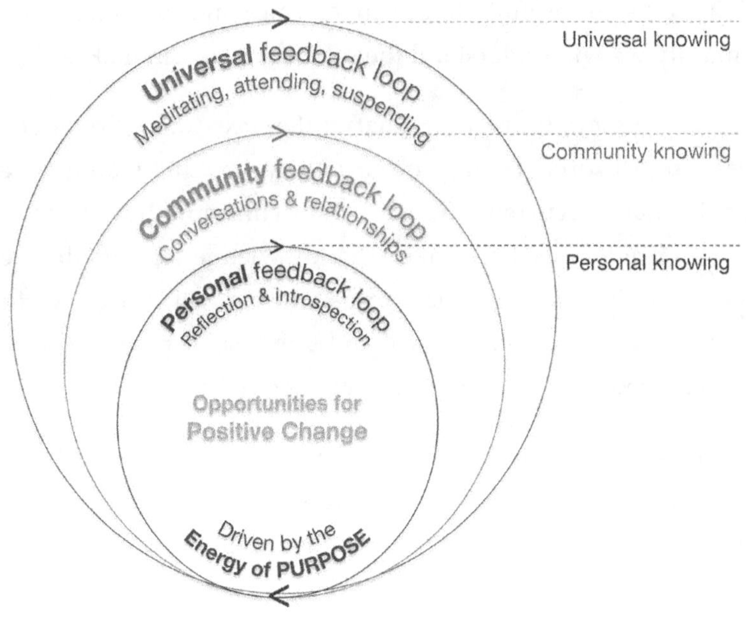

Figure 50: Personal feedback loops

Imagine if...

Imagine if we were the difference we could make.

Our real potential as human beings is to live our life on purpose. We release that potential by creating the outcomes that manifest our unique purpose; a purpose that expresses the truth of who we are; a purpose that only we have the capacity to manifest. That purpose is our raison d'être and our potential to make a unique contribution to the world we live in.

If we are confident about our purpose in life, we can accept the risks of an uncertain future and frame our life as an opportunity for learning. If we have a positive learning orientation, we will view the challenges and change we encounter as opportunities to make a difference.

And, if we listen carefully to our inner voice and the voice of our community we will understand the difference we can make.

Once we commit to making that difference 'then Providence moves too. All sorts of things occur to help one that would never otherwise have occurred' (Goethe). We will know how to make the difference we need to make. The knowledge and intelligence we need will be made available to us and we will experience the full support of our personal, local and universal communities. We will be enabled to be the difference we need to be.

If we focus our attention on living a purposeful life, we will have the capacity to know what we need to know to be the person we are meant to be. Being that person is the difference we are meant to make!

Imagine if the difference we make could change the world.

If we are committed to a life on purpose, we will choose to co-create our future with the communities of people with whom we have a shared purpose. Within those communities our authentic presence will enhance their collective capacity to create the outcomes that manifest our shared purpose. By collaborating with our communities to co-create a shared future we will be helping to build communities of purpose that create equitable-shared value for their constituencies. We will be making a difference that has the potential to change the way that many (most?) communities (and organisations) work.

By being who we are meant to be, we can make a difference that can change the way our world works!

Acknowledgements

I would like to acknowledge the influence of Nick Udall and Nic Turner[59] through their enlightening writings about purpose and human potential. I am also indebted to Danah Zohar and Ian Marshall[60] for their encouraging discussion about spiritual intelligence; and to Ken Robinson[61], Michael Michalko[62] and Robert Fritz[63] for their writings about creativity.

16 | My Participation

My opportunity for contribution is to be who I am. What I do with my life will echo in eternity.

Figure 51: Individual contribution

Each of us is a unique strand in the intricate web of life and here to make a contribution.

Deepak Chopra

Do I make a difference in my communities?

How often do we reflect on the way we participate in our communities, the communities with whom we share a common interest or purpose? Do we ever pause to consider how we add value to these communities; to ask 'How does my presence in each community make a positive difference for me and my community?'. Within our personal communities (our life-partnership, our family and our friends), what is it that we contribute to make those communities a better place for all participants? Within our local communities (our workplaces and social spaces), how does our participation create equitable-shared value for us and the other members of those communities?

For those communities in which we are positively engaged in pursuing a shared purpose, we will be helping to create outcomes which manifest that purpose. We will be co-creating community contributions that are also consistent with our own purpose. Given the nature of purpose is concerned with selfless service to others, our contributions to those communities will reflect selfless service. The positive value of our presence within 'our communities' will be the service we provide, not just for our own benefit, but also for the benefit of others in our communities.

For those communities where we cannot identify the positive mutual value of our participation, then either we are not participating as we could (or should), or our lack of engagement may suggest that they are not really our communities after all. As we have discussed previously, our knowing will reveal the reality of our community connection and presence. We will know if our participation can and should change, if we can and should make a difference to this community. We will know whether we can be of service in a way that is mutually beneficial to our own wellbeing and that of the community.

Our potential to make a positive difference to our communities is to be of service in a way that demonstrates our commitment to our shared purpose and contributes to the creation of shared benefits for the community. Therefore, to reflect on how we participate within each of our communities, to consider if and how we add value to each of these communities, we simply need to respond to the question 'how do I serve my community?'

Answering this question for each of our communities (personal, local and universal) will not only challenge the nature and quality of our contribution to those communities, it will also challenge the validity and reality of our community presence. Understanding how we do, or do not, serve our communities may well cause us to question why we belong to a particular community or to reconsider how we can best serve each of our communities. The understanding that will flow from considering this question will almost certainly reveal new opportunities for personal learning, including opportunities to think about our purpose and/or new ways of being present in our communities.

For each of your personal and local communities consider the following questions:

- What is the nature of my service to the community?
    - Is it purposeful (consistent with my life purpose)?
    - Is it community aligned (consistent with the community's shared purpose)
    - Is it essentially selfless (primarily motivated for the benefit of others)?
- What is the quality of my service to the community?
    - Am I passionate about what I do in the community?
    - Does what I do make a positive difference to the community?
    - Is that difference acknowledged by the community?
    - How do I know that it is the best service that I have to offer?

These are questions that should be addressed in conversation with our communities. Seeking their open and honest feedback is essential to qualify our own reflections and self enquiry. Taking time to listen to the voice of our communities is the focus of our next discussion on the authenticity of our community presence.

If we are living purposefully we will choose to belong to communities where we enjoy a shared purpose. Our participation in those communities will reflect our efforts to help them to succeed, to be congruent communities that manifest their shared purpose. Our contribution will also be a manifestation of our own purpose and thus assist the development of our own congruence. If we choose to make a difference by helping our communities to succeed we are also making a difference in our own life.

Is my community profile authentic?

We have already discussed the challenge of being truly present in our communities and relationships. And we have briefly considered the options of leaving, hibernating or changing the communities and/or relationships where we feel that we do not really belong. But, what about the challenge of being present in those communities and relationships where we feel that we do belong? It is one thing to know that we are in a community or an important relationship where we have a shared purpose and where there is the potential to co-create mutual benefit. It is quite another thing to openly and honestly reveal our true presence, to be an authentic member of that community or an authentic participant in the relationship. To know (to honestly believe) that simply by being who we are, we can make a positive difference to our relationships and to our communities.

Being **authentic** means being true to our purpose; creating a presence in our life that is a genuine reflection of our core purpose; a presence where our actions (our doing) are consistent with who we are (our being).

Achieving an authentic presence in our communities (and our relationships) is important for two reasons. Firstly it enables us to act purposefully, to release our true potential for the benefit of others. And secondly it ensures our own longer-term wellbeing by enabling us to be ourselves within our community environment, to be who we really are and not who we are supposed to be.

As we have discussed previously, if our presence within our communities is continually managed or masked so that we can fit in, we are adopting a fabricated lifestyle that can put our physical, mental and spiritual health at risk.

350

If we are disabled from presenting the real us, we are denying ourselves and the community (or relationship) the benefit of our full participation. By not sharing the full potential of who we are, we are diminishing the opportunity to contribute to the positive development of our communities (and relationships). And we are also diminishing the potential of our communities (and our relationships) to be an enabling and positive force in our life, to assist our own pursuit of a purposeful and joyful life.

Our community profile is a reflection of our perceived presence within the community, how the community views our participation in terms of our behaviours and the contributions we make. If our community profile is authentic, our participation (our actions) within the community will be a true reflection of who we are (our purpose). To reveal the truth of our community presence – to understand the degree of alignment between who we are and the way we operate within our communities – we can simply rely on our own reflective enquiry or we can engage our community in conversation to inform us about their perception of our presence.

The simplest way to access the community knowing about our presence is to seek feedback through our meaningful relationships within those communities. These trusted and respectful relationships provide a safe place to begin conversations about our community profile. These are conversations that will seek to reveal if what we do in the community is a true reflection of who we are. We are asking our community for candid feedback on how we show up. We are seeking open and honest answers to the deeply personal question 'Who do you see that I am?'.

For most people, a community conversation about their authenticity will be a challenging event.

If we are genuine in our intention to explore our presence within our communities, we will need to be open and honest about who we really are, why we participate in those communities and what we see as the real issues for our ongoing productive engagement. Initiating and sustaining a genuine community dialogue about the truth of our connection with our communities can be both intellectually and emotionally challenging for all involved. However, the feelings and behaviours that surface during such a personal conversation will reveal valuable insights about the reality of our presence, and how that presence is perceived by our community.

To assist our reflection on our presence within our communities, and to prepare for our community profile conversations, we could consider the following questions:

- What is the nature of the purpose or intention that I share with this community, and why is it important to me?

- Do I have a presence within this community that encourages others in the community to be open and transparent, to say what they really think?

- Do I have a presence within this community that values other community members, a presence that listens carefully (attentively, respectfully and thoughtfully) to what they say?

- What do I understand to be the value of my participation in the community; what are the outcome benefits for me and for other community members? What is the difference I make?

- Do I have a presence within the community that openly welcomes difference, diversity and dissent? Is it a presence that expects to be informed by genuine difference? Or is it a presence that is mostly suspicious of difference and expects to avoid, assimilate or discount it?

- How do I envisage my future role in this community; how will my participation help to create a positive future for the community? How will my continuing presence in the community enable me to live purposefully?

These are all questions that challenge the nature of our community presence. They challenge us to reflect on why we belong to the community and how our presence is mutually beneficial to us and the community. But they also challenge us to think about how we live our life generally, how we show up on a daily basis in the universal community to which we belong. These questions pose the more fundamental and general question 'Am I living my life purposefully?'.

Our communities will have a sense of who we are from our living presence within them. They will know from our interactions with them and the contributions we make if that presence is consistent with, and supportive of, our shared purpose. But for our community profile to be authentic, our presence within that community must also be a manifestation of our own life purpose. Only we will know the real truth of that. While our perception of our community profile may be positively endorsed by community feedback, the final judgment on the authenticity of that profile is ours alone to make. Only we know if our presence in that community is also an integral part of our own life on purpose.

Do I collaborate with my communities?

By definition, the people that comprise our communities are committed to a common intent or purpose that we share with them. They are therefore motivated to co-create outcomes that manifest that intent or purpose and in so doing generate mutual value outcomes.

This commonality and mutuality of interest is the basis of the meaningful relationships that interconnect us within our community and which have the potential to help us live purposefully.

Our community relationships also provide a framework for collaborative action. They provide a way of understanding and engaging the collective energy and capacity of the community to pursue those elements of our purpose that we share with our community. It is through these relationships, and the information sharing networks they enable, that we have the opportunity to know our community; to understand their collective capability and how we can collaborate in the pursuit of our shared purpose. We can only come to understand our community if we are open to its voice. It is by listening through our relationships, the nodes of our community network, that we are able to 'know' our community. And it is through purposeful dialogue with our community that we engage their collective energy and capability in the collaborative pursuit of our own purpose.

Collaboration, which we have previously defined as 'the effective interaction of...people...who share a common interest or purpose...to pursue a shared-value outcome' is enabled by successful conversations that create the possibility for genuine dialogue. If we are serious about collaborating with our communities we will create the opportunity for community conversations that explore the potential for co-creating our future together.

Those conversations require us to be authentic participants, to 'show up as who we are to talk about something we really care about'. We must have the intention to collaborate and the intention to co-create a purposeful shared-value outcome.

To reflect on our intention to collaborate with our communities, focus on some of your personal and/or local communities and consider your response to the following questions:

- Can you be authentically present in conversations with this community? Can you share your own life purpose with them?
- Are you prepared to openly share all of your relevant knowledge and understanding with these communities?
- Do you genuinely believe that you can learn from these communities? Can you enable them to learn from you?
- Are you prepared to serve this community? Is your real intention to give, take or exchange value with this community?
- Could you really admit this community as a co-creative partner in your life journey?
- Do you acknowledge the potential of your community to assist your life on purpose?

Of course, these questions also test the nature of our connection with these communities. Once again we are checking on the validity of our shared purpose or intent and revisiting the question 'Is this my community?'.

We may have the intention to collaborate, but for collaboration to be possible, we also need our conversational interactions with our communities to reflect that intention. To reflect on your recent conversational experiences with your personal and local communities, consider your response to the following questions:

- When was the last time you engaged in conversation with one of these communities about your shared purpose?
- What was your intention in initiating or participating in the conversation?

- o   What did you intend that dialogue to generate?
  - o   Did you have a mutual benefit outcome in mind?
- How did you engage your community in this conversation?
  - o   Did you create a context that enabled and encouraged their active and positive participation?
- Was it a genuine dialogue where you listened to understand and contributed thoughtfully for the benefit of the community?
  - o   Did you contribute in a way that served your community?
  - o   Or was it a 'talk down' where your thoughts and opinions dominated the conversations?
  - o   Or was it a 'take down' where your critical voice refused to admit the different and diverse voices of your community?
- Was it a positive dialogue which benefited all of the participants, including you?
  - o   Were the outcomes generally purpose-aligned for you and your community?
- Do you have successful conversations within your communities?

I suggest that we can look to the outcomes of our community conversations for the answers to these questions.

If these conversations were largely successful, then we intended to enable a dialogue that would engage our community in the pursuit of our shared purpose. We intended to create a context that would enable us to leverage the collective capability of our community to generate outcomes that manifest that shared purpose, to engage our community in co-creating the future together. Our intention was unselfish and collaborative and concerned with co-creating outcomes for the greater good of the whole community including ourselves.

If we cannot see the creation of purposeful shared value as an outcome of our community conversations, then I suggest we probably failed to create a context for those conversations that was based on the commonality and mutuality of our community connections. We simply did not intend, consciously or unconsciously, to create the context for a purposeful dialogue with our community. We did not intend to genuinely engage our community in the collaborative pursuit of our own life purpose.

If we are endeavouring to live our life on purpose, a purpose that is concerned in some way with service to others, then our collaborative interaction with our communities (who share our purpose), must have the potential to help us live purposefully. Our connection with these communities will be purpose based and our service contribution to them will be a manifestation of that purpose. This is a win-win situation for us and the community – we not only have the opportunity to create shared purposeful value for ourselves and the community, we have the opportunity to enlist their help to co-create that value. We have the opportunity to energise and engage the collective capability of the community in the pursuit of our life purpose.

Each of us is a uniquely individual member of the universal community and of the personal and local communities with whom we choose to share our life journey. The knowledge and wisdom of those communities, and their collective energies and capabilities, are available to enable and sustain our life purpose. By choosing to collaborate with our communities to co-create our life on purpose, we are contributing to each of those communities in a way that co-creates our future with them.

Is my life on purpose?

Who we are is defined by our life purpose. Who we appear to be is defined by what we do. Our physical presence in the world is evident in the way we live our lives, in the actions and behaviours that reflect our participation in the community at large, and in the outcomes that we create. The degree to which 'who I am' is consistently reflected in 'what I do' speaks to the authenticity of our presence, the degree to which we are really living our life on purpose.

In the predominantly materialistic world in which we live, many people are defined (some happily and some unhappily) by what they do and not by who they really are. The mental models on which these people base their life, often prioritise doing over being. They are focused on creating and sustaining a presence in their life that preferences their physical and material wellbeing over their spiritual wellbeing. For these people, success is measured primarily in terms of the things that represent their physical presence in the world, such as status, money, possessions, health. Their life is not balanced by a spiritual agenda that aligns their actions and behaviours with their life purpose. They have chosen, consciously or unconsciously, to be defined by what they do and not by who they are.

For people with an understanding of who they are, who are aware of their life purpose, their presence in the world will be influenced by knowing that purpose. For some people their presence is their life purpose. The truth of who they are is essentially manifest in what they do every day. Their presence in the world is an authentic representation of their true self. These people are constantly and consistently living their life purpose.

However, for many people who endeavour to live their life on purpose, aligning what they do with who they are, creating and sustaining an authentic life presence, is a constant challenge. They may be clear about their purpose, but living that purpose is constantly challenged by changing life circumstances and priorities. They are on a lifetime learning curve, balancing the tensions between their physical, social and spiritual presence in the world, constantly checking and realigning their 'doing' with their 'being'.

Often these people are trying to 'construct' a purposeful life, trying to plan and manage their presence to create the outcomes that manifest their purpose. But trying to construct a purposeful life can be a fraught process. It assumes that we can plan and implement our future based on what we already know. It assumes that we can predict the future impacts of the decisions we make and that our purpose will somehow be manifested by the outcomes that we choose to pursue. Such a construction process overlooks the possibility that we can be purposeful in anything that we choose to do, and that we can be who we are meant to be wherever we find ourselves. It forgets that being purposeful is essentially about being who we are rather than being what we do.

This does not mean that purposeful life planning is a waste of time. But it does remind us that such planning is only useful when it can accommodate the wonderful complexity of our life journey, and provide a dynamic framework that enables us to create our presence rather than construct our future. Useful life planning provides a flexible and agile framework which maintains our focus on purpose and allows our life to unfold in a purposeful way. It is essentially a set of creative process guidelines. I suggest that the six essential factors for achieving individual congruence could provide a relevant set of planning guidelines.

Consider the possibility of always framing our responses to life's ongoing challenges and opportunities within our individual congruence framework.

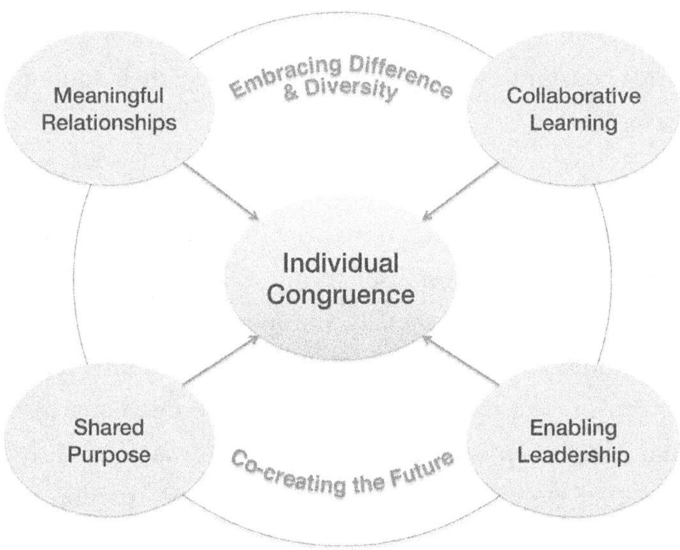

Figure 52: Life planning framework

If we use our congruence framework as our life planning guide we will remain firmly focused on our purpose. Our responses to life's challenges and opportunities will reflect the self leadership ethic of selfless service to others. We will preference responses that make our relationships more meaningful and build community. We will use our capacity for learning (and creativity) to engage our vocational and spiritual knowing and encourage collaborative learning to enable the positive integration of difference and diversity. And we will seek to co-create our purposeful presence with our communities, those people who share our purpose and ambition for the future.

It is no surprise to confirm that individual congruence is essentially the achievement of an authentic (purposeful) presence in our life.

We enable our life to be purposeful by embracing our true purpose as the mindful intention for our life – by holding our unique purpose as the focal frame within which we allow our life to unfold. By continually focusing our attention on our purpose we will begin to see our whole life through a purpose filter, screening out those elements of our life that inhibit or disable our purpose, and accentuating the opportunities to become more purposeful. And as we increase our focus on our purpose we will become more attuned to our spiritual knowing, the knowing that revealed our purpose and can continue to enlighten and support our life on purpose.

Imagine if...

Imagine if our presence within our communities was authentic.

We create an authentic presence within our communities by always acting and behaving in ways that are consistent with our core purpose. An authentic presence enables each of our communities to see who we really are, to understand why we want to belong, and to appreciate our potential to contribute.

By being authentically present we are revealing how we can be of service to our communities, but we are also enabling our communities to understand how they can be of service to us. We are creating the context and the opportunity for a genuine collaboration with our communities and the possibility of co-creating a shared future.

Co-creating a shared future means collaborating with our communities to create outcomes that manifest our shared purpose and create equitable-shared value for that community.

An authentic presence enables us to develop the meaningful relationships and networks, which facilitate our collaborative engagement with our communities. These positive, trust-based relationships also enable us to engage the collective capacity of the community in the pursuit of our own purpose. By being authentically present in our communities we not only create the context and opportunity for a shared future, we also secure the motivation (shared purpose) and the means (collaborative engagement) to co-create that future with our community.

By collaborating with our communities to pursue a shared purpose and create 'equitable-shared value for all', we are helping to build collaborative communities of purpose. These communities care about the wellbeing of their people. They acknowledge the potential of their people to co-create a better future together and they foster a culture of shared leadership and collaborative learning to enable that future to become a reality. These are the congruent communities that can change the way our world works!

Imagine if everyone could be authentically present in their communities, then perhaps we could imagine a world where congruent communities of purpose were the norm – a world where people everywhere collaborated in a generous and selfless way to co-create a shared future in which the 'self evident truth that all men are created equal' was the current reality.

Imagine if being ourselves was more than enough.

Our true purpose expresses the essence of who we are. If we can discover our purpose and make it the inspirational force in our life, then who we are will become evident in what we do. Our inner being will be aligned with our outer world and what we choose to do will be a manifestation of our deepest intention for our life.

If we can embrace the truth of who we are, we will have the confidence to let our life unfold. We will be able to access the inner strength and wisdom that we need to maintain a purposeful presence in our society. Our commitment to live on purpose will create a positive context for integrating the change and difference we encounter in our life. We will create a life that is the expression of our purpose. We will be who we are meant to be.

But the truth of who we are is not just about us. Our true purpose in life will not be selfish. It will embrace our humanity and the importance of community in our life. Our deepest intention for our life will include our concern for the wellbeing of the people we care about and those that care about us. If we have the courage to share our truth with these people, we can build communities of people who share our purpose and ambition for the future. With those communities we can co-create a future that manifests our shared purpose. By embracing the truth of who we are, we not only release our potential to create our life on purpose, to be who we are meant to be. We also help our communities to release their potential to create a shared future.

In so doing we are also helping other people to live their lives on purpose. We are co-creating a future with our community, which is more than enough for us. We are co-creating a purposeful future for others which will extend beyond our own time.

17 | My Wellbeing

Congruent people enjoy the health, wealth and wisdom that enable and sustain their purposeful life.

Figure 53: Individual wellbeing

What lies behind us and what lies before us are tiny matters compared to what lies within us.

Ralph Waldo Emerson

> **Wellbeing** is one of the Congruency Framework's five factors. Our individual wellbeing is dependent on our capacity to access the physical, intellectual, social and spiritual capital that enables us to be healthy, wealthy and wise individuals, and to be **sustainable** members of our communities.

How do I improve my wellbeing?

To begin this discussion we need to talk about what we mean by wellbeing and consider how it is interconnected with the related concepts of wellness and quality of life. There do not seem to be any universally accepted definitions of wellbeing, wellness or quality of life. So I have selected the following evidence-based definitions to set a context for our discussion. They present three interrelated concepts or constructs of wellbeing, wellness and quality of life, which enable us to think about a more holistic, integrated definition of wellbeing.

Martin Seligman offers a positive psychology-based definition of **wellbeing** as a construct comprised of five elements:

- positive emotion (our happiness and life fulfillment)
- engagement (our level of life engagement)
- meaning (belonging to and serving something bigger than ourselves)
- positive relationships (a focus on others)
- accomplishments (our life achievements)

This definition references the psychological and social dimensions of wellbeing, but does not include the physical dimension which is an important element in many alternative definitions.

Expanding our definition to include physical wellbeing brings the typically more holistic concept of wellness into view.

Jane Myers and Thomas Sweeney define **wellness** as:

> *...a way of life oriented toward optimal health and wellbeing, in which body, mind, and spirit are integrated by the individual to live life more fully within the human and natural community.*

Their model of wellness, which is based on this definition, also has five factors or dimensions:

- creative self (thinking, emotions, control, positive humour, work)
- coping self (realistic beliefs, stress management, self worth, leisure)
- social self (friendship, love),
- essential self (spirituality, self care, gender and cultural identity)
- physical self (exercise, nutrition)

But this definition also has a relatively limited view of the physical health dimension and so we look to a quality of life perspective to admit the broader environmental aspects of wellbeing.

The World Health Organisation defines **quality of life** as:

> *...an individual's perception of their position in life in the context of the culture and value systems in which they live and in relation to their goals, expectations, standards and concerns.*

It is a broad-ranging construct affected in a complex way by the person's:

- physical health (physical wellbeing, functional ability and mental health etc.)

- psychological state (psychological wellbeing, morale, life satisfaction and happiness etc.)

- personal beliefs (spirituality, religion, personal values etc.)

- social relationships (family, social networks and support, level of recreational activity, contact with organisations etc.)

- their relationship to salient features of their physical and socio-economic environment (personal autonomy, work satisfaction, standard of housing and living, mobility, access to facilities etc.)

The following schematic (Figure 54) presents a view of these three frameworks and shows some of their more obvious interconnections. The first point to note is that all three frameworks are anchored around the need for a clear sense of self. Our wellness and wellbeing stems from a positive sense of identity and purpose, the essential spiritual self from which we derive our understanding of *'belonging to and serving something bigger than ourselves'*.

And our quality of life is influenced by our deeply personal (spiritual, religious, ethical and other) beliefs. Clarity of purpose (who we are), and a commitment to that purpose, as referenced by dimensions relating to positive participation in our world (e.g. engagement, coping self) is proposed as a primary prerequisite for achieving a strong sense of wellbeing. I would call this being **purposeful** and agree it is the central factor influencing our sense of wellbeing.

All three frameworks also admit the importance of positive relationships to enable and support the social self. The need for relationships which provide friendship and love, relationships that nourish us and enable us to nourish others, are clearly important for our wellness, quality of life and our wellbeing.

Thus I would argue that **meaningful relationships**, which enable and sustain our positive social networks (and our collaborative frameworks), are an important enabler of our wellbeing.

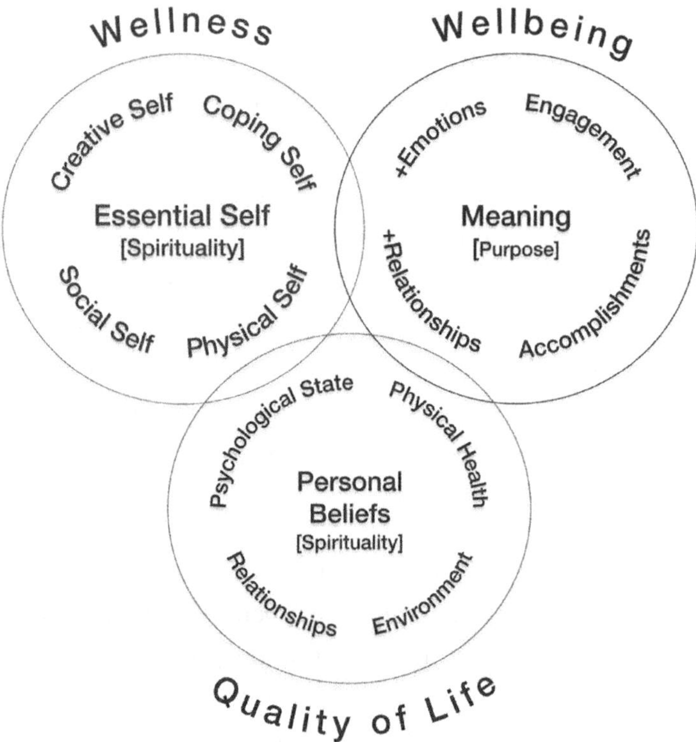

Figure 54: Constructs of wellbeing

The Seligman model suggests that our wellbeing is not only dependent on meaningful engagement (positive participation) but also on the accomplishment of positive outcomes. It is not just about being purposeful; it is also about knowing that we are making a positive contribution. This is how we build our self worth and achieve life satisfaction.

We have previously discussed that we make our positive contribution by acting in a way that is consistent with who we are; by being authentically and purposefully present in our communities; and by collaborating with others to co-create mutual-value outcomes. To maintain an authentic presence in our communities we must be prepared to respond purposefully to changes within – and feedback from – those communities. We must see the changes and challenges in our operating environment generally as learning opportunities; opportunities for personal growth and opportunities to refine and refresh our presence within our communities. This includes change that presents as difference, diversity or dissent within those communities.

As we have observed previously, to successfully negotiate change and to engage and leverage the difference and diversity we encounter requires a positive **learning orientation**. Our capacity to learn, to see new ways to manifest our purpose, is fundamental to maintaining an authentic presence in our communities. It is through collaborative learning that we co-create the mutual-value outcomes that affirm our positive presence in our community and our own sense of self worth which is fundamental to our ongoing wellbeing.

Finally, good physical health is a factor in both the wellness and quality of life models, and all three frameworks also include a focus on mental health (positive psychological or emotional state).

And, although good physical health is not a focus of the Seligman wellbeing model, it is included in other wellbeing models and in many wellbeing definitions. It seems all too obvious that the state of our health generally, both physical and mental, is an important wellbeing factor. Also, as our quality of life definition makes clear, our health is significantly influenced by a range of physical, socio-economic and environmental factors that reflect our state and standard of living.

Therefore, to sustain our wellbeing we also need good physical and mental health supported by a positive physical and socioeconomic environment – what I will call our **situational wellbeing**.

Figure 55: Wellbeing and congruence

The above diagram presents a visual integration of these three definitional perspectives of wellbeing and highlights the following five conditions that are essential for our wellbeing, wellness and quality of life:

- being purposeful (spiritual wellbeing)
- having meaningful (social) relationships (social wellbeing)
- enjoying meaningful (community) engagement (occupational wellbeing)
- having a positive learning orientation (intellectual wellbeing)
- enjoying positive (physical and mental) health (situational wellbeing)

The diagram also shows how this integrated model of wellbeing is aligned with the Congruency Framework and highlights the connections with our essential conditions for congruence:

- Our **sense of purpose**, our sense of who we are and why we are here, is the essential element which underpins and enables both our **spiritual wellbeing** and our congruence. In the same way that purposefulness is central to our individual congruence, our spiritual wellbeing provides the foundation stone for our overall wellbeing.

- The **positive relationships** with others that are essential to our **social wellbeing** are the same meaningful relationships that build the social networks which enable our communities and sustain our individual congruence.

- The positive **learning orientation** that supports our **intellectual and emotional wellbeing** is essentially the capacity for collaborative learning that enables us to positively negotiate change and integrate difference to release our potential and maintain our individual congruence.

- The **positive engagement**, which supports our **occupational wellbeing** and affirms our sense of self worth, is the purposeful contribution to our communities that flows from our enabling self leadership. Leadership that is concerned with selfless service to others and affirms our positive presence within our communities.

- And the **positive physical and mental health** that enables our **situational wellbeing** is essential to our individual sustainability and, therefore, our capacity to present as a congruent person within our communities and to live our life on purpose.

Thus, improving our overall wellbeing is essentially about developing our individual congruence and creating and sustaining the situational wellbeing for that congruence to be present in our life. Therefore to improve our wellbeing we need to:

- become more purposeful, being purposefully present within our communities

- build better (meaningful) relationships that nourish us and enable us to nourish others

- grow our capacity for positive (collaborative) learning, improving our ability to engage with difference and negotiate change positively

- enhance the contributions we make to our communities, to increasingly manifest our purpose through our participation in the life of those communities

- develop and sustain good health, developing our physical and mental capacity and creating the environmental conditions to sustain our physical presence within our communities

The previous four chapters (my purpose, my potential, my people and my participation) have focused on thinking about our key congruence factors (purpose, relationships, learning and contribution).

Because of the alignment between congruence and wellbeing, all of those discussions are also relevant to thinking about the related wellbeing dimensions of purposefulness, positive relationships, positive engagement and positive learning. The questions those discussions pose, and the conversations they encourage are intended to help us think about how we can improve our congruence and therefore our wellbeing. But, those discussions do not traverse the fifth dimension of wellbeing – our situational wellbeing.

So, now we need to focus on thinking about how we develop and sustain the physical and mental health and the environmental factors (including related socioeconomic factors) that enable our situational wellbeing:

- How do we improve our capacity to be physically and mentally present in our communities?
- How do we improve the environmental factors (relationships, shelter and sustenance) to enhance our physical and mental presence?
- Are we as fit and healthy as we could be?
- Do we feel energised and excited about our life?
- Do we operate from a space and place that enables and encourages us to be who we are?
- Can we focus and maintain our attention on what matters most?
- Are we happy and at peace with ourselves and others?

Figure 56: Dimensions of situational wellbeing

Do I have a healthy attitude?

Our overall sense of wellbeing is significantly influenced by our level of individual congruence. If we have a high level of congruence we will know who we are, we will be centred and grounded by a strong sense of individual purpose, which enables our spiritual wellbeing. We will enjoy positive and meaningful relationships that nourish our social wellbeing. We will have a propensity for learning and a positive attitude to change that enhances our intellectual and emotional wellbeing. And our contribution of selfless service to our communities will create the positive engagement that secures our occupational wellbeing.

The more congruent we are as individuals, the more confident we will be about who we are and our potential to make a difference. We will have a positive and purposeful attitude to our life which is anchored and energised by a deep sense of spiritual wellbeing. We will see our life as an exciting opportunity to manifest our true purpose, to be present within our communities in a way that enables the co-creation of a better future for all. We will be highly motivated to live our life on purpose, to be the best that we can be, and to be of service to others. We will be committed to living our life on purpose.

This positive attitude to life will influence the way we think about our health. We will be strongly motivated to make sure that our health enables our purpose – that we have the best possible physical and mental capacity to allow us to make a positive contribution to our communities. And we will also be motivated to manage our environment in a way that is consistent with our life purpose and enhances our physical and mental capacity.

Leaving aside the impact of genetics, the onset of a serious disease and disabling accidents, there are two critical factors that affect our ongoing physical health – our diet and our exercise regime. If we are purposeful in the way we manage our diet then we will ensure that the food and drink we consume is only what we need to enhance and sustain our physical health and wellbeing. We will avoid eating or drinking to excess and consuming food, drink and any other substances that are harmful to either our physical or mental health. We will be ever mindful that maintaining a quality diet is important to enable and sustain our physical and mental capacity to pursue our life purpose.

Being purposeful about the way we exercise our body requires that we maintain a fitness regime that is appropriate to our physical and mental condition – a regime that is focused on ensuring that our physical and mental capacity can sustain our life purpose. In addition to strengthening our physical capabilities and preventing the onset of a range of diseases, we know that physical exercise also enables our mental health. For example, physical exercise enables us to cope better with stress and anxiety; reduces the risk of depression; improves our memory and our mental dexterity; and being physically fit improves our sense of self worth. We also know that physical exercise that engages our mind as well as our body (e.g. yoga, tai chi) refreshes and energises both our physical and mental health, and also potentially our spiritual wellbeing.

Developing and sustaining our mental health also requires an exercise or fitness regime. Our brain needs a regular workout to sustain our capacity to learn, to be creative and to find innovative ways to negotiate change and respond to life's challenges. We need to train our mind to be relaxed, to be fully aware of our life situation and to enable our connection with our inner self. Our mental health will be enhanced by practising some form of meditation, participating in activities that engage all of our senses, seeking out challenging opportunities to learn new things, and finding ways to make interesting new social connections. We need a mental exercise regime that helps us to remain grounded and centred by our life purpose, enables us to build and sustain productive social relationships and sharpens our capacity to learn.

Having a healthy attitude implies that we have a constant focus on ensuring that our physical and mental presence enables rather than disables our life purpose. We will be ever mindful of our diet and our level of physical fitness, always conscious that what we consume and how we exercise has a significant influence on both our physical and mental health.

Our attitude and approach to our physical and mental health will be authentic, entirely consistent with our core principles and values and always in alignment with our intention to live our life on purpose. Thus a healthy attitude is essentially a purposeful attitude.

Our physical and mental wellbeing is also influenced by environmental factors. Our state and standard of living is generally dependent on:

- the quality of our social frameworks, the relationships and social networks that nourish and support us
- the nature and quality of our shelter, the space and place we occupy
- our access to sustenance, the means to access the food, medicine and the services we need to sustain our life
- the level of personal freedom we enjoy

We have already discussed at some length the importance of positive relationships and supportive social networks as a contributing factor to our individual congruence and therefore to our overall wellbeing.

And the discussion that flows from our next question 'do I have all that I need?' will include a focus on sustenance. So let's discuss briefly what we mean by having a purposeful focus on the space and place in which we live.

To begin, let's remind ourselves that in theory we can be congruent anywhere. We do not need to be in a particular place or space to be ourselves, to be purposeful and authentically present in the world. Nevertheless, the location and nature of our space can obviously have an impact on our overall wellbeing.

Our location will clearly influence the nature of the communities we can interact with and, therefore, it can influence our opportunities for participation and learning. Our location may also determine the quality of the food, medicine and other services that are available to us. And the nature of the physical space we occupy can affect our attitude, how we feel about ourselves and our relationships with others. It can also affect our motivation to seek out opportunities for social interaction and learning.

I accept that many people will not have the ability to relocate or substantially change the nature of the physical spaces they inhabit. And some people, who have the means to change their living and/or working circumstances, may choose not to because of other physical, emotional or social constraints. But irrespective of where we live, or the nature and quality of the spaces we occupy, it is how we think and feel about our place and space that will finally determine its impact on our wellbeing.

Integrating our place and space in a purposeful way requires that we have a positive attitude to discovering and realising its potential to assist our purpose. If we have a purposeful focus then we will be able to see our current location and space as an integral part of our life journey.

We will know how to 'be' in our place and how to integrate our spaces in a way that enables our life on purpose. We will find ways to engage with our location, and shape and realign our public and private spaces, so that we maximise the opportunity to enhance our overall wellbeing.

For example, we can perform 'space cleaning' or decluttering as some would call it. This is where we refine the physical contents of our space by removing those things that are either inconsistent with, or distract us from, our purpose.

We can then reshape our clean space by adding new things or by emphasising those things that assist our purpose focus and help us to become congruent individuals.

We can also 'clean' our social spaces in a similar way by refining our social connections, letting go of relationships and connections and divesting responsibilities that are not assisting our purpose. We can turn down the level of social noise by filtering our contacts and communications, focusing our media attention and reducing unnecessary electronic communications (notifications, twitters, emails etc.) to create a 'quieter' place for our life on purpose. And we can reshape our social space by developing new relationships and connections, taking on new responsibilities and amplifying the communication channels that support and enable our purpose.

We may not be able to easily change the physical attributes of our public spaces, but we can affect the social and physical ambience of those spaces by the way we occupy them. By choosing to be authentically present in those spaces we can influence how the space operates and feels for ourselves and others. By simply choosing to be ourselves we will inhabit the space in a way that is purposeful. We will make the space positive and enabling for ourselves and for others who interact with us. The critical factor in the way we respond to our space and place is our attitude.

For individuals who are focused on living their life on purpose, their attitude to life will be purposeful in every respect. They will be excited about who they are and their potential to make a meaningful contribution to their community. They will understand that their ability to be fully present in their communities, to make their unique contribution, is enabled by being well.

Therefore their attitude to the enhancement of their overall wellbeing will be positive and purposeful, and they will act to ensure that their wellbeing can support their life journey in ways that are consistent with who they are. A healthy attitude to our wellbeing comes from being purposeful.

Do I have the wealth I need to be well?

What doth it profit a man if he gains the whole world and suffers the loss of his own soul?

Matthew 16:26

This is a discussion about sustenance. If we are to be congruent individuals, we need adequate resources, or the means to access those resources, to sustain our life as physical, social, intellectual and spiritual beings. We need the resources to discover and understand our purpose, nourish our relationships, enable our learning and our community engagement, and enjoy good physical and mental health. We need the means to develop and sustain our overall wellbeing.

Our capacity as individuals to own or access the resources we need to sustain our physical, social, intellectual and spiritual life depends on how wealthy we are. It depends on how much 'capital' we have to invest in developing and sustaining our wellbeing. This wealth cannot be simply measured in terms of our 'material capital' or the amount of money and/or physical possessions that we control. The wealth we need to be well includes non-monetary and other forms of capital that are necessary to also sustain our social, intellectual and spiritual wellbeing.

Our overall wellbeing is dependent on our collective wealth, on having the spiritual, social and material capital we need 'to be well' – the meaning of the Olde English term 'welthy' from which the word wealth is derived.

Our **spiritual capital** is the wealth we accrue by knowing who we are, why we exist, and our true purpose in life. It is the value we derive from knowing our place in the Universe, understanding the deeply held beliefs that guide our life journey, and acknowledging our responsibility to live our life on purpose. Within the context of our discussion about congruence, our spiritual capital is the internal resource that powers our life purpose.

Our **social capital** is the wealth that accrues from our ability to interact positively with other people, to create the meaningful relationships that build and sustain our social networks and communities of interest. It includes our ability to engage positively with difference and diversity, our capacity to collaborate for mutual benefit (including our ability to participate in collective learning and co-creative endeavours), and to successfully navigate change.

For the purposes of this discussion it is helpful to consider the constructs' of human capital (or intellectual capital) and cultural capital as subsets of our social capital:

- **Human capital**, which is typically defined as the value attached to our level of intellectual capacity, knowledge and experience (our intellectual capital), is in my view an integral part of our capacity for adaptive learning and, therefore, can be considered as part of our social capital.

- And the notion of **cultural capital**, which seems to include the knowledge and experience that relates to our ethnicity, language and gender, and the values and practices of our communities, can also be considered as part of our social capital. It is an aspect of our ability to socialise and to engage productively with others and our communities.

Our **material capital** is the wealth that represents the amount of economic (or financial) and other physical (non-human) resources that we own or control. Our physical resources include what some writers term our **natural and constructed capital**, our ability to access the worlds natural resources and create value by utilising those resources to construct assets and to provide services. In this context natural resources can include both the materials and substances that occur in nature and the 'live capital' which is the non-human species of life that inhabit the earth.

The means to improve our overall wellbeing, the capital we need be welthy, to enhance our quality of life and to be well, is clearly a mix of the spiritual, social and material capital that comprise our **'true wealth'**.

As we have already observed, our pathway to individual wellbeing is essentially the same as our pathway to individual congruence. Our journey begins with the clarification of our purpose on which all the other elements of our congruence (and the dimensions of our wellbeing) are dependent. And our clarity of purpose is dependent on our level of spiritual capital, the degree to which we understand and acknowledge our place in the universe and are committed to living a purposeful life. Therefore, our level of spiritual capital, which 'powers our life purpose', is the most important resource to enable our wellbeing.

And so the question 'do I have all I need?' must first address the questions 'do I know who I am?', a question we have already addressed in our previous discussions about 'our purpose' and 'our potential'.

If we do not understand who we are, and/or we are not living a purposeful life, our presence will lack the authenticity that enables meaningful relationships. Our relationships will lack the co-creative intimacy and collaborative endeavour that flows from a truly shared purpose. The quality of our social capital will be low. We may be successful in expanding the reach and membership of our social networks. But if these networks are not supported by relationships built on a shared purpose and the generation of mutual benefit, they will probably be shallow and self serving. They will not engender the mutual trust and goodwill that enables our congruence and wellbeing

Increasing our social capital, our ability to interact positively with other people, is about building the productive (meaningful) relationships that enable our networks and communities to work together for a shared purpose. Building these relationships is dependent on our ability to engage our communities in successful conversations, to facilitate a genuine dialogue about a shared purpose that generates opportunities for the co-creation of mutual value.

We also need a capacity for learning which embraces difference and diversity and encourages collaboration and the co-creation of win-win outcomes. To reflect on how we can develop our capacity for learning and our ability to develop meaningful relationships, you should refer to our earlier discussions about 'our potential' and 'our people', in particular our response to the questions 'How do I release my potential?' and 'Are my relationships meaningful?'

To grow our spiritual capital we must activate our spiritual intelligence through which we access the spiritual knowing that will reveal and enable our life purpose.

We do this by reflective enquiry, conversational and meditative practices that unlock our vocational and spiritual knowing, and access the wisdom of our personal, local and universal communities. Our earlier discussions on the questions of 'What is my unique purpose?' and 'How do I know what I know?', provide a framework for thinking about engaging our spiritual intelligence to clarify our life purpose.

To create a context for our discussion about the adequacy of our material capital, we need to consider the interconnections between our spiritual, social and material capital. In particular, we need to understand the relative importance of these different capital elements as sources of sustenance for our overall wellbeing.

One observation is that our level of spiritual capital, the most important source of sustenance for our wellbeing (and congruence), is not particularly dependent of our level of social or material capital. It seems entirely plausible that provided we have enough material and social capital to be alive, reasonably healthy, and relatively independent, we could know who we are and be committed to a life of purpose.

We do not need a substantial amount of material possessions or the social support of multiple communities to be clear about the meaning of our life. We could be part of a tiny impoverished community, or lead some form of monastic life, or be a recluse, and still be living a purposeful life. However, in the absence of adequate material and social capital our quality of life would become very dependent on our level of spiritual capital. And to be happy in this state, our presence as a spiritual being would need to transcend our social and material presence.

Figure 57: Dimensions of 'true wealth'

Another observation is that our level of social capital has a critical dependency on our level of spiritual capital and some dependency on our level of our material capital.

As we have already observed, our commitment to live a purposeful life is fundamental to developing the relationships that will enable and sustain our wellbeing and congruence. To develop an adequate level of social capital is, therefore, dependent on having a reasonable level of spiritual capital.

We could argue that provided we have enough material capital to be alive and well, we can build the meaningful relationships and supportive networks, the social capital we need to enable our purposeful presence within our communities.

However I acknowledge that we may also need to invest in relevant geographical, mobility or communication resources to enable the conversations and learning opportunities that grow our social networks and develop our capacity to build community.

We also need to know that our capacity to be well, to learn and to sustain our social networks is reasonably secure for the duration of our lifetime. And so, for us to have sufficient social capital, arguably the second most important sustenance for our wellbeing (and congruence), we need an adequate amount of material capital to enable and sustain our ongoing physical and mental capacity to learn and to contribute to our communities.

Thus, I think we can argue that:

- Our spiritual capital is the primary source of sustenance for our wellbeing, and that we can grow our spiritual capital without requiring a substantial investment of our social or material capital.

- Our social capital is the second most important source of sustenance for our wellbeing, and growing this capital has a critical dependency on our level of spiritual capital and has some degree of dependence on our investment of material capital.

- Our material capital is the least important source of sustenance for our wellbeing, subject to:
    - a primary requirement to support our physical existence, to have the means to access adequate food, shelter and necessary health services, to be alive and well and able to function as an effective participant within our communities for the duration of our lifetime

- o   a secondary requirement to provide the necessary infrastructure; to enable us to develop and sustain our capacities for learning and building community

It is important to remember that this prioritisation of our wealth focus assumes that we intend to live our life on purpose (as we have defined it) and to enjoy the congruence and wellbeing that will enable us to manifest that purpose within our communities. If that is our intention, then our answer to the opening question 'Do I have the wealth I need to be well?' will be informed by our reflection on the questions that follow. If we do not intend to pursue a life on purpose, then I think these questions still have the potential to engage us in interesting and reflective conversations, with ourselves and perhaps others, about our life perspectives and priorities.

- Do I have the spiritual capital I need to be well?
    - o   Do I know my purpose in life and do I accept the responsibility to live my life on purpose?
    - o   Do I make time for purposeful reflection, to understand the truth of who I am, to appreciate my unique potential and to observe my real presence? Is my life purposeful? Is who I am consistent with what I do? Is my life presence authentic? Is my life contribution the best it can be?
- Do I have sufficient social capital to be well?
    - o   Do I have a purposeful presence within my communities? Is that presence based on a shared purpose and concerned with selfless service to others?
    - o   Are my relationships meaningful? Are they based on commonality of purpose and energised by the co-creation of mutual value outcomes?

- o Do I make time for learning? Do I embrace difference and diversity as learning opportunities.

  - o Do I encourage and value open feedback from others? Can I work collaboratively with others for mutual benefit?

- Do I have enough material capital to be well?

  - o Do I have access to the basic food and shelter that I need to be a fully functioning participant within my communities? Can I access the medical care that I need?

  - o Do I have access to the resources I need to enable my ongoing learning and development (my continuing education) and to facilitate my contribution to my communities?

  - o Do I have enough material capital to feel reasonably secure about my lifetime access to the food, shelter, medicine and education that I need to be a fully functioning member of my communities?

Throughout this discussion I have been conscious of the many people and communities in the world who live below the poverty line. These are the millions amongst us who do not have adequate shelter, and struggle continuously for the means to sustain their physical and mental health. For these people, their standard of living is mostly decided by the organisations and governments who control the development and distribution of the world's resources. Their hope for a brighter future is relying on those of us that already have enough to share some of what we have. Their hope must be that we can build a congruent world where they can expect to be included in a real community. A community that cares about who they are, and the difference their purposeful presence can make in our world.

Their hope is that you and I will become more congruent people and influence the development of more congruent communities.

Am I a sustainable person?

Sustainability is [achieving] the optimal balance of [our] natural, economic, and social systems over time.

The Florida Center for Community Design and Research

Our sustainability as individuals cannot be defined simply in terms of our ability to access the resources that enable us to be physically and mentally healthy enough to achieve longevity. I suggest that sustainability is not so much concerned with the unpredictable length of our lifetime as it is with the quality of that lifetime – the degree to which our needs as physical, social, intellectual and spiritual beings are being met. Individual sustainability is dependent on achieving an optimal balance of our physical, social, intellectual and spiritual presence on the planet during our lifetime. In other words, it is concerned with the quality of our overall wellbeing over time.

Therefore to answer the title question 'Am I a sustainable person?' we need to consider and assess all of the dimensions of our wellbeing – our spiritual, social, intellectual, occupational and situational wellbeing.

But we know from our previous discussion that our overall sense of wellbeing is directly linked with our level of congruence and that developing our congruence will improve our wellbeing. The more congruent we are, the greater our sense of wellbeing and the more sustainable we become.

Therefore, we can assess our level of individual sustainability by assessing our level of individual congruence. We can change our title question to 'Am I a congruent person?'

The Congruence Framework provides a context for thinking about how we can become a more congruent person. If we embrace that thinking we are choosing to frame a way of living that will enable us to be a congruent individual – a person who lives their life on purpose. We can use the framework to help us create a more congruent life by embracing its five congruence factors as attitudes and making them integral to the way we live our life.

- The **purpose** attitude – always purposeful in all that we do; discovering and living our unique life purpose; and embracing a self-leadership ethic of selfless service to others.

- The **people** attitude – continually building and sustaining the meaningful relationships that enable community; co-creating communities of purpose that care about the wellbeing of their people.

- The **potential** attitude – appreciating our capacity for knowing what is true, having a positive learning orientation, embracing difference and diversity and always being open to new ideas.

- The **participation** attitude – having an authentic presence within our communities, making a difference by always being who we are, and co-creating purposeful outcomes that represent equitable-shared value for our communities.

- The **wellbeing** attitude – living our life from the inside out; creating the spiritual, social and material capital we need to enable and sustain the other four attitudes.

By using these five attitudes to frame our life we will focus our attention on being who we are meant to be, and on doing the things that enable us to be that person. We will be focused on becoming a welthy congruent person.

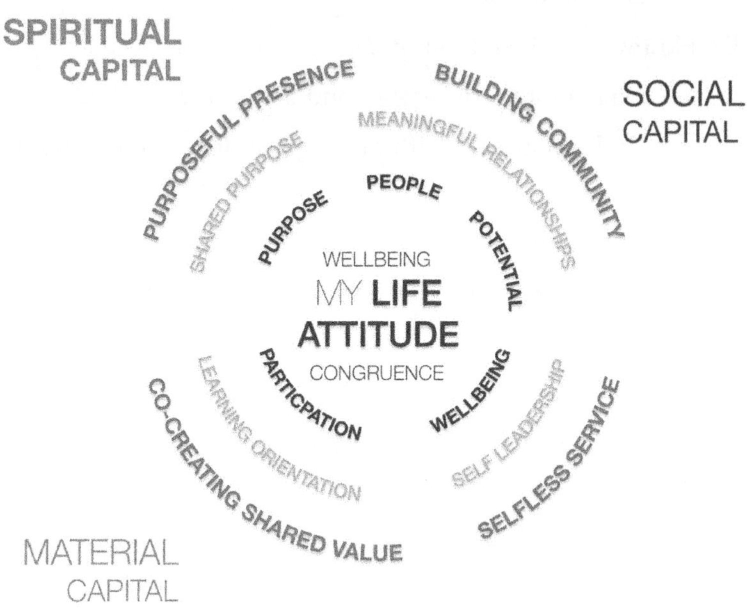

Figure 58: A congruent life attitude

We can address the question 'Am I a congruent person?' by examining our life for the presence of each of the five congruence attitudes. If we reflect honestly on our recent life history and ponder the following five essential questions, we will know how congruent we are. We will also know where we need to make the changes that will release our true potential to be joyful, to lead a happy, peaceful and fulfilling life.

- Am I joyful?
    - Do I know and live my life purpose?
    - Is my life presence authentic?
- Do I love my people?
    - Are my relationships meaningful?
    - Do I build community?
- Do I know what I could know?
    - Do I embrace difference and diversity?
    - Do I collaborate with my communities to co-create my future?
- Do I make a difference?
    - Is my life about selfless service to others?
    - Is my life presence my life contribution?
- Do I have all that I need to be myself?
    - Do I create the spiritual and social capital I need?
    - Do I have a healthy attitude to my life?

These are all questions that we have explored in our discussions about the application of the Congruence Framework to our individual lives. They are not the only questions we could ask, but these questions touch the six keystones of congruence. And if we respond to them honestly they will focus our attention on the areas of our life where there is an opportunity to become more congruent.

We can also apply the learning that flows from this exploration of our congruence in a practical way by creating a 'purpose guide' – a simple visual reminder of the things we need to focus on to keep our life on purpose.

Our purpose guide consists of our core purpose statement encircled by a set of concise action statements (guiding principles) that are focused on what needs to change in our life.

Figure 59: Purpose guide schematic

We can use this visual mapping of our congruence journey to focus our thinking and reflection and guide us towards our life on purpose. It can be our 'life plan', a focusing agenda for our daily reflection, and a framework for thinking about and prioritising our life. This simple-purpose guide can also map the alignment between our personal and community agendas. It provides an elegant way of framing the strategic blueprints of our communities and organisations.

Community and organisation purpose guides enable us to see at a glance how we are aligned with their purpose, and how we can be engaged with the activity focus that expects to manifest that purpose.

Imagine if...

Imagine if I had all that I needed to be myself.

Imagine if I was healthy, wealthy and wise enough to be who I am.

First, I would need to be wise enough to know who I am, to know and appreciate my real self.

I would need to know my life purpose and to understand how to make that purpose meaningful for myself and the other people in my life.

Then I would need to be wealthy enough to be who I am. I would need the internal strength to be authentically present in my life, and the support of a caring community of family, friends and colleagues to nurture my life journey.

And I would need to be healthy enough to be able to do the things that fulfil the expectations of my purpose. I would need to have the physical and mental capacity to make a difference in my lifetime for the people I care about.

And so...

If I spend time in reflective meditation I can access the wisdom I need to know who I am. If I know who I am, I will understand my purpose in life, and I will 'know' that my opportunity to be joyful is to live my life on purpose.

If I decide to live my life on purpose, then my presence within my communities will be an expression of my purpose.

The authenticity of that presence will enable me to build the meaningful relationships with 'my people' that will nurture and support my life journey. I will be enabled to co-create my future in the present with the people I care about and who care about me.

If I decide to live my life on purpose I will have a positive life attitude, which will enable and encourage me to be physically and mentally healthy. I will want to be as healthy as I can be, so that I can manifest my purpose and be fully present in my communities.

And the material wealth, the physical possessions and means of sustenance I need to be alive and to participate in my communities, will be no more than I need to live my life on purpose. If I have more than I need then I can share with others, and if I do not have enough I can expect my community to help.

Once I make the decision to live purposefully, then as Johan van Goethe reminds us:

> *... the moment one definitely commits oneself, then Providence moves too. All sorts of things occur to help one that would never otherwise have occurred. A whole stream of events issues from the decision, raising in one's favour all manner of unforeseen incidents and meetings and material assistance, which no man could have dreamed would have come his way. Whatever you can do, or dream you can do, begin it. Boldness has genius, power, and magic in it. Begin it now.*

Imagine I am a congruent person.

If I am a congruent person I will know who I am, I will know and embrace my true purpose in life.

I will be confident and comfortable being who I am and not who I am supposed to be. I will be living my life from the inside out. I will be the joy, peace and happiness that I feel. And I will be the unconditional love that connects me in a shared purpose with 'my people'.

If I am a congruent person I will enjoy meaningful relationships with my people. I will live within a community of friends who value my diversity and appreciate the difference I can make. I would expect to share my life purpose within a welcoming and caring community where relationships are built on mutual trust and respect and a genuine concern for the wellbeing of all.

If I am a congruent person, I will be the difference that I wanted to make in the world. My presence in the world would be an unfolding manifestation of my life purpose, a presence enabled by, and co-created with, the people I care about. An authentic presence, which speaks to the truth of who I am, and reflects a life of selfless service to others.

If I am a congruent person I will smile at all the people I meet. My life would be the success that Ralph Waldo Emerson imagined when he said:

> To laugh often and love much; to win the respect of intelligent persons and the affection of children, to earn the approbation of honest critics; to appreciate beauty; to give of one's self, to leave the world a bit better, whether by a healthy child, a garden patch or a redeemed social condition; to have played and laughed with enthusiasm and sung with exultation; to know even one life has breathed easier because you have lived – that is to have succeeded.

Acknowledgements

I would like to acknowledge Gill Ereaut and Rebecca Whiting[64], Martin Seligman[65], Jane Myers and Thomas Sweeney[66], and Sam Spurlin[67] for their thoughts on wellbeing and wellness; Dottie Billington[68] for her writing about life attitude; and Danah Zohar and Ian Marshall[69] (again) for their thinking about spiritual capital.

Concepts and terminology

Ambition – *Refer to* **Organisational ambition** *and* **Individual ambition**.

Assets include all of the monetary, intellectual and infrastructural assets which are owned, controlled or managed by the organisational community and available for deployment in pursuit of their shared purpose.

Authentic conversations occur when the participants are all able to be who they really are and say what they really think about a topic they care about.

Authentic individuals are people who are true to their purpose. They create a presence in their life that is a genuine reflection of their core purpose and in which their actions (their doing) are consistent with who they are (their being).

Authentic leaders are positive people who know who they are (self aware). They are true to themselves (self regulated), motivated by deep personal convictions (independent), are without bias or prejudice (hold balanced opinions) and behave in a manner consistent with their personal values and beliefs (authentic action).

Brand: An organisation's brand is intended to express the intrinsic value of the organisation (who the organisation is and what it stands for) to all its stakeholder communities, not just to its customer community. It is a construct designed to facilitate an emotional and functional connection with the organisation's primary value proposition. 'Branding' an organisation is, therefore, concerned with increasing its presence within the hearts and minds of its stakeholder communities.

Collaboration can be broadly defined as the effective interaction of two or more diverse and independent (autonomous) participants, who share a common interest or purpose, using an agreed set of generated or negotiated processes (rules or guidelines) to pursue a shared-value outcome. By working together, collaborators can share their collective capability (resources, knowledge, intelligence and experience) to co-create a 'more valuable' outcome.

Collaborative learning is a relationship among learners that requires positive interdependence, individual accountability, and interaction to complete a common task. It is a process of constructing knowledge and meaning through interaction with others.

Collaborative learning provides a framework to engage the collective organisational community in the co-creation of its future. It enables organisations to embrace difference and diversity as non-threatening learning opportunities, and to engage the collective intelligence and creativity of stakeholder communities to navigate change. Collaborative learning promotes organisational congruence by enabling the development of positive and productive (meaningful) relationships within and across stakeholder communities.

Collaborative space is a social context which enables and encourages positive interactions between individuals and groups. This context promotes learning outcomes by providing the opportunity for effective knowledge sharing and dialogue about the mutual interests or concerns of participants.

Collective leadership is seen as a way for individuals, leaders and organisations to interact cohesively in order to achieve common goals. It attempts to embrace a multi-faceted definition of leadership which accepts a mix of different models or styles as applicable to different organisations and situations.

A **Community** is a social entity bound together by a common interest and perceived as distinct in some respect from other communities and the larger society within which it exists. The community's common interest is the primary source of its identity and coherence. This interest sustains the interpersonal relationships (social ties) that enable the joint actions of the community and provides a focus for engaging the community's diversity.

Community of purpose is a social entity bound together by a shared purpose, which is the primary source of its identity and coherence. This shared purpose sustains the interpersonal relationships (social ties) that enable the joint actions of the community and provides a focus for engaging the community's diversity.

Community wellbeing is dependent on the collective 'health, wealth and happiness' of the community. It reflects the degree to which the social (health, welfare, education etc.), cultural (identity, diversity, values etc.), economic (prosperity, employment, food, shelter etc.), and environmental (physical and natural environment) needs of the community are being met.

Complexity leadership encompasses three intertwined leadership roles – **adaptive leadership**, **enabling leadership**, and **administrative leadership**. This blended leadership model is considered appropriate to focus and facilitate the dynamic relationship between the controlling (administrative), adaptive, and enabling functions of an organisation.

The **Congruence Framework** is an organising framework with five factors, each of which provides an influencing focus for organisations (communities or individuals) designing and implementing operating models that enable and sustain organisational congruence.

- The **purpose factor** has a leadership focus and is concerned with aligning and engaging the organisation's stakeholder communities with a shared purpose, and fostering shared enabling leadership that encourages an organisational ethic of selfless service to others.

- The **people factor** has a community focus and is concerned with building the meaningful relationships that increase community (and individual) engagement and enable genuine collaboration.

- The **potential factor** has a learning focus and is concerned with encouraging collaborative learning to embrace difference and diversity and promote positive response to change.

- The **participation factor** has a contribution focus and is concerned with promoting the co-creation of equitable-shared value (mutually-beneficial) outcomes for stakeholders.

- The **wellbeing factor** has a sustainability focus and is concerned with providing access to the frameworks, systems, and resources that enable growth and sustain the collective wellbeing of the organisational community.

Congruent individuals are people who live their lives on purpose. They seek to co-create an authentic presence with and within their communities that integrates and aligns who they are with what they do. They have a learning orientation that welcomes difference and diversity, and continually seeks opportunities for personal development and renewal. And they develop and sustain their communities of interest by building meaningful relationships that are based on selfless service and the generation of mutual value.

Congruent organisations (or communities) are accordant groups of individuals who embrace a shared purpose. They enjoy enabling leadership which promotes selfless service to others; encourage the development of meaningful relationships that create community; and foster collaborative learning to embrace their difference and diversity. They seek to co-create a future which manifests their shared purpose and creates equitable-shared value for all their stakeholders.

Creative capacity is our ability to imagine (to see the possibilities for different futures), to create (to explore the potential of new solutions), and to innovate (to risk new ways of being present).

Culture – *Refer to* **Organisational culture**.

Dialogue is *'a conversation with a centre not sides. It is a way of taking the energy of our differences and channeling it towards something that has not been created before...it is a conversation in which people think together in relationship.'* (William Isaacs)

Emergent leadership is a shared behaviour that emerges as required to guide and influence the complex interactions of an organisational community adapting (self-organising) in response to its changing circumstances. These emergent leadership behaviours are viewed as an integral part of an operating culture that exists at all levels and localities within the organisation.

Enabling leadership is about contribution through service. It fosters organisational cohesion around a shared purpose; creates a positive and ethical organisational climate and builds meaningful relationships within its stakeholder communities. Enabling leadership encourages participation and collaboration to discover, co-create and deliver relevant and valuable outcomes for all stakeholders; and always acknowledges the potential of the organisation's people.

Frameworks – *Refer to* **Framework competencies, Organisational frameworks** *and* **Organising frameworks.**

Framework competencies refer to the governance, management and operating systems that enable an organisation's people to create, manage and deploy its resources (monetary, intellectual and infrastructural assets) to co-create shared-equitable value for the organisational community.

Individual ambition is essentially a glimpse of our individual purpose manifested, that is, a future view of our presence in the world as an expression of our life on purpose.

Individual purpose expresses the truth of who we are, our deepest understanding of why we exist, and our most treasured intentions for our life.

Individual wellbeing reflects the degree to which the physical (including economic and environmental) social (including cultural), intellectual and spiritual needs of an individual are being met during their lifetime. It is dependent on the individual having a positive attitude to life and access to the material, social and spiritual capital that is necessary to develop and sustain their physical, mental and spiritual health.

Intelligence is defined simply as our ability to learn and understand, which we use to access and make sense of what we know, and to create meaning relevant for our context. There are four basic kinds of intelligence:

- **Physical intelligence**: the innate or instinctive capacity of our physical human form to learn and adapt to complex changes in its operating environment.

- **Rational intelligence**: our ability to make meaning through reasoning which is often equated with our intellectual capacity (IQ).

- **Perceptual intelligence**: our ability to make meaning by using our senses; to make sense of our environment through what we see, hear, smell, taste and feel (PQ).

- **Spiritual intelligence**: our ability to find meaning and purpose in our lives, the ability to 'see' and understand our interconnectedness with the Universe (SQ).

Joyful is a wonderful entanglement of peacefulness, happiness and love. Being joyful is about revealing who we really are – the truth of us. It is about being our authentic self. Being joyful is the expression of a deep inner sense of wellbeing that flows through us when we are truly present, when we are living our life on purpose.

Knowing can be loosely defined as possessing knowledge, information, or understanding; the state of being aware or informed. Our capacity for knowing reflects our ability to integrate all of our knowledge and intelligence to create meaning relevant to the achievement of our life purpose. There are two primary dimensions of knowing:

- **Vocational knowing**: encompasses the knowledge and intelligence we need to live within and contribute to our community and do our life's work.

- **Spiritual knowing**: the knowing we need for being truly present and to live a purposeful life. This is the knowing that reveals our true purpose; the knowing that unfolds and guides our life journey; the knowing that releases the real potential we have to live our life on purpose.

Knowledge *'is a fluid mix of framed experience, contextual information, values and expert insight that provides a framework for evaluating and incorporating new experiences and information.'* (Davenport and Prusak). *Refer also to* **Organisational knowledge** *and* **Personal knowledge**.

Learning centre is a concept, construct, or force within the organisation which continually energises its community learning program. It may be realised differently in each organisation, but the expected outcome is energised leadership of the organisational learning agenda. The role of the learning centre is to engage the collective knowledge and innovation potential of the organisational community in the design and implementation of proactive and positive responses to derivative and disruptive change opportunities. *Refer also to* **Personal learning centre**.

Learning organisation: A community of individuals and groups that can operate as an integrated 'whole' (systems thinking) to successfully adapt to change and sustain the pursuit of its shared purpose for the future ('shared vision'). A learning organisation has a capacity for collective learning (derived from 'personal mastery') that is enabled by genuine dialogue ('team learning') and an ability to embrace new ways of thinking ('mental models'). It has leadership that embraces its shared purpose, encourages a collective view of its capacity for organisational learning, and fosters the dialogue and thinking which enables that learning.

Life on purpose means that our presence within our communities is a true manifestation of our individual purpose; it is the outcome of co-creating an authentic presence with and within our communities that integrates and aligns who we are with what we do. By choosing to live our life on purpose we are choosing to reveal the truth of who we are, to align our inner 'being' with our outward presence in the world; we are choosing to be congruent.

Material capital is wealth that represents the amount of economic (or financial) and other physical (non-human) resources that we own or control. Our physical resources include what some writers term our natural and constructed capital, our ability to access the worlds natural resources and create value by utilising those resources to construct 'assets' and to provide services. In this context natural resources can include both the 'materials and substances that occur in nature' and the 'live capital' which is the non-human species of life that inhabit the earth.

Meaningful relationships continually acknowledge the value of their participants. They find their meaning in a strong mutual interest or shared purpose. These relationships are nurtured within an atmosphere of mutual trust and goodwill. They welcome conversations that embrace difference and diversity, promote understanding, and encourage learning and collaborative engagement to co-create outcomes that generate equitable value for all participants.

Organisations are a community of their stakeholders, actively engaged in the coordinated pursuit of a common goal and perceived as distinct in some respect from other organisations and the society within which it operates.

Organisation culture is a complex set of explicit and implicit practices and behaviours (or social practices) that affect the way the organisation operates and interacts with its stakeholder communities. These behaviours are the manifestation of shared understandings, norms, beliefs and symbols which have developed over time and are considered by the organisation to be valid or 'correct'. The beliefs derive from a set of (usually tacitly held) core values or assumptions.

Organisational ambition articulates a qualitative future state of the organisation that is a manifestation of its core purpose. It reveals the future potential of a journey in pursuit of the organisation's shared purpose.

Organisational frameworks refer to the organisation's governance, management and operating systems including the associated policies and practices.

Organisational knowledge is the collective knowledge of an organisation's stakeholder communities. It includes organisational intelligence (environmental, market, customer, business, process and product or service etc.) and intellectual capital (cumulative individual and group knowledge and experience). It is a collective asset that includes both the codified and tacit knowledge (know-how) and experience of the individuals and groups that comprise the organisational community.

Organisational operating models are usually defined by a schematic, which illustrates the structural relationships between various business or operating units and internal and external stakeholder groups. It also incorporates and a set of guidelines that detail how the model is intended to work.

Organisational purpose is the reason the organisation exists. It articulates the organisation's primary value proposition (it's 'why'), its equitable contribution to its collective stakeholder community. Organisational purpose is beyond profit and expresses a raison d'être that inspires all of the organisational community to engage in manifesting its true presence. It sustains the organisation by shaping its strategic agenda and guiding its purposeful response to change.

Organisational responsibility could be defined as four interrelated and interdependent accountabilities, which together provide a principle-based conceptual framework that can be applied by any organisation (or community) to reflect its particular circumstances:

- **Building sustainable communities**: Improving the social, cultural and economic viability of those communities and the sustainability of the physical and natural environments within which they operate.

- **Making societal contributions**: Pursuing and manifesting a shared purpose that is concerned with creating value for the society within which it operates.

- **Co-creating equitable-shared value**: Ensuring that the organisation's stakeholders have an equitable share in the value they co-create with the organisation.

- **Enabling good governance**: Establishing and maintaining organisational governance frameworks that ensure that its leadership, management and decision-making processes are authentic, ethical, open and transparent, and enable the co-creation of purposeful and equitable shared-value outcomes.

Organisational resilience reflects the capacity of an organisation to successfully navigate change and is influenced by four key factors:

- **Responsiveness**: The change orientation of the organisation, its attitude to change which is influenced by its leadership and culture.

- **Knowledge**: The change awareness of the organisation, its capability to anticipate, recognise and understand the change opportunities and learn from its change experiences.

- **Resourcefulness**: The change adaptation capability of the organisation, its ability to successfully negotiate the change opportunities in a way that adds value to the organisation.

- **Confidence**: The change appetite of the organisation, the ability of the organisation (and its stakeholder communities) to continually energise and resource change initiatives and sustain the impacts of ongoing and disruptive change.

Organising framework: A conceptual model designed to frame, structure, systematise, or give character to a situation or group of entities. It is essentially a way of thinking about the organisational structures and processes that influence how entities operate.

Personal knowledge can be divided into four interrelated sets of knowledge, each of which can be broadly defined as follows:

- **Inherited knowledge** includes our innate or genetic knowledge that we acquire from our birth parents.

- **Learned knowledge** includes both our rational and sensory knowledge, and experiential knowledge that we have acquired by using our reasoning and perceptual abilities.

- **Intuitive knowledge** refers to the knowledge gained from our insights, the truths and facts that we apprehend directly and apparently independent of any process of sensing or reasoning.

- **Universal knowledge** refers to our access to the dimension of knowledge that exists in the wider Universe of which we are part, and which we have the capacity to know.

Personal learning centre is a concept or construct used to describe the capacity we have to utilise our knowledge, intelligence and creativity to continually adapt to changes in our environment in a way that sustains our life on purpose.

Personal operating model. The natural ecology of a personal operating model is people as living organisms; participating with and within their communities of interest; each making a contribution according to their unique purpose; continually increasing their knowledge and expanding their potential to adapt to change; and renewing the resources that enable and sustain their wellbeing.

Purpose: *Refer to* **Organisational purpose** *and* **Individual purpose**.

Resilience: *Refer to* **Organisational resilience**.

Staff are an integral part of the organisational community and play a vital role in the development of inter- and intra-community relationships. They are not a resource or (human) capital to be used up in delivering value to other stakeholders.

Stakeholder community refers to a community of organisation stakeholders typically defined by their primary organisational role – e.g. shareholders, customers, suppliers, staff, etc. Collectively, these individual communities represent the organisation's stakeholder community. But it is also useful to refer to them as 'stakeholder communities' to remind us that an organisation is comprised of multiple distinct communities of stakeholders.

Social capital is the wealth that accrues from our ability to interact positively with other people, to create the meaningful relationships that build and sustain our social networks and communities of interest. It includes our ability to engage positively with difference and diversity, our capacity to collaborate for mutual benefit, including our ability to participate in collective learning and co-creative endeavours and successfully navigate change.

Spiritual capital is the wealth we accrue by knowing who we are, why we exist, and our true purpose in life. It is the value we derive from knowing our place in the Universe, understanding the deeply held beliefs that guide our life journey, and acknowledging our responsibility to live our life on purpose. Within the context of our discussion about congruence, our spiritual capital is the internal resource that powers our life purpose.

Successful conversations occur when two or more people (or communities) enter into dialogue about a common interest or shared purpose and co-create outcomes that manifest that interest or purpose and create equitable value for all participants. Successful conversations are also authentic conversations in which participants are all able to be who they really are and say what they really think about a topic they care about.

Sustainable organisations are those equipped to maintain the longer-term engagement of their stakeholder communities in the pursuit of their shared purpose, and to continually manifest that purpose by co-creating equitable-shared value for those communities. Sustainable organisations assume a collaborative responsibility for the wellbeing of their stakeholder communities. They pay responsible attention to the social, cultural, economic and environmental needs of those communities to ensure that they continue to co-create contributions that enhance the overall wellbeing and sustainability of the entire organisational community.

Sustainable individuals have the necessary physical, mental and environmental capacity to access the level of material, intellectual,

social and spiritual capital they need to live their life on purpose –
to be congruent people.

True wealth refers to our capacity to own or access the resources
we need to develop and sustain our physical, social and spiritual
life. It comprises the mix of material, social and spiritual capital
that we need 'to be well' – the meaning of the Olde English term
'welthy' from which the word wealth is derived.

Wellbeing: *Refer to* **Community wellbeing** *and* **Individual
wellbeing**.

List of figures

List of acknowledgements

In addition to the author acknowledgements at the end of each chapter, here is a list of the particular texts that have informed this discussion.

---

[1] Stephen P. Robbins. *Organisation Theory, Structure, Design and Application*. 1990

[2] K. M. MacQueen et al. *'What Is Community? An Evidence-Based Definition for Participatory Public Health'*. 2001

[3] Rajendra S. Sisodia, David B. Wolfe, Jagdish N. Sheth. *Firms of Endearment; How World Class Companies Profit from Passion and Purpose*. 2003, 2010

[4] Amie Southcombe. *Proposed Model of Individual-Organisational Congruence in a Knowledge Intensive Context*. 2009

[5] Lloyd C. Williams. *The Congruent Workplace*. 2002

[6] Mark Esposito, Lloyd C. Williams. *Moving Beyond Human and Organisational Congruence*. 2010

[7] Marvin L. Bouillon et al. *Economic Benefit of Goal Congruence and Implications for Management Control Systems*. 2006

[8] Jeffery T. Polzer et al. *Capitalizing On Diversity, Inter in Small Work Groups*. 2001

[9] John P. Kotter. *Leading Change*. 1996; *The Heart of Change*. 2002

[10] Nikos Mourkogiannis. *Purpose: The Starting Point of Great Companies*. 2006

[11] Richard R. Ellsworth. *Leading with Purpose: The new corporate realities*. 2002

[12] Christopher A. Bartlett and Sumantra Ghoshal. *Beyond Strategy to Purpose*. 1994

[13] Jerry Porras and Jim Collins. *Built to Last*. 1994, 1998

[14] Joel Kurtzman. *Common Purpose: How Great Leaders Get Organisations To Achieve The Extraordinary*. 2010

[15] Christine Arena. *The High Purpose Company*. 2007

[16] Peter Block. *Community: The Structure of Belonging*. 2002

[17] Paul Born. *Community Conversations*. 2012

[18] C. Otto Scharmer. *Theory U, leading from the Future as It Emerges*. 2009

[19] Jamie Showkeir and Maren Showkeir. *Authentic Conversations: Moving from Manipulation to Truth and Commitment*. 2008

[20] William Isaacs. *Dialogue: The Art of Thinking Together*. 1999

[21] Peter Senge. *The Fifth Discipline: The art and practice of the learning organization*. 1990

[22] David A. Garvin. Amy C. Edmondson, Francesca Gino. *Is yours a learning organisation?*. 2008

[23] Nathalie Greenan, Edward Lorenz. *Learning Organisations: Report prepared for the OECD's Innovation Strategy*. 2009

[24] Pierre Dillenbourg. *What do you mean by 'collaborative learning'?* (Chapter 1). 1999

[25] Amy C. Edmondson. *Teaming: How Organisations Learn, Innovate and Compete in the Knowledge Economy*. 2012

[26] Daniel Bishop, Alan Felstead, Alison Fuller, Nick Jewson, Tracey Lee and Lorna Unwin. *Connecting Culture and Learning in Organisations: A Review of Current Themes*. 2006

[27] S.P. Lopez, J. M. M. Peon, C. J. V. Ordas. *Managing Knowledge – the link between culture and organisational learning*. 2004

[28] Margaret Wheatley and Myron Kellner-Rogers. *What Do We Measure and Why?*. 1999

[29] Peter Block. *Stewardship: Choosing Service over Self Interest*. 1996

[30] Mehrdad Baghai and James Quigley et al. *As One: individual action, collective power*. 2011

[31] A. Gregory Stone, Robert F Russell, Kathleen Patterson. *Transformational versus Servant leadership: A Difference in Leader Focus*. 2003

[32] Brien N. Smith, Ray V. Montagno, Tatiana C Kuzmenko. *Transformational and Servant Leadership: Content and Contextual Comparisons*. 2004

[33] Fred Walumbwa et al. *Authentic Leadership: Development and Validation of a Theory-Based Measure*. 2008; Bruce J. Avolio, William L. Gardner. *Leadership Development: Getting to the root of positive forms of leadership*. 2005

[34] Gregory G. Dess and Joseph C. Picken. *Changing roles: Leadership in the 21st century*. 2000

[35] Donde A. Plowman and Dennis Duchon. *Dispelling the Myths about Leadership: From Cybernetic to Emergence (in Complexity Leadership Part 1: Conceptual Foundations*, Ed. Mary Uhl-Bien). 2008

[36] John Kay. *Obliquity*. 2010

[37] Jerry Porras and Jim Collins. *Built to Last*. 1998

[38] Martin N. Davidson. *The End of Diversity As We Know It*. 2011

[39] Yasar F. Jarrar and Mohamed Zairi. *Knowledge Management: Learning for Organisational Experience* (ECBPM). 2010

[40] Jeff Dyer and Hal Gregersen. *The Innovator's DNA*. 2011

[41] Michael H. Hugos. *Business Agility : Sustainable Prosperity in a Relentlessly Competitive World*. 2009

[42] Venkat Ramaswarmy and Francis Gouillart. *The Power of Co-Creation*. 2010

[43] Rob Cross and Robert J. Thomas. *Driving Results Through Social Networks*. 2009

44 Peter Senge, C. Otto Scharmer, Joseph Jaworski and Betty Sue Flowers. *Presence*. 2005

45 Liisa Valikangas. *The Resilient Organisation*. 2010

46 Timothy J. Vogus and Kathleen M. Sutcliffe. *Organizational Resilience: Towards a Theory and Research Agenda*. 2007

47 Jeremy Hope, Peter Bunce and Franz Roosli. *The Leaders Dilemma: How to build empowered and adaptive organisations*. 2011

48 Adam Werbach. *Strategy for Sustainability: A Business Manifesto*. 2009

49 Constance Helfat et al. *Dynamic Capabilities: Understanding Strategic Change in Organisations*. 2007

50 Wayne Visser. *The Age of Responsibility*. 2011

51 Marcel van Marrewijk. *Concepts and Definitions of CSR and Corporate Sustainability*. 2003

52 Stephen R. Covey. *The 7 Habits of Highly Effective People*. 1990; *Principled Centred Leadership*. 1990

53 Eckhart Tolle. *The Power of Now*. 2004

54 Wayne W. Dwyer. *The Power of intention*. 2010

55 Charles Guignon. *On Being Authentic: Thinking In Action*. 2004

56 Mike Robbins. *Be Yourself, Everyone Else is Already Taken*. 2009

57 Rupert Spira. *Presence, The Art of Peace and Happiness (Vol 1)*. 2012

58 Jan Frazer. *The Freedom of Being At Ease with What Is*. 2012

59 Nick Udall and Nic Turner. *The Way of Nowhere*. 2011

60 Danah Zohar and Ian Marshall. *Spiritual intelligence: The Ultimate Intelligence*. 2000, 2012

61 Ken Robinson. *Out of our Minds: Learning to be Creative*. 2011

62 Michael Michalko. *Creative Thinkering: Putting your imagination to work*. 2011

63 Robert Fritz. *The Path of Least Resistance* (revised). 2010

[64] Gill Ereaut and Rebecca Whiting. *What do we mean by 'wellbeing'? And why might it matter?*. 2008

[65] Martin Seligman. *Flourish* (version 2). 2011

[66] Jane E. Myers and Thomas J. Sweeney. *Counseling for Wellness: Theory, Research and Practice*. 2005

[67] Sam Spurlin. *The Pyramid of Wellbeing: A Framework for Happiness and Success*. 2011

[68] Dottie Billington. *Life is an Attitude: How to Grow Forever Better*. 2000

[69] Danah Zohar and Ian Marshall. *Spiritual Capital: Wealth we can live by*. 2004